Friendship in Politics

In today's society, friendship and politics are most commonly viewed as distinct and mutually opposed concerns. Politics tends to be seen as general and impersonal, to do with Power and Hierarchy. Friendship, by contrast, is generally conceived as particular and intimate, relating to Equality and Fraternity. On this view, friendship may corrupt politics, and politics override friendship. Ancient thought, however, as in Greece and Rome, tended to bring the two together, locating friendship as the moral foundation of the political.

This view of the two as linked, moreover, has tended to obtain significance across the world, especially in early social systems. But is that view sound? Ought not Friendship to be dismissed by moderns as primitive, inefficient, nepotistic, as Freud suggested? Or ought it to be promoted as a vital moral constraint on Power and the consuming egotism of rulers, as Plutarch and others have recommended?

This book seeks to answer, directly and indirectly, by supplying analyses of the concept, critical reconstructions of some crucial modern accounts, for example Kierkegaard, Arendt and Schmitt and concrete accounts of the actual play of friendship both within and between states. It throws light on the place of friendship in politics, by connecting theoretical questions to empirical answers.

This book was previously published as a special issue of the *Critical Review of Social and Political Philosophy*.

Preston King is a visiting professor in the Leadership Center at Morehouse College (Atlanta), and in the philosophy department at the University of East Anglia (UK).

Graham M Smith is in the Department of Politics and International Relations at Lancaster University.

Friendship in Politics

Edited by Preston King and Graham M. Smith

LONDON AND NEW YORK

First published 2007 by Routledge

2 Park Square, Milton Park, Abingdon, Oxfordshire OX14 4RN
711 Third Avenue, New York, NY 10017

Routledge is an imprint of the Taylor & Francis Group, an informa business

First issued in paperback 2018

Copyright © 2007 Edited by Preston King and Graham M. Smith

Typeset in Times by Genesis Typesetting Ltd, Rochester, Kent

All rights reserved. No part of this book may be reprinted or reproduced or utilised in any form or by any electronic, mechanical, or other means, now known or hereafter invented, including photocopying and recording, or in any information storage or retrieval system, without permission in writing from the publishers.

Notice:
Product or corporate names may be trademarks or registered trademarks, and are used only for identification and explanation without intent to infringe.

British Library Cataloguing in Publication Data
A catalogue record for this book is available from the British Library

ISBN 13: 978-0-415-42081-5 (hbk)
ISBN 13: 978-1-138-99315-0 (pbk)

Printed in the United Kingdom
by Henry Ling Limited

Contents

Notes on Contributors   vii

Introduction
Preston King and Graham M Smith   1

Part I: Theorizing Friendship in Politics

1 Friendship in Politics
  Preston King   9

2 Friendship and the Political
  Evert van der Zweerde   31

3 Friendship as a Reason for Equality
  Daniel Schwartz   51

Part II: Thinkers on Friendship

4 Kierkegaard: Responsibility to the Other
  Graham M. Smith   65

5 Carl Schmitt on Friendship: Polemics and Diagnostics
  Gabriella Slomp   83

Part III: Friendship Within States

6 Friendship and Revolution in Poland: The Eros and Ethos of the Committee for Workers' Defense (KOR)
  Nina Witoszek   99

7 Civic Friendship: A Critique of Recent Care Theory
  Sibyl A. Schwarzenbach   117

Part IV. International Friendship

8 Friendship, Mutual Trust and the Evolution of Regional Peace in the International System
  Andrea Oelsner   141

9 The Institutionalization of International Friendship
  Antoine Vion   165

  Index   183

Notes on Contributors

Preston King is Professor of Political Philosophy, with current appointments at Fisk University (Nashville) and Morehouse College (Atlanta), CEO of CONANDEAG, Chair of the Political Philosophy Research Committee of IPSA (International Political Science Association), founder and co-editor of *CRISPP*, Professor Emeritus at Lancaster University, and author of such books as *The Ideology of Order, Toleration, Federalism and Federation and Thinking Past a Problem*.

Andrea Oelsner is Lecturer at the Department of Politics and International Relations of the University of Aberdeen. Her main research interests lie in the areas of international security and theories of international peace, constructivism in international relations, and Latin American politics. She is the author of *International Relations in Latin America: Peace and Security in the Southern Cone* (Routledge, 2005).

Daniel Schwartz is Lecturer in Politics at Aston University, Birmingham, UK. He has previously been a postdoctoral fellow at the Dept. of Politics and the Truman Institute of the Hebrew University of Jerusalem, Israel and the Chaire Hoover of Université catholique de Louvain, Belgium. He writes about scholastic and neo-scholastic political and ethical thought, nineteenth century political ideas in Latin America, and contemporary luck-egalitarianism. Recent publications include *Aquinas on Friendship* (Oxford: Clarendon Press, 2007) and 'Francisco Suárez y la Tradición del Contrato Social', *Contrastes: Revista Internacional de Filosofía* 10(2005)119-138.

Sibyl A. Schwarzenbach is Associate Professor of Philosophy at The City University of New York (Baruch College & the University Graduate Center). She has written numerous articles in social and political philosophy, ethics, legal, as well as in feminist theory. She is editor of (and contributor to) *Women and the United States Constitution: History, Interpretation, and Practice* (Columbia University Press, 2003) and her book *On Civic Friendship* is forthcoming (2006).

Gabriella Slomp, Dott. Fil. Siena (Italy), PhD (London School of Economics), is Lecturer in Political Theory at the University of St Andrews. Her main interests are Thomas Hobbes, Carl Schmitt and just war theory. Her main publications include: *Thomas Hobbes and the Political Philosophy of Glory* (Macmillan, 2000) and *Carl Schmitt and the Politics of Hostility, Violence and Terror* (Palgrave, 2007).

Graham M. Smith is Lecturer in the Department of Politics and International Relations at Lancaster University. He has special interests in nineteenth- and twentieth-century political thought and his research explores the relationship between human and political ontology.

Antoine Vion is Assistant Professor at the Mediterranean University (Aix-Marseille 2), and member of the Institute of Labour Economics and Industrial Sociology (UMR CNRS 6143). He has already published several historical studies about the construction of international friendship movements in post-war Europe (*Contemporary European History*, 2002; *Revue française de science politique*, 2003). More generally, his research aims at understanding the processes of internationalization of social activities through different studies on direct foreign investment, standardization, and related issues.

Nina Witoszek FitzPatrick is a writer and professor of cultural history at Oslo University. Her latest publications include: *Philosophical Dialogues* (1999), *The Postmodern Challenge: East and West Perspectives* (1999) and *Culture and Crisis* (2002).

Evert van der Zweerde is in the Department of Social and Political Philosophy of the Radboud University in Nijmegen, Netherlands, where he directs a Centre for Russian Humanities Studies. His main publications include: *Soviet Historiography of Philosophy* (Kluwer, 1997), '"Civil Society" and "Orthodox Christianity" in Russia: a Double Test-Case', *Religion, State & Society*, 1999, and 'All Europeans Are Equal ... But Aren't Some Less European than Others? (Reflections on Europe and Orthodox Christianity)', *Journal of Eastern Christian Studies*, 2005. With Gerrit Steunebrink, he published *Civil Society, Religion, and the Nation; Modernization in Intercultural Context: Russia, Japan, Turkey* (Rodopi, 2004). He specialises in political and social philosophy, meta-philosophy, and Russian (including Soviet) philosophy.

Introduction

PRESTON KING* & GRAHAM M SMITH**

*Leadership Center, Morehouse College, Atlanta, Georgia, USA **Department of Politics and International Relations, Lancaster University, UK

This volume is concerned with friendship as a dimension of politics, both domestic and international. Friendship can be viewed as *non-political*, especially where we take political relationships to be oppositional, driven merely by power and interest. If we take politics to be about nothing more than power – who gets what, when, how (as Harold Lasswell put it, under the influence of Machiavelli) – the emphasis is upon ego, the individual, in headlong pursuit of desire, stripped of moral inflection. We shall likely infer from such an orientation that amity and fellow-feeling can have little place.

By contrast, friendship can be viewed as *indispensable* to politics. For we may take political relationships to be combinational, mobilizational, dipped in authority, meaning consent, thus pointing towards fellow-feeling sufficient to bind agents one to another in common affection and loyalty. This bonding may emerge at any point along a scale that runs from cronyism, to 'log-rolling', to the spirituous unity of 'good old boys', to *noblesse oblige* among weathered elites, to companionable and likeminded Fabian reformers, and to the fraternal 'utopianism' of movements like those of the Owenites and the Society of Friends.

The definitional question is a trying one, since observers seem free to fix friendship as either wholly alien to politics or, on the contrary, as its most salient trait. Ought then friendship to be peremptorily incorporated into, or sharply excised from, what we mean by politics? The paradoxical answer may be 'both'. Suppose we articulate politics as always expressing some antipathy along the lines of 'Us v. Them'. If so, the first term of the antipathy is itself expressive of an internally affective tie. Can there be an 'us' (even where ranged against 'them') that repudiates some affective community among those who make it up? The essay by Preston King commits to friendship as essential to politics and seeks to identify what are or ought to be its key features in a modern setting.

This is not the place for fuller exploration of the issue. However we do need, over the horizon, some fuller and more coherent construct of friendship, bracketed upon a sensitive delineation of its various types. One question is whether any community ('us') is necessarily defined in opposition to some other and also whether any such

---

Correspondence Address: Graham M. Smith, Department of Politics and International Relations, County South, Lancaster University, Lancaster, LA1 4YL. Email: g.m.smith@lancaster.ac.uk.

opponent ('them') is necessarily to be construed as an enemy. Another key question, assuming politics to be oiled by some variety of affective bonding, is how political life may be improved or corrupted by some forms of friendship by contrast to others. If we develop a fuller picture of the varieties of friendship, then we may be better placed to locate and encourage those varieties that more nearly help than hurt. Evert van der Zweerde concentrates directly upon the conceptualization of friendship as either essential, or essentially alien, to politics, and seeks a way to transcend that polarity.

If we wish to cast the die, by way of accepting politics as somehow inseparable from some variety of friendship, we can do so in two ways already adumbrated. First, we may construe politics as alliance-formation in the pursuit of power. It will not matter that the Allied element standardly pits itself against the Axis contestant in enemy-recognition mode. A 'band of brothers', whose mutual amity emerges from confronting a common opponent, share a real bond, no matter that bond's origin or cause. The amity of a cohort is not contradicted by an enmity that is deflected elsewhere.

Second, politics can be conceived as tied to friendship, in as far as politics involves bonding, and in as far as this bonding need not *necessarily* be prompted by the sole urge to unite against a common opponent. Agents may bond, whether from intuitive fellow-feeling, or in order to achieve some existential goal they share. To love the neighbour, to act in unison, to build the village school, to irrigate our common valley, to assemble under a common religious inspiration, or to advance the cause of science (and of knowledge so conceived): each of these may have an internal, affective spring, without being prompted by an external, dyspeptic dislike. Members of a group may be internally bound in ways that have nothing to do with threats from, or even the existence of, other groups. Thus any group, A, where marked by an internally affective bond, need not perforce be opposed to or even aware of the alternative groupings, B or C.

Let us (for the moment) characterize politics as the 'thing' of the state, and the state as nothing if not hierarchy. Aristocratic and monarchical regimes are plainly hierarchical. Arguably, democratic regimes are only marginally less so. Karl Popper claimed that the distinctive effect of democracy is to ensure regime change by nonviolent means – not to eliminate hierarchy. The voter, however sovereignly equal on entering the ballot box, does not re-emerge from the affair as free as air. The equality of the vote, even if it achieves a government to a voter's liking, still confirms – it does not overthrow – the overarching system of rule. The equality of the ballot box is designed, at day's end, to put some person or party in power. It thus confirms, it does not destroy, the hierarchy, the inequality. If politics is to do with the management of this state (conceived as a hierarchy), then it is also to do with superintending, not eliminating, the inequality that is the primal feature of state structures.

How then can we square, if at all, the inequality of status built into state forms, with the apparent equality of status caught up in various types of friendship? How can it be possible for political (hierarchical) relationships to be friendly (equal) relationships? If the heart of friendship is equality, and the essence of the state is inequality, and if politics is all about the management of the state, can the political realm handily accommodate any meaningful 'friendship'? How can those who are in politics, who exercise control over the state – commanding others, which means being significantly unequal to them – co-exist on genuinely 'friendly' and equal terms with those they command? In this, we confront a clear challenge regarding how politics, and its power structures, can cohere with friendship.

Again, of course, friendship comes in different forms and degrees, in just the way that equality does. If we take different types of equality, we see that one sort always excludes another. For example, equality of opportunity excludes equality of result and vice versa. Treating patients strictly by turn (equality of one sort) excludes treating them strictly by order of urgency (equality of another sort). Promoting congressmen to chairs by length of tenure or seniority (one equality) excludes promoting them by intelligence or otherwise (alternative types of equality). As suggested earlier, an equal right to vote is married to the creation of unequal access to power.

We may assume in parallel that types of friendship differ and clash, such that some are not compatible with others. On that reading, the question becomes less whether friendship has a place in politics, but what place, and what sorts of friendship. In that way we may begin to redirect concern from the logic of the idea of friendship, to the ethical notions that do or ought to inform it. A key element in this ethic is less to define politics and friendship than to identify appropriate types of political friendship, and the extent to which it may be proper to engage with them.

There are always inequalities between any two or more individuals – and so with friends. Friends are always unequal in some department, the enumeration of which – perhaps height, weight, skill, wealth, warmth, generosity, prudence and so on – can have no term. If that is so, then equality, in any abstract or absolute sense, cannot be a condition for friendship. Presumably there must be something held in common between friends, else they would not be 'friends', and we might loosely call this something equality. Nevertheless, we shall not insist that this 'thing' held equally between friends, extends to *identity* (meaning, lack of other significant differences).

Attention thus moves away from the abstraction – viz, whether equality as such is compatible with friendship – to a more specific concern with the particular type(s) of equality that friendship may require. This connects in turn with the question of the impact of certain types of friendship upon politics, up to and including effect upon the stability of the state. Enmity between social strata – whether we call these strands classes, races, ethnic groups, clans, tribes or whatever – can destabilize states. Can friendship, in some egalitarian way, play a role in inhibiting this? Daniel Schwartz explores the question whether friendships across social strata may serve to diminish social inequality between them.

In this collection, only two recent thinkers are attended to in detail: Kierkegaard (in the nineteenth century) by Graham Smith, and Schmitt (twentieth century) by Gabriella Slomp. Kierkegaard raises the question, less whether friendship in politics is possible, than whether it ever transcends selfishness, and thus achieves any genuine moral worth. Kierkegaard challenges the morality, rather than the 'politicity', of friendship. Kierkegaard's negative conclusion may be described, in sum, as a rejection of the classic Greek notion of mutuality among friends. It is an approach that characterizes the autonomous reciprocity and equality of friends as shallow and inadequate, to be displaced by some notion of the priority of universal adoration and common submission to God. On this view, the frame moves from love of the equal (another mortal) to love of the all-powerful (a transcendent God). The question this may raise is not really whether friendship is a good thing, but who (Who?) is a worthy recipient.

With a switch of priorities, from human to divine friendship, the question is directly raised whether so unequal a relationship as that between 'man' and God can be passed off as friendship. Another way of putting this is whether the love of human for human is worthy unless redefined as a sublimated love that each may entertain for the Almighty. We may ask whether Kierkegaard withdraws from friendship because it is selfish or because he embraces a theology of submission to an omnipotent creator-god. By extension, if love of the Other can be dismissed as inferior to love of God, maybe politics generally (burdened by crass want and impulse) can equally be dismissed as inferior to the otherworldly politics of the Final Ascent (as famously detailed by St Augustine's *City of God*). If friendship, as love of the Other, is self-interested, it may follow that love of God is no less self-interested – given that the ultimate aim, after all, is eternal salvation. To demean friendship on grounds of selfishness may require that we dismiss love of God for the same reason.

Schmitt raises the question, not whether love of the Other should be replaced by love of God, but whether, in politics, there can be any love of the Other at all, however inferior this love may be. From a Schmittian perspective, the heart and soul of politics lies in enemy-recognition, in identifying those over whom one has power, and who in turn threaten one's possession of power. If we promote such a perspective, then we may be tempted to regard the essence of politics as enmity, and so bracket friendship as entirely alien terrain. On the other hand, as Slomp argues, we may, in this, miss the fact that, even if the enemy is vital to such a construction of politics, there is no politics that can be constructed in complete abstraction from the process of alliance-formation. More than that, in politics, positive valence among allies has to be at least as important as negative valence among enemies.

Indeed, to have only enemies is arguably not to be political anyway. To be bereft of friends in a landscape that swarms with enemies seems a terminal move and not a sustainable and ongoing engagement. To be such an isolate seems *pro tanto* to enact a brisk and certain self-negation. If there can be no enemy-recognition without alliance-formation, then the latter must somehow matter, and may be of the utmost importance. The conclusion here is that, even where we take the most extreme view of politics – Schmitt's view is usually read as extreme – where this excludes amity, we can readily see, not just that it is inadequate, but that it self-destructs, apart from constituting a likely misreading of Schmitt in the first place.

We may then accept that friendship of some sort is indispensable to politics, and that this implicates, not just dyads, but wider relationships. Friendship is always intimate, even where it acquires a political complexion. But since it may give rise to nepotism and cronyism, as is commonly remarked, we are standardly tempted to seek to avoid it. But this raises the question whether such evasion is genuine and effective, or whether by contrast – as with the 'war on drugs' and so many other prohibitions – it only drives what is disdained (but in great demand) underground, turning erstwhile sunlit episodes into more atrophic, reptilian transactions. Nina Witoszek provides a striking and deeply engaging example of a 'friendly circle', intimate and intellectual, intensely political and highly effective, that served to transition Poland from a mere communist dictatorship into a vibrant electoral democracy.

The Polish example raises the question whether a wider friendship in politics, of the type Witoszek details, is merely the exception, or whether (for being viewed as somehow 'impolitic') it is commonly kept from public view in a more deliberate way. For reasons that require closer inspection, the only commanding types of friendship publicly celebrated in electoral democracies tend to be trite intra-familial cases, especially husband–wife teams – Ike and Mamie, Jack and Jackie, Lyndon and Lady Bird, Bill and Hillary, Tony and Cherie, etc. What is also widely remarked is the tendency for the retiring politician, not ostensibly burnt out by rebuke and rejection, to implausibly proclaim love of family, and the desire to have more of this, as the root cause for abandoning the public sphere. The implication of this may be that the public sphere is an entirely non-erogenous zone, quite bereft of affection, sustained or not – so that the only place to take up the slack is elsewhere, maybe underground.

When we inspect social relations in many more economically advanced states, especially the United States, we note a growing gap between rich and poor, inadequate social provision, whether to do with medical insurance or pensions or homelessness. The market stresses liberty, autonomy, property, self-promotion. Meanwhile the vulnerable fall between the cracks and are often viewed as deserving their discomfort. We also note something else – viz a difficulty in valuing the critical importance of the care and affection that may be extended by one person to another, but not directly aimed at generating a material product. A market-based system, as reflected first in the writings of figures like David Hume and Adam Smith, finds it increasingly difficult to value persons other than in terms of what they produce. From this perspective, such professions as nursing, teaching, and child-care, such dispositions as respect, recognition, affection, all occupy decreasing ideological space, since it cannot be clear what they are 'good for'.

In so far as women especially – but not women alone – have traditionally been responsible for so much of care, their status (where continuing to perform as carers) has tended accordingly to be lowered. That diminution of status, moreover, attaches to all those who engage in the extension of care to their fellows. Loss of status threatens to envelop entire ethnic or national groups, especially in the global South, where these have been incorporated into expanding market systems. They may be affected thus, whether they remain at home to service holiday sites for Northern holidaymakers, or are suctioned into the geographic North as casual, unskilled and ill-paid migrant labour. Sybil Schwarzenbach enters the lists as a proponent of 'public care', as over against mere 'productive labour', and views some broader embrace of civic friendship as essential to incubating 'a general and public concern' of citizens for one another.

Friendship is important as a matter of domestic politics. However, its arc of intimacy doesn't just cut up within borders; it cuts across them too. The autonomy imposed upon the individual by a domestic theory of market production has its parallel in the autonomy imposed upon the state by an international theory of realism or neo-realism. If an individual is expected to produce and bring to market a product that expresses and validates autonomy, such an outlook inhibits placing a value upon, and so being friendly with, others who do not or cannot do the same. If individuals are unable to respect and combine with others save on the basis of money (product), their relational dilemma is that they cannot combine meaningfully even with their peers. For the implicit object of each associate becomes the business of accessing the other's product, not the associate qua person.

Similarly, if the state is expected to promote what are advocated as its permanent interests, then the emphasis must relentlessly flow to its autonomy, such that it can have 'no permanent friends'. Hence the 'security dilemma' of sovereign states: If the state takes the view that it must always ultimately seek to help itself, and so relentlessly build its own power (especially military), then - should it succeed - it cannot but excite the fear and antipathy of other states, thus circularly undermining the security it first sought. If, *per contra*, the state fails in this security-driven lurch for power, then it magnetizes (by the same token) the predation of fellow-states, on the view that the motivation of each of these is the same.

Andrea Oelsner, internationally, like Schwarzenbach, domestically, seeks to get round the difficulty. In Oelsner's case, this is done by reference to the construction of mutual trust. This trust is claimed to involve an underlying concept of transnational community, blunting the very notion that there can be war between states where their vertical alignments are cut across by fundamental horizontal transactions. If then the citizens of different states cease to be packaged as mutually excusive communities, their moral and social entanglements undermine the state's capacity to radically marshal one citizen-bloc against the other. Antoine Vion is concerned with the extension of this process through such applied means as town twinning and cultural institutes, having the effect of cutting across the verticality of state hierarchies and achieving more intimate, horizontal, transnational connections.

In sum, this volume explores the presence of friendship in politics. It kick-starts the discussion on how and in what forms political friendship, domestic and international, can and should be instituted. Friendship here is not just regarded as a matter of affective ties, i.e. as solely a matter of emotional connections. For friendship on any ongoing basis is always shored up by moral principles of some kind – questions of equality, loyalty, respect, independence – that establish the basis on which social and political relations are and ought to be maintained. The subject of friendship in politics is not one that has been unduly fashionable. We may expect nonetheless that future work will build on the helpful initiatives supplied by contributors to this volume.

Acknowledgements

The editors wish to thank the ECPR for sponsoring the workshop on friendship in Granada in April 2004, and to Oleg Kharkhordin who co-convened that workshop. There were many insightful comments and discussions in Granada and in addition to thanking all the participants we would like to extend a special thank-you to Heather Devere and Elizabeth Frazer. We would also like to thank those who have helped with the editorial process including Richard Bellamy, Carla Turner and Deltrick Johnson.

Friendship in Politics

PRESTON KING
Leadership Center, Morehouse College, Atlanta, Georgia, USA

Friendship in an Ancient Setting

Friendship means different things. Though we shall find common ground among these differences, we shall also accept that the meanings of terms are not somehow naïve and self-imposed matters of fact. Meaning is attributed by agents, who, in turn, are burdened by purpose. As purpose varies, so do the key terms by which it is communicated. So what we mean by 'friendship' will not change willy-nilly, 'over time'. That is to say: changes of meaning and application do not occur simply because clocks are ticking (chronology). Nor is the mind, in its rococo internal workings, forced to execute an 'about-face!' merely due to changes in external material conditions. Nor does it much help to think of 'context' imposing change – as distinct from changed thinking itself changing 'the' context. New thinking, whatever may trigger it, is itself both precondition and cause of new outcomes.

It may be desirable that a change of circumstance, understood as a change in problem or project, should occasion new thinking. Yet the desirable and the desired are not a happily married number. The acreage between them poses a problem for ordinary folk, but no less for people with power – perhaps especially and increasingly for people *in* power. Elites, for being elites, tend to have a direct investment in the status quo. They do not readily embrace transformative ideologies. With whatever tolerant reluctance, they are not averse to manipulating supposedly democratic public opinion where that serves their purposes. This may be especially crucial in the increasingly successful pursuit of concentrated ownership and management of the media. So a change of 'objective' conditions cannot be counted on to secure, directly or immediately, large shifts of perspective – save of course in the long term (and we know what happens in the long term).

People are disposed to cling to their overviews with admirably religious intensity. Contradictory evidence will not reliably shake the faith. British military leadership did not think to kit out soldiery, seeking to subdue guerrilla colonials in 1770s America, in less conspicuous regalia. The French *État-major*, in the lead-up to the Second World War, unhappily (again) prepared itself for trench warfare, not Blitzkrieg. The mindset of the generals, we are advised, is always to fight the previous war. The Hoover administration's best plan for beating back the Great Depression of 1929 lay in even more slavish adherence to failed *laissez-faire* policies. The calcified thinking of the George W. Bush administration (2000–2008) in the face of global warming is scarcely the most dramatic illustration of our impressive indisposition/incapacity to adapt. A majority of Israelis, infected by a Wild West mentality, and in league with America's religious right, have long persisted in the thought that they can make a home for themselves in the Middle East by bombing and displacing the Muslims around them. These Muslims, similarly, seem no more flexible in their thinking – though that may be less relevant in face of their inability to bring effective power to bear.

Hence we are to expect, no matter that we deplore, the persistence of settled ways of thinking. Nothing is changed by the fact that it is inept to the point of actual or near-extinction – as among ancient Easter Islander fisher-folk and pre-Columbian Maya farmers. In the end, it is difficult to elicit why thinking changes. At least we know that to account for it in terms of notions like 'time', or 'context' or the emergence of new 'material conditions' is at best simplistic, if not plain false. The mind follows its own route, logical or illogical. It notices what it notices, whether what is noticed is critical or trivial. Minds interact, too often imitatively, since minds tend to confirm what other minds affirm – no matter that the facts seem (often) to protest.

The meanings and applications of a concept like friendship, if we go back as much as two and a half thousand years, significantly diverge from current meanings and applications. And we observe this as a matter of fact, not as a matter of course. All early thinkers were obsessed with notions of friendship far more sustained and intense than ours. The question is how we explain this. The answer is ultimately uncertain, but that is all the more reason to explore their circumstances with a view to clarifying what may be in play for us.

The scale of early states was small, as in 'town', with population density low. The basis of production was agriculture, with significant pockets of hunting and fishing.

Subsistence was the norm, every man and woman a handyman (on the model of Levi-Strauss' *bricoleur*). Work was unremitting, diurnal and hard, done by slave and free, using rough tools, no 'machinery', nor even a robot – the oddity of unemployment lurking over an impossibly distant horizon. Commercial exchange was essentially conceived in the mode of 'home' economics, as by Aristotle. Trade was occasional (on market days), not ubiquitous; the appetite for it was not insatiable. Travel was animal, as by human foot, or by donkey, camel, or horse – thus slow. Communication was febrile, the volume of interaction with neighbours restricted. Tourism (to adapt the arcane formula of Secretary of Defense Donald Rumsfeld) would have been an 'unknown unknown'.

The known world consisted basically of neighbours and kin. Societies were largely self-enclosed, knowledge of the wider world given up (in major part) to fable, in which the alien was truly alien, in the manner of the Cyclops. But then such a monster as this was progeny of the gods, meaning that the alien, even, was touched by divinity. The circle leads back, from bizarre otherness to mundane self, the latter thus infected with some intimation of its own magical possibility. There is tension in the ancient setting, between (a) the imagination of otherness, frightening but exciting and (b) the apparently enclosed community of neighbours and kin, reassuring, if a touch boring.

Socio-political relations were built around the constitutional or ideological theory of the 'blood' knot. That does not mean that biological kinship dictated socio-political relationships, only that these were commonly justified in the language of kinship. Viewed purely as a genetic datum, kinship unites no one – for reasons that can only be touched on. On evolutionary theory especially, but as also with most world religions, one is kin to all the world. On that assumption, if kinship imposes obligation, it must be to humanity as a whole – and beyond that to life as such.

The counterargument is that kinship does not obligate to *everyone*, only to kin who are *close*. The question this raises is: On what objective grounds do we decide which kin are 'close'? If kinship only generates obligation in some degree, then what is that degree? Is it to the eldest brother, but not to the second, or third? Is it to the first cousin, but not to the third ... or the thirtieth? Does the mother's side count, or only the father's, and if both in some degree, then in what degree? The gambit of grounding social obligation in kinship, being unpersuasive, is standardly deflected by a turn into the alley of choice.

The pitch in relation to choice tends to be that parents are obligated to look after babies since it is by parental choice offspring are sprung. But of two things one: either parents are obligated to progeny (a) because they chose them or (b) because they bore them. And if obligation is due to choice, then it is not due to biology. Suppose one chooses to adopt the progeny of others, and suppose it is the choice that binds. In that case, it follows one is just as obligated as if one had oneself engaged in the original coupling (assuming we are not to do with the blander sin of test-tubing).

If now we scan the position from the ascending side – with regard to grounding such an obligation as that to 'honour thy father and thy mother' – we may conclude that progeny owe fealty either (a) because parents 'begat' them (biological), or (b) because parents nurtured them (implicitly contractual). The first type of argument (obedience owed in exchange for procreation) tends to derive its strength from conflation with the second. For where the biological parent is withdrawn (abandonment, adoption) or demonstrably inept (gross neglect, serious maltreatment) the notion that s/he is owed a duty quite shrivels up. Once the notion of filial obligation shifts from dependency upon 'life' to dependency upon care, we observe a transition from a biological to a contractual ground. The crucial point about this second type of argument is not so much that it is specifically contractual as that it is inescapably non-biological.

So biological imagery in socio-political argument, whether now or then, is no more than that: imagery, metaphor. Let us then abandon further elaboration. The summary point is that we are not to see emphasis on 'blood' ties in the ancient world as a matter of genetic relations (on the order maybe of a 'selfish' gene) somehow directly dictating political allegiance. Biological kinship, real though it be, serves as nothing more than a limiting type of constitutional or ideological grid, on which autonomous socio-political relations, rights and duties, are enacted. It is not the genes – the actual biology of kinship – that dictate allegiance. Rather it is the allegiance that finds it convenient to package/present itself as kinship.

The relevance of relatedness by biology, or the theory of such relatedness, is that it does and is designed to heighten the sense of intimacy marking the relationship between the persons involved. For A to remark of B that she is 'flesh of my flesh', or 'bone of my bone' is a metaphor for proximity; it is the *ne plus ultra* of an indelible intimacy. It is an appeal to a connection, a demand for affection, a solicitation of loyalty. It does not matter that close relations often detest one another or that the bloodiest conflicts tend to be fratricidal – not least where siblings compete for the supreme power in a royal household.

We noted earlier that *spatial* and *productive* intimacy is a feature of the ancient world. Now we may add to this, via the centrality of kinship, both the fact and the ideology of a *genetic* proximity. In this world, human relations are intimate on every level. That sense of personal (not impersonal) exchange, as in Buber's 'I and Thou', extends to the governance of divinities. For ancient gods were not just plural, they were local. They were not indifferent to locality and particularity, since they were themselves ancestral and exclusive. Gods could be jealous, had favourites, were capable of, and could be moved by, emotion, and were in various ways bound by the human or part-human flotsam and jetsam that they themselves spawned.

On the one hand, intimacy and mutual exposure were untrammelled. On the other, custom was rigid and traditional authority unbridled. Government was limited in terms of its reach. But those who governed could do much as they liked within their remit. Privacy was a near impossibility. Individuality moreover was dangerous. One's defence lay not in a Weberian bureaucracy, but in a complex of kin and near-kin, of friends and allies. Hence a great emphasis upon observing custom, speaking well and effectively, retaining the loyalty of the extended family, being kind to strangers, and cultivating intense and reliable friendships extending beyond the family. Utterly intense trans-familial bonds offered relief from the cloying web of family. They also offered prospective protection against the perilous ups and downs of command in small states as also against the oppression marking later empires (St Augustine's 'great robber bands').

Certainly, the denizens of early systems were not capable of anomie; they were not diverted by radio, television, mobile phones, video games, nor by much in the way of foreign travel and other such forms of detachment and evasion. They were not cut off from one another by mutual ignorance or what we call privacy and individualism. Intimate, personal friendship was widely promoted as vital in part simply because, in the circumstances described, it was genuinely possible, and enjoyable, and profitable. One could no more do without the loyalty of family and friends then, than most of us can do without a pension or state-funded education now. In settings where virtually all relations are intensely personal, where what matters is who you are, not what you know, a person so cavalier as to dispense with close and intimate ties must appear not a little foolish, perhaps indeed a fool. Friends worth the name require a great deal in the way of time and attention. But moderns either do not have the time, or do not take it. They fall back upon their washing machines, dishwashers, cars, banks, telephones. By such means they are well able to divorce the practicalities of self-maintenance from intimacy and to insulate such intimates as they have from one another. Moderns may well 'network', but they (we) do not explore the souls of one another, and usually consider it socially inept (intrusive) to attempt it.

Modernity, so far from representing civilization, would appear – at least from an ancient perspective – to represent a new barbarism. Modernity is nervous in the face of self-revelation. Self is meant among us to be self-subsistent. Thus the probing Other comes to be represented more as peril than prospective ally. Promoters of self-enclosure, we fear self-disclosure. There is an exception to this (at one end) among some of the most ambitious who can make money from declaring what no one else will and (at the other end) among the poor and destitute who may flail and flash uninhibitedly since the space they have fallen into gives no cause to care. But there is a difficulty where those who directly command in modern conditions, cannot know themselves, and have no legitimate means of knowing one another.

The difficulty is, without significant self-disclosure, there can be no real moral development. The self that is hidden is a sustained lie to itself. The virtue of friendship, despite other limitations, is that it may develop in the subject a degree of self-awareness, self-understanding, self-acceptance and – by extension – an abstract empathy that carries wider political implications. The modern's self-disclosure is perhaps exhausted by confession of catechist to priest in some obscure cubicle. Perhaps it reaches its limit at the quay of the psychiatrist-boatman who purposes, for a substantial fee, to navigate one through stream of consciousness into self-awareness. But otherwise such revelations may be taken as a sign of weakness, as also dangerous.

If modernity is more concerned with liberty than friendship, and with liberty indeed as the flip side of power (devolved), then self-disclosure may be precisely what moderns are compelled to avoid. All who would exercise power over others require a degree of distance from them. The modern politician, in a democratic state, may wish to appear an ordinary person, and even accessible in a populist way, but cannot afford to give too much away. How relevant is friendship to politics in modernity? How much genuine disclosure and intimate but politicized bonding can we and ought we to sustain? If the friendships of the ancients cannot be our own, what can we learn from them that may be of value in our own time?

Ten Aspects of Friendship for Modernity

In what follows, friendship of some sort (its varieties are not properly attended to) is assumed to be irretrievably linked to politics. If one says (at the extreme) that politics is merely about obtaining and maintaining power, and that it turns round recognizing and creating enemies, it remains that even this process dictates some form of combination among those who either do, or aspire to, command. This then raises the question of the type(s) of bonding that characterize politics, and how far it may be reasonable to speak of – and even to recommend – such bonding as 'friendship'.

To begin to respond to that question we need, first, to develop a basic, outline construct of friendship that takes proper account of modern conditions and needs. We also require a construct that is roughly consistent with key insights of ancient writers, given that later writing on the subject is (in sum) exiguous, impoverished and, not least, besieged. We need a grid that maintains an overt connection between friendship (a) as an intimate dyadic tie, (b) as somehow expressive of a broader political ethic and (c) as connected to the brute fact of socio-political networks. This grid should enable us to plot a logical progression from the intimacy of the private circle to the public disclosure involved in open forums.

First, and fairly obviously, friendship is never to do with an agent or subject taken singly. It concerns some type of *relationship*, whether (a) interactive, as between subject and subject, or (b) unilateral, as from one subject to another – though (a) is the more common construct.

Second, the key initial component in the relationship turns round a basic sentiment of *affection* – one dimension of which is care or *caritas* – of one for another or others (putting aside for now the question whether the affection is interactive or unilateral).

We need not initially be too restrictive regarding the *depth* or *character* of this affection. At one end, it may be plainly *carnal* – involving longing, sexuality, even intercourse. At the other, it may be severely *intellectual*, or radically political and mobilizational, venting itself via various expressions of concern and support, perhaps moral, material or psychological.

Affection has an enormous range – from mawkish to morbid. Swathes of it can be ruled out as 'infatuation', obsession, neurosis and even cunning, as among ardent stalkers, mewling fans and other such idolaters. The affection often expressed by supporters for favoured politicians need not be any more or less rational than that of howling teens for pop stars. It can be difficult to judge whether any affection is genuine or false, perfectly apt or entirely vicious. What is meat for one is the poison of another. Young people today abide far longer in the care of their seniors than used to be. Similarly, the old grow older than they used to do. Thus those with seniority and power today are well positioned to sit upon young passion, seeing it as an inconvenience.

Affection – for all of being inept or imprudent – remains what it is, among young or old. An individual of independent mind or means will likely be far more indifferent to the negative judgements of peers. The conformist or placeman, by contrast, steeply dependent upon the support and guidance of others (parents, patrons, backers, whatever), enjoys far less leeway. At the end, what affection is, and whether it is genuine, and appropriate, may be best left to whoever owns it. In any of its forms it may grow cold or, by the same token, flower in what appear unlikely beds (like those of the arranged marriage).

Certainly we do not prove that affection is false simply by showing that it may wane (for whatever reason: absence, fatigue, overexposure, disappointment, etc). It would be perverse to demonstrate that Roman Empire never was by reference to the fact that it declined. Affection, tenacious or fleeting, may be excited by almost any cause. It may spring from delight in another's performance or skill. Witness and admire a student sailing through an exam; a lecturer conveying an idea with economy and wit; a singer making intelligent and elegant use of a limited voice. (Admiration and affection are sometimes hard to distinguish.)

Attraction to another may be rooted as much in difference as in similarity. One may be drawn to those who differ by their difference, to the foreigner by foreignness, and to the vulnerable by vulnerability. One may be drawn to others as much because they stand apart as because they blend, because they excite or console, because they protest or acquiesce. Who is to say what may not open a window to affection? It may be exotic, like beauty and wit. It may be banal, like sociability and 'company'. It may be valuable, like an elegant frock and diamond-freighted cleavage. It may be curious, like idle curiosity. Indeed, it may be moral or immoral – like honesty and directness, or flexibility and guile, or ruthlessness and rottweiler tenacity.

Affection may prompt its owner to do almost anything: physically to embrace; merely fondly to gaze upon; but then to avoid or altogether abandon (the poor mother surrenders the child to another in hopes of giving it a better life). Affection may prompt one warmly to look after the recipient, like a nurse, or coolly, like a benefactor. It may excite support, as of an endearing rascal, perhaps a magician, politician, preacher, CEO or some similar con or fun artist(e). So affection or endearment is a perfectly *positive* phenomenon *in se*, despite the fact that it may be expressed unhappily and even perversely. It is highly variable regarding those to whom it is directed, the causes that may excite it, and the beneficial/nefarious consequences that come in train.

Third, this relationship of affection may either be reciprocal or unilateral. To say that a friendship is *reciprocal* is not to claim any specific degree of reciprocity – not at least beyond some necessary minimum. In reciprocal friendship, some type of affection is both given and returned. The threshold of that return is whatever satisfies the genuine need of one who extends affection. Reciprocal affection remains a circular engagement, though the *thickness* of the circle varies, taking account either of the number of persons entering it or of the quantity/quality of the affection they reciprocate. The lover and the beloved, the mentor and apprentice, the star and the fan may well not, in the fullest sense, be 'friends', but are locked none the less into a circle of affection, however thick, however thin.

Unilateral affection, by contrast, at least in one of its key dimensions, can be described as instancing the generalized trait of 'friendliness'. Friendliness in a person is like the essence of a flower distilled as perfume: it gives itself up to the open air, without restriction to some narrow and predetermined target. Unilateral affection may be expressed in any number of ways. It may take the form of help to strangers, anonymous assistance to the distressed, or the unrequited love of known benefactors – as with a devoted mother or father, or of the attentive philanthropist. Parents often do for children in ways the latter cannot possibly return. Carers constantly attend to the needs of those who are in ill-health, often just because ... they *care*. A good teacher attends to the needs of pupils without the least sense that these beneficiaries may somehow ultimately reward the silent affection of the benefactor. Many agents entertain affection for their region, their environment, their people or indeed for people at large, and unilaterally give themselves up to the business of defending and improving these. Such action lies well beyond any prospect of return. Unilateral affection, then – that which is only given and never received – is socially real and often morally appropriate.

Fourth, friendship, as a circle of reciprocal affection, is (in one sense) *bounded*. For it is *intimate* and has obvious *numerical limits*. The sky is not the limit with regard to the numbers who may be friends. And yet, though there is a limit, it is impossible properly to specify what it may be. Earlier writers standardly claim that those who have lots of friends, by the same token have none, which is often true. For some may traffic with many without particular affection for any. Nonetheless, it is obvious that some have a greater capacity for friendship than others. Bill Clinton is very likely one of these. But since modern elites do not celebrate friendship, it is difficult to know if and how far they practice it. Thus, though we can say that the friendship of reciprocal affection is necessarily limited, we cannot say with equal confidence what its upper numerical limits are. There are those who have a genuine gift for friendship and are well able to sustain a wide range of reciprocal intimacies. By contrast, many seem able to sustain only the narrowest ties, and some – even where they devoutly wish it otherwise – may sustain none at all.

The friendship of reciprocal affection is bounded, consistent with the agent's capacity for it. An exclusive friendship in which there is none but the single other may of course flourish. But it is just as likely to prove desultory, desiccated, stultifying – both morally and imaginatively. (That is reported to have been the case even for Walt Disney and his angularly negative wife.) Friendships with several may revive or reinvigorate the one; and it may be much the same with friendships across cultures. To have friends only within the family or church or society or race or state is often hard to avoid. Still, it likely hints at stultification, sometimes to the point of immorality, and even civic irresponsibility. Simultaneous relations are not necessarily shallow. Exclusive relations are not necessarily deep.

Affection for friends may be much the same as affection for cities: if you know only one you may know it well; but if you have knowledge of others, you may learn more of your own, and appreciate it better. In any event, any circle of mutual affection, whether those engaged are few or several, remains bounded. That is to say, a friendship circle requires focusing upon some, and for that reason is not in itself a universal alliance. As the focus of a friendship circle is upon its members, it is in such degree exclusionary – unless of course there is something in the local that is itself universal, and unless other connections of a relevant sort spiral out from it.

The self is not just a given; it is a work in progress. It can be an orchid. It can be a weed. It requires cultivation. Absent some kindly human presence – as cases of feral children show – the self *in se* can be no more meaningfully human than an embryo. The self is responsive to affection, and sensitive to enmity. The self knows itself in the mirror of others' regard. The attentiveness of that regard is not everything, but matters hugely. The self can never be properly explored in the absence of the other. If 'hell is other people' (Sartre) – and it sometimes is – there is a circle beneath hell marked by the complete absence of others. The feral child is simply unaware of the waste to which its isolation consigns it. The self profits from the other, if it is lucky, and it can profit the other, if it is attentive.

A part of the moral concern of every person must be with self-improvement. That in turn is a condition for social and political improvement. An enhanced knowledge of the world, and of self in the world, is the ground of an improving capacity for dealing with others. That knowledge always starts in a small circle; it is not an option without society; it is dented and endangered by denial of affection from some concrete source (as distinct from 'society' at large). The affection of some friendship circle, however limited, seems indispensable to growth and to a wider moral sensibility. In this sense small circles may be universally important, by way of grounding personality, generating a sense of self, of self-worth, and of the worth of others. Such intimacy may be located in caring homes, in foster families, in schools with small classes, etc. In sum, the local contains within itself the germ of its negation – which is to say that it is never exclusively parochial.

To say that reciprocal relationships are intimate, is not the same as saying they are private rather than public. Take the case of the novelist who appears before her public at a reading in a small bookstore, and who enjoys, by virtue of the reciprocal and interactive character of this function, a certain intimacy with that assembly. This gathering, despite access and proximity, is nonetheless public. Its intimacy – smallness of scale and interactive structure – in no way diminishes its character as a public event.

In parallel, the wider public that reads the author's books may do so in private, but without intimacy. Observe the sequence of solitary individuals – in a cloistered study, on a library lawn, in the cabin of a plane, lounging on some beach – where the relationship of author to reader is unilateral and non-interactive. The world the novelist reveals to the unknown reader may not appear at all anonymous or impersonal. It may, on the contrary, strike the reader – just like the small, live audience – as intensely personal. The reader's access to the author may appear as vivid and direct as can be. Thus the relationship that is anonymous, at arm's length, unilateral, nonreciprocal, though it is not circular or interactive, and though in that sense it is not intimate, may all the same be private and intensely significant. That consideration has wider significance regarding the prospective value and impact of unilateral friendships or generalized friendliness.

Reciprocity, and the intimacy peculiar to it, place limits (however indeterminate) on the numerical extent of a friendship. Where an agent has many dyadic friends, these, though perhaps well-placed in turn to be friendly, yet need not be, and sometimes cannot be, due to some lack of congruence between them. These serial amities, of A to B and A to C, all help to define A, but do not allow the inference that B & C are necessarily bound reciprocally one to another. The friendship of A both to B and to C thus does not mean that B & C enjoy any direct, reciprocal friendship themselves. In modern settings, B & C are likely never even to meet. All the same, though the 'friend-of-a-friend' syndrome does not directly generate ancillary dyads, it does contain some more general disposition towards friendship. That disposition reveals itself in unilateral friendships and in networks of friends, though these are totally inconsequential unless marked and buoyed by some fairly plain and robust common ethic.

On the reciprocal view, friendships are always intimate, even where diffuse. If reciprocal friendship is always dual and intimate, then though there may be friendship within groups, there is no friendship of groups. On the reciprocal view, there may be friendship within, but not of, the mass. Reciprocal friendship does not come *en masse*. There is no dyadic friendship as of all citizens, or of all nationals, or of any group too large to accommodate reciprocity. The state, nation, region, city can never enjoy friendship of this type. Friendship, however, does not end in dyads, though that is normally where it begins. Dyadic friendship has a universal substratum, as in the example that it sets, the ethic that underlies it, the unilateral offshoots that spring from it, and the generalized friendliness it can bestow upon society at large as a regnant morality.

The particular knot of dyadic friendship contains the germ of its own sublimation. This germ is the element of affection for another or others, of caring for these, of seeking their happiness and well-being, of being welcoming and kindly – even should one reach the point where these dispositions are not reciprocated, or cannot be reciprocated, or where reciprocity is simply not sought. We draw nearer to the idea of friendship as a mass phenomenon, within society as a whole, when we concentrate upon this abstracted germ of affection, this unilateral offshoot, this generalized species of *friendliness*, in which the reciprocity itself is grounded.

We do not learn the reciprocity – 'Do unto others as you would be done by' – from the solitary self. The ill-nurtured self may have no self-respect or self-love; thus one cannot teach it respect for others on that basis. Positive reciprocity is grounded only in an already socialized and reciprocal existence. Its beneficiary, already dipped in affection, already confident and respectful of self because a recipient of past or present trust and affection, can extract from that experience a germ of friendliness, that may now be rendered unilateral, which is to say abstract. This friendliness is sometimes private, sometimes public; it is sometimes domestic, sometimes international. It is aimed at the other who may not be seen or heard. It may be directed even at future generations without the least expectation or possibility of return or gain. Friendliness is a morality learned from circles of friends – whether located within or beyond the family. The loss or denial of mutual friendship to any agent may in turn prejudice the prospects of friendliness in that agent. Yet even a *memory* of a friendship may suffice to keep the morality of friendliness abroad.

Fifth, reciprocal friendship is in some fashion an *equal* relationship. It is equal in that there is some minimum of affection shown by one friend and returned in some form by the other. The reciprocal relationship, though dyadic, also accommodates links to one, several, or many, but not directly to a mass – except by example and the complex circuitry of influence. Friendships, however, are only equal *in some respects*. They are always unequal in others. If we intend by 'equality', the elimination of all difference whatever between A and B, then we are confounding equality with identity. *Equality* presupposes the distinction, A, B, which can be read off either as 'A & B' or as 'A or B'. That is to say, equality presupposes a similarity between two persons, such that they may both combine and part without prejudice to the distinctiveness of each. *Identity*, on the other hand, hypothesizes the merger, AB, such that there is no difference, and thus no option either to combine or separate. Taking identity as absolute, and accepting that equality is not identity, we shall accept that equality is never absolute, anywhere, including the equality in friendship.

Every reciprocal friendship is, in different senses, equal and unequal, though the balance (or imbalance) can vary hugely in any given case. There may be friendship between the experienced and the inexperienced, old and young, rich and poor, parent and progeny, sound and lame, teacher and taught, mentor and mentored, yellow and brown, black and white, Muslim and Jew, Montagu and Capulet, Republican and Democrat. That is to say, there may be notable inequalities between the parties to a friendship without prejudice to the core equality that gives the relationship wings. But the more the inequalities (of other types) outweigh the equality (of shared mutual affection), then the more likely is the friendship to retreat from mutual affection, to unilateral affection, and possibly end in loss of affection altogether.

What we shall not wish too simplistically to claim is that, (a) the more equal the parties, the more stable shall be the friendship, and (b) the less equal, the more unstable. For the key element in the reciprocal friendship is some exchange of affection. And if that is great and mutual it will outweigh by far all other concerns. If most friendships tend to be between relatively equal parties, that does not appear to render these relationships, in our age, any less brittle. All the same, a large part of the foundation of mutual affection, where it is sustained, lies in mutual understanding.

Large inequalities of various sorts (especially wealth, position and experience) may readily generate clouds of incomprehension that soak affection to the point of drowning it. At the heart of friendship lies mutual affection, but at the bottom of such affection there lies in turn mutual openness and accessibility. If the one party cannot know the other, or loses touch with the other, due to some great gap in rank or power, then this may turn the relationship more into one of propitiation than friendship proper. If there is some equality of affection in mutual friendship, based upon some *res publica* – in the sense of interpersonal knowledge of and between one and the other – then friendship of a reciprocal sort between the worshipper and her God seems excluded. Large inequalities, in this way, tend not to accommodate friendship, properly speaking, but lose ground to a type of patron-client relationship, which remains reciprocal, but is far from equal.

If then great power tends to exclude reciprocal friendship and to feed dependency, it does so by virtue of veiling one prospective friend from another. It does so by sharply diminishing common knowledge and common exposure. It does so by replacing knowledge that is certain (or deemed certain, because personally attested to) with the indirect knowledge of rumour and conjecture. Thus the intuitive rapport based on a common world possessed in common may give way to reticence in judgement and even fearfulness of judgement. To lose the capacity for free and unflustered exchange must corrode the prospect of reciprocal friendship. If there are great and growing gaps between strata in a society – races, classes, sexes, clans, tribes, religions – there may emerge in parallel a diminished ability to forge mutual friendships across these strata.

The two intuitive options, where reciprocity is valued, must either be to diminish stark social cleavages, or to assimilate exemplary agents from lower into higher strata. The former is the option of every welfare state. The latter is the procedure historically followed in England, after 1888 in Brazil, and increasingly from 1965 in the United States. Both policies have much to recommend them and neither is a panacea. There is no question that a generalized friendliness in society can check the downside of stark social cleavage. On the other hand, stark social cleavage may tend as such to exclude the prospect of friendliness across strata. The great question is whether concentrated power must be checked to enable the emergence of societies based on principles of friendliness, or whether this generalized friendliness is itself an effective means of corroding vast concentrations of power.

It makes perfectly good sense, however, to entertain the possibility that reciprocal friendship may both establish and subvert social inequality. Let us take the second, or more paradoxical, of these possibilities. Let us say that elite agents need allies to secure, maintain and grow power. We know that friendship can merge with cronyism. If agents are friends, enter into alliance, and exploit personal connections to further their own good at the expense of the public, we can think of this as friendship – on the model of cronyism and nepotism, undercutting equality. That is, the collusion of a few, equal between themselves, may generate a power or wealth that distances them from the many, and indeed sets them above the rest. Hence one type of equality – in this case nefarious – may undercut another sort, perhaps more virtuous.

We can then see that an alliance, hypothetically between two or more equal parties, can subvert justice, and pervert the judicial process so that it is not equally fair to all citizens. Suppose a man is wantonly murdered by armed elements within the police and the investigation of this affair is choked off by officers within the force who act as 'brothers' and even threaten to go on strike should prosecutions be brought. Here we can see three things in play: (1) an equality in friendship among a small number who pervert justice; (2) an ideal of more comprehensive equality between the citizens or residents of the jurisdiction in question; (3) defeat of equality of the first by means of an equality of the second. If then friendship must be held to involve an equality, it is clear this must be *equality of some particular type* – not some notion of *equality as such*. Reciprocal friendships will simultaneously affirm (some) equality while generating (some other) inequality – meaning inequity. It goes without saying that reciprocal friendships promote some sort of equality. The question is 'what sort'. The distinction we shall look for is that between types that are fair and types that are not – between the equitable and inequitable.

It will not hurt yet again to stress the contradictoriness internal to equality, so that we keep the fuller picture in view. If voters go to the polls to elect a government, they are all equal at the point of voting. But the morning (or week or month) after, what the equality of the vote has thrown up is a government with (unequal) power over its erstwhile competitors. In education we may aim for equality of outcome ('no child left behind'), especially in the earliest years, where we seek to attain universal basic literacy and numeracy. But in education we may equally aim for equality of opportunity ('careers open to talent'), especially in later years, where the object is to train specialists in advanced skills and where only a small number will be fit to do these jobs.

Equality of outcome and equality of opportunity each has its place in the determinate context x or y – these being different contexts. But both of these are types of educational equality and the one is inconsistent with the other, taking account of the goals aimed at. In one case the concern is to bring all equally to a certain level. In the other case, it is to allow all to compete, fairly, but only in order to bring the best to the fore, and (alas) to exclude the rest. Equality of outcome defeats equality of opportunity and vice versa; both may be needed on different occasions. In schools, in corporations, in governments there will always be some place for both. Yet it is always necessary to choose between them, in any given setting, at any given time, in respect to some determinate end. In choosing one over the other it will never be the case, and can never be the case, that one is just choosing equality full-stop. The different types of equality are mutually contradictory. Thus to embrace equality as such, indeed to promote equality as some species of unqualified absolute, would be foolish, since all it would amount to is the embrace of an elaborate self-contradiction. In practice then equality is always a matter of choosing some particular type of equality, and – by the same token – rejecting some other.

If we bring the discussion directly back to reciprocal friendship, we can see that the latter involves a particular type of equality. Friendship is not necessarily good or bad for that reason. Any type of equality may serve good or bad ends. It may be deployed appropriately or inappropriately. And so it is with the equality engaged in reciprocal friendship. The question is whether such friendship lends itself *of necessity* to injustice of a wider sort, or not. It is obvious it *may* do. It is not obvious it *must* do. We readily see that friendship may be misused. The problem is to explore how the morality of the thing can be got to avoid such errors. The key question here may be to distinguish between friendship as brute affection, as distinct from affection enfiladed with some presumption of worth, including moral worth.

Let us now hypothesize that affection is in part a response to what is admired. Let us follow this up by winnowing out any assumption that there can really be such a thing as *brute* (wholly unreflective) affection. We may now then be entitled to suppose that affection, in different ways, (a) can be modulated, (b) will be modulated, and (c) ought to be modulated in some degree as a function of moral performance. No *perception* can be regarded as unmediated by some attribution of value (or disvalue). Thus no fact (the supposed item *perceived*) can be taken to be unmediated by the attribution of value or disvalue. And we seem entitled to extend this train of reasoning to affection. Thus we shall avoid the temptation of ever conceiving affection as bare matter of fact.

Sixth, even reciprocal friendship involves an *asymmetrical sharing*. In friendship between A and B, we know A and B share something. The least we know is that A is drawn to B and vice versa: they share a mutual attraction. We know that the substratum of this attraction, in the case of each of the parties, may itself somehow diverge. A may say, 'I like B due to B's calmness under fire'. By contrast, B may say, 'I like A due to A's fastidious attention to detail'. Or A may be shy, and likes it that B is bold. Or B may be outgoing, and likes it that A is a homebody. So A and B may be drawn to one another, and share a mutual attraction. But the trait in B that A admires may wildly diverge from the trait in A that B admires. In this there is mutual attraction and a common bond that is generated by divergent properties. Let's call this asymmetry a Type-One Divergence (Tod1).

Let us now consider a more challenging type of asymmetry. Suppose that A and B are drawn to one another, not by different and overlapping features, but by some feature that seems to be identical for both parties. This may be that A and B discover a mutual compatibility in their shared love of music, or of political engagement, or sport, or the quiet life, or of some cultural datum, like language, or of some broad cultural mesh (they may both be Jewish or Anglo or Amish or Argentine or American or African-American or Antipodean and so on). Here then we again identify a shared feature. But in this case there seems to be no divergence at all, in that the parties to the relationship converge in their admiration of a trait that is the same for both of them. Thus A and B view their relationship as more unitary than complementary, knotted by some seamless Guardian nod. Let's then call this a Type-Two Divergence (Tod2), for the reason that it is (a) different to Tod1, (b) at least *less* divergent than Tod1 – though (c) possibly not divergent at all.

It cannot take long for the position at Tod2 to be seen to fray. One is not identical with one's friend. One's friend (so far) is not a clone of one's self. Any relationship, from casual meeting to enduring alliance, implies separateness, or separability. For there to be 'partners', they must be mutually distinguishable. A can only befriend B on condition A and B are distinct. The very term 'pal' or 'partner' implies a relationship and that someone *else* is in it. If A and B share *one* wretched cigarette or candy bar, each consumes a *different* part of the shared bar. If A and B stand back to back, or side by side, they enjoy different fields of vision. If A suffers trauma, and B is unaware of the fact, it is A who is the immediate victim, not B. And if A and B share a love of music, and attend some given concert, some unavoidable divergence is built into how and what they experience. A may be particularly attentive to the lead singer, B to the backing group; their levels of attention move up and down, differently; and however close the patterns of focus in A and B, they are never identical.

We reach the conclusion, even for Tod2, that what is shared in friendship always involves some degree of divergence and non-identity. Even where the object of the mutual attraction is in some sense the same, it can be seen that this is not quite so. It is never the case that what attracts A to B is exactly identical to what attracts B to A – no matter that the divergence is greater in some cases (Tod1) than in others (Tod2). As regards men and women, this notion is commonly captured thus: '*Vive la différence*!' But the particular example does not matter. There is always some genetic and phenotypic difference, no matter how similar the friends A and B may appear. There is always some positional and experiential difference, no matter how proximate A and B are. There is always psychological difference, never mind the level or intensity of accord. Thus we are not entitled to assume, wherever A fondly beholds B, that A sees exactly what B sees when B, in turn, fondly beholds A – however much wedded both may be to the notion that each is to the other 'another self'.

Seventh, the friendship relationship, reciprocal or unilateral, is not just abstractly psychological but is, more precisely, somehow *moral*. Let us take a variety of cases that fall under the description of friendship. Let's concentrate on straightforward dyadic relationships – such as two companions, or a mate and her partner, a worker and co-worker, a soldier and her buddy, a child and his playmate, a mother and her son, a father and his daughter, and so on endlessly. In so many of these relationships, that are marked by affection, even if there is some significant power gap, we commonly remark some sense of a reciprocal duty owed by one to the other, even if duty is not the defining aspect of the relationship. For one may have a duty to a person one dislikes; and one may like a person to whom one owes no duty. What the exact morality of friendship may be – the rules on which it is based – is another matter; but that friendship is grounded in morality, and in the rules attaching thereto, is not easily avoided.

Eighth, the moral character of the relationship between friends is voluntary and *contractual*. Morality is as a matter of course relational. Its exercise must depend upon some supposition of free will. Agency is implicit in any morality, including that attending friendship. Many moral duties are externally imposed, assuming capacity – as where we rightly feel obliged to lend assistance to the hit-and-run victim whom we do not know, or rescue some stranger from drowning, or go the help of a visitor set upon by thugs. If it is an externally imposed duty that one ought to seek friends – and it is – that duty does not extend to seeking the specific friendship of A or B. Any such specific attachment, as to A or B, is freely assumed; and no sooner is that relationship (of affection and reciprocity) in place, than some obligation of particular care and concern arises from it.

The obligation to the friend, like any other, is based on some notion of free will. But the obligation to the friend is voluntary in a specifically *contractual* sense. Though the contractual element in friendship is usually implicit or *sotto voce*, it is also often enough rendered explicit, at the extreme in declarations of support, or allegiance, or marriage. So the contours of a friendship may be expressly chiselled by the parties themselves. Alternatively, the vessel holding it may be a balloon of ready-to-hand social conventions into which the friends lightly step for the ascent. In as far as friendship is an affective relationship, of a reciprocal, intimate and voluntary (or contractual) type, borne along by a strong moral updraft, the question arising concerns the direction and nature of that morality.

Ninth, the element of first importance in the content of friendship as a moral matter is the specific morality of *tolerance* of divergent judgement. Whatever imagery we affect relating to the notion of friends as one, as united, as some indissoluble whole, we always return to their necessary alterity. Friendship based on the assumption of some granitic unity of outlook is quite unsuited to modernity. Individuals are highly diverse; and if anything, fortunately or not, they are growing more so. To expect to encounter and to live with people, whose views are exactly congruent with our own, borders on the simplistic gravitating towards the absurd. It is based on the assumption of an epistemologically closed universe, an assumption today rendered wholly inapplicable. Different parts of the world intermingle, knowledge is both vast and uncertain. In such a world of flux, intelligent friends cannot, for a start, expect to know everything. Increasingly they specialize in different directions to increase the range of knowledge they can bring to bear between them. If they cannot expect even to know everything (that matters), then they cannot begin to think – if they *think* – that they can possibly *agree* upon everything (that matters).

The notion of a *fully achieved* friendship seems a vacuous aspiration. The idea that one can lose oneself in another person, as opposed to losing oneself full-stop, seems misplaced. A friend is one in whose company one is comfortable, but not lost. The aspiration caught up in supposedly fully achieved friendship – as simple merger, the elimination of difference between self and other – may not only be illusory but perverse. Where marriage is purveyed as simple merger, it tends to translate as absorption – usually (but not always) of the woman by the man and/or his family. A total unity, including a total unity of opinion, is repugnant, even were it desirable. Typically where the vote is 70% or more for a given candidate, we know straightaway that the election is rigged.

Unanimity of opinion is either a function of repression or self-delusion or both. We know that actual unanimity of opinion exists in no large cohort. We also know that there is widespread fear in large systems among individuals that they may suffer for being different or for expressing difference. There is fear they may be singled out, cut off, boxed in, and constituted as vulnerable minorities. But if difference is inescapable, unless we allow it to be repressed, then in friendship as elsewhere we have to allow it to surface by removing fear of truthful expression – even where we dislike the result.

As something is always shared in friendship, there is then also some residual unity. But it need not be unity of opinion, such as that Picasso was a great painter and Dali was not, or that G.W. Bush was a lousy president and Clinton not, or that Popper was a major philosopher and Russell not quite, or that Elvis Presley could not cut a lyric by contrast with Paul Robeson or Frankie Sinatra. In any intellectual association, and most others, some expression of opinion comes with the turf. If a friendship is marked by mere conformity this suggests that it is pre-argumentative, which also means untested in any adult way, and thus likely not long sustainable. The question in friendship cannot be, 'Do we agree?', but rather, 'Can we affectionately and amicably mediate difference?' A 'friend' who insists on agreement is like a comic and his straight man, a cowboy and his sidekick, a star and her fans, the populist politician and her fanatical base, or the dodgy holy man – rabbi, priest or imam – who encourages dogmatic and exclusionary belief as the supreme and sole virtue.

Unity as shared affection is crucial to reciprocity in friendship. Unity as conformity of opinion is stifling and spurious. One of the very most important things a person can seek is to understand the world, scientifically and morally. One of the most appealing means to this is through the friendship of those who assist in the quest. The largest body of extant writings on friendship comes to us from the ancient Greeks. These people were in no way 'irreligious'; they were awash with priests and gods; they also privileged the integrity of rational discourse; belief and reason were not seen as opposites (as with Kierkegaard and many who follow him). Belief, like hypothesis, can be seen as a necessary beginning, not an end. To treat it as an end ... is a dead end.

Indeed, how, *on grounds of faith*, can one choose between Jove and Jehovah, Allah and the Buddha, Confucius and Augustine, nuclear fission and nuclear fusion? All faith, all revelation, is equally dogmatic, and each of its expressions can only recommend itself. Beliefs relentlessly differ, and one cannot satisfy the hunger of resolution merely by heaping on more belief. Differences of initial belief, if resolvable, are resolved by reason. If reason is ungodly, then so is faith. For if some all-powerful being has created human nature; if human nature is thus divinely endowed; and if our nature is a mix (as it is) of belief and reason; then reason too should be viewed as a divine gift, sacrilegious to repudiate. If the ancient Greeks could take some such view, rejecting neither belief nor reason, then it may be presumptuous of any contemporary to spit upon their lead.

It is often argued that Judaism is a community sustained by bonds of faith mediated by unceasing rationality – argument. While it is difficult to follow exaggerated claims that the oldest part of the Christian Bible – for Jews the Torah – shows Abraham and Moses genuinely quarrelling with God, it is not hard to make a more modest case. For there remains a hugely creative tension in Judaism (one sees some of this in the Book of Job) that much orthodox Christianity, and especially Protestant fundamentalism, shamefully lacks. It is one thing to view the Bible as perfectly true, and another to assume that truth to be perfectly transparent, that it can be got at without sustained reflection and argument, or that such argument can ever be deemed closed.

One attractive view of the Jewish idea is that man is made in the image of Jehovah, is given a holy text (the Torah), is endowed with reason as a means of eliciting the truth of that text, such that learned religious argument remains ever vital to achieving understanding of Jehovah's will. To be able to nail (through argument) some signal error in standard interpretations of the Torah becomes hugely important, not as an isolated intellectual accomplishment, but as a closer approximation to the will of God. So in the mainstream of the Jewish theological tradition, argument is not reprehensible, is not ungodly, is not quashed. (If this portrait is accurate, all well and good; and if it is not, then it ought to be.)

We cannot say that there is parallel openness to rational debate within the Catholic and Protestant hierarchies in relation to such ontological concerns as biological evolution and stem-cell research. The point of this in any case is that there are no grounds for maintaining that religion must perforce exclude rational argument, even of the most insistent type. Those who defend their religion in irrational terms only demonstrate the inanity of their defence. Those who attack all religion as necessarily irrational prove less than impressive as historians of ideas.

The application of these considerations to the morality of friendship seems clear. A reciprocal friendship, one that is ongoing, must mediate epistemological difference, not view it as destructive and out of bounds. The object of friendship cannot be simply to agree. It is to be joined in a process of common rationality, which is pursued as far as it has to be, without prejudice to the affection by which parties to the pursuit are bound. The key component of friendship, in the face of divergent understandings, does not then turn round simple agreement or disagreement. It turns round shared affection and amicable pursuit of resolution. This pursuit may on occasion be relinquished by both sides (they 'agree to disagree') should disputatiousness undermine affection itself. And that is why the ninth feature of friendship, the morality of *tolerance*, matters so hugely. It involves prioritizing an underlying mutual affection over a perhaps irresolvable difference of perception or understanding, whether merely empirical or deeply metaphysical. And it involves drawing back from any tendency ever to equate the friend with, or reduce the friend to, some judgement s/he makes, and from which one's own judgement diverges. It involves the friend, A, never acting against the friend, B, by withdrawal of affection, in virtue of B arguing counter to some thesis as entertained by A.

Tenth, the practice of friendship can have a beneficial impact on society at large. Although relations of reciprocity are not mass relations, they nonetheless point well beyond dyads. Though reciprocal friendship is always an intimate relationship, it may indirectly impact society as a whole. (1) The moral example extracted from reciprocal friendships may be replicated by other dyads. (2) The moral example of selflessness, commitment, tolerance and rationality internal to the dyad often transcends it. (3i) Reciprocal friendships may spiral off into interlocking chains of friendly networks, and dyads thus linked may achieve some greater good. (4) Reciprocal friendships contain the germ of unilateral friendships – of a generalized friendliness. So it is a mistake to see dyadic friendship, the most intimate of friendship's forms – within or across gender, whether carnal or ascetic, determined by age or not – as devoid of a wider political impact.

Yet there can, properly speaking, be no *mass* of friends, no *pile* of pals, no heap of *close* relations, no total and indistinct unity of all citizens. There can be no family or city or region in which everyone is equally a personal friend to everyone else. This cannot be. Nor should we aspire to it. The outcome otherwise must be much the same as with our joint-stock companies – today's corporations. These were promoted in the nineteenth century and earlier as democratic in the sense of being owned by the shareholder and thus subject to owner control. Today, instead of that, a small number of managers, with vastly concentrated powers, have positioned themselves to do pretty much as they wish, domestically and beyond, all in the name of millions of dispersed, anonymous and anaesthetized holders of shares, who are in most respects quite out of the loop. There is no solace in the thought that such corporations as Enron and Worldcom are quite typical. But there is sense in the thought that all such should be checked and balanced.

We have no need of a regime of instant intimate friends, giving rise as it must to the Leviathan-manager. We have no need for a joint-stock company of followers hoping and pretending to be close to a gate-keeper they can never know. We have no need of yet another Leader of homogenized little people, the Leader who, now in the name of Friendship, stands in stiletto heels on a herd of bent backs (the neo-modern version of backstabbing), urging them along. We have no need of a society-wide corporation of friends, subject to some supreme manager – who knows no one in particular, yet claims to speak for all; who is humanly cut off from others, but professes to know their pain; who is on a footing of equality with none, yet speaks for a universal friendship beyond achieving. It would be all too easy to establish distant and impersonal control in the name of friendship. Who could speak against it? Anyone who did would be no 'friend'. But no nation or state, though friendships may suffuse it, is capable of maintaining direct relationships – let alone reciprocal friendships – between each citizen and all her peers. To erect institutions that pretend to achieve this would point towards the ultimate in despotism.

If one could be a friend to all, inclusively, that would be well and good. Such indeed would be the condition, following Aristotle, on which we could entirely dispense with the formality of justice. But a homogenized and massed friendship – that eliminates dyads, obliterates distance, turns friendliness directly into friendship – is an impossibility. A dyad is, as a matter of course, intimate even if not always or necessarily private. And friendliness, as important as it is to oil the machinery of social interaction and to forge political cohesiveness, is not itself friendship. Particulars, like friendship dyads, give rise to universals, like friendliness. But such emergent universals do not in turn wipe out the particulars in which their continued existence is grounded. Friendship cannot characterize all social interactions as such – given that it starts by attending to what is small, local, particular. But that cannot be an excuse for omitting friendship in at least one or some cases and friendliness in most others. Thus does one transmit a spirit of kindliness throughout society. The spirit of unilateral friendliness, which is how one builds 'a kinder gentler society', is learned best from the practice of dyads.

Friendship itself is an ultimate in desirability. And it ought to be the ultimate check on despotism. Dyadic friendship generally, the small field in which one expresses sustained affection and practices care – not only or even especially marriage – ought to be regarded as the nub of civil society, applying checks and balances to one another, and ultimately to the apparatus of government as a whole. Unilateral friendships – a generalized disposition towards friendliness – ought to be viewed as the universal moral imperative deriving from these dyads. They ought to become the constitutional bedrock of civil society in the Open Society. Children ought to be encouraged to have friends, no less than adults. They ought to be taught to cultivate at least one or two others, without regard to future material gain. They ought thus learn to relate and to be related in a civilized and disinterested way. Everyone should be taught to care for someone, to mentor someone, to be on the qui vive for another – no matter difference or sameness, as of age, gender, condition, race, nation etc.

It was observed of a famous sociologist of the last century, that he had a tragic flaw. It was an obsession with keeping his own counsel. He was attributed the view that friends should always be treated as if one day they will be enemies and enemies as if one day they will be friends. It is good counsel for a steady life, but counsel, too, perhaps, for a fairly empty one. It is the perfect ground for authoritarianism. It is the ground for a shift from a Lenin to a Stalin. On this view, no one to whom one relates has special standing, and all are blandly and flatly integrated into the regulatory machine of control – whether family, school, corporation, or state. On game theory it makes some sort of sense: I may give you my trust, but then you may proceed to violate it, thus I should not trust. It becomes foolish ever to trust. By the same token, one is not to be trusted.

A large group is united in different ways. The only way in which it should not be united – and this applies to the globe as a whole – is by entire surrender of private judgement to some person, leader or class. Friendships give citizens confidence and (paradoxically) independence. Friendships should be knitted together on the basis, not of unreflecting conformity, but of amity and rational reconciliation. This orientation excludes any notion of social 'mass'. A friendship regime of dyads and networks, informed by rational discourse and – where rationality fails – by supple give and take, leaves no room for notions of 'the mass' (*las masas*) or 'the crowd' (*la foule*). Such dyads and friendly networks, plus the morality of amity, rationality and compromise these bring with them, may supply the skeletal integrity of last resort to city, region, nation, and state. If a good society – meaning civil society – has a constitution, then friendship is it. Friendship networks, moreover, reach well beyond any given country. Indirectly, they tie communities together worldwide. Such dyads and networks are less like a pile of marbles, pebbles or coins, and more like a chain. The chain, in which A links with B and B in turn with C and C in turn with etc., is a set of serial connections. Each of its links is distinctive in that the rapport of A to B is not that of B to C. Thus there is strength to the whole in that each member is both bound and free, committed yet independent, caught up in a chain but not overwhelmed by a mass.

The model of a friendship society is more chain than mass. It is not a hierarchy and is not a pile. It provides for significant individuality, linked to an irreducible degree of sociality. Modernity has lots of folk, and the problem now is to turn them into knots of folk, mutually gnarled particulars, friendly combines, conversing and debating, working together, relating one to another, interacting one with the other, attending to people they know, and getting to know people they don't. We need such interactions – laced with affection, respect, mutuality, tolerance and rationality. Modernity needs to update friendship, cleansed of illusion and false starts. There is, all the same, a very long way to go in the quest to create for it the central space it deserves in human life – and in politics.

Friendship and the Political

EVERT VAN DER ZWEERDE
Radboud University, Nijmegen, Netherlands

'Quonam enim modo quisquam amicus esse poterit si, cui se putabit inimicum esse posse?'

Cicero, *Laelius de Amicitia* (Cicero 2001: xvi, 59)

'Nichts kann dieser Konsequenz des Politischen entgehen.'

Carl Schmitt, *Der Begriff des Politischen* (Schmitt 1963: 36)

'Persons of many friendships ... are thought to be real friends of nobody (otherwise than as fellow-citizens are friends).'

Aristotle, *Nicomachean Ethics* (Aristotle 1994: 1171a, 16-21)

On the face of it, politics and friendship are opposites. Politics is a sphere of suspicion, dirty hands, and hidden agendas, where 'friends' are the last thing to rely upon. Friendship is about sincerity, trusting someone else as you trust yourself (Seneca 2002: 11), freedom, and having nothing to hide – not even your agenda. As Cicero put it, 'true friendships are very hard to find among those whose time is spent in office or in business of a public kind' (Cicero 2001: xvii, 64). Friendship and politics, moreover, appear as mutually destructive: political disagreement is a major threat to friendship, and within politics friendship, bordering on favoritism, is suspect. Politics is a necessary evil; friendship to is a good one does desires, but doesn't *need* (Seneca 2002: 47).

At the same time, there are grounds for viewing political and friendship as linked. Apart from Jacques Derrida's *Politiques de l'amitié*, two authors come to mind. One is Aristotle, whose *filía politikè* as 'that which appears to keep the polities together' in the *Nicomachean Ethics* (Aristotle 1994: VIII, i, 4, 23f) and the *Politics* is as classical as it is complicated. The other is Carl Schmitt, whose *Begriff des Politischen* as dividing into friend and enemy is as challenging as it is controversial (Schmitt 1963: 26f). The *prima facie* objection that Aristotelian friendship (an affective relationship between individuals) and Schmittian 'friendship' (a forced alliance between collective actors) have nothing to do with each other is, I believe, a little too facile. If Aristotle had a point with his notion of 'political friendship', as its frequent invoking by communitarian critics of the liberal-democratic political order suggests, and if Schmitt also had a point, as the frequent invoking of his concept by left-wing critics of that same order suggests, then the conflict between their conceptions may shed light on the deadlock in political philosophy: a widespread dissatisfaction with the existing liberal-democratic order, combined with a lack of viable alternatives.

For Aristotle and Seneca, friendship – *filía / amicitia*[1] – was of great importance within the context of the *polis* or the republic. Aristotle linked the polity not to life – *to zèn–* but to the *good* life – *to eu zèn* (Aristotle 1990: 1252b30f), leaving the choice between the two forms of 'life accompanied by virtue ['*o bios airetōtatos*]', namely *bios politikos* and *bios teoretikos*, undecided (Aristotle 1990: 1324a27, 1324a32f, 1325a17). In both good forms of life, friendship – the friendship among those who take care of the common good, and the friendship among those who discuss philosophical topics – plays a major role. What Aristotle and Seneca say about friendship is intuitively convincing, but their notion of friendship is at odds with modern politics. The aim of this essay is to explore this apparent conflict.

Forms of Friendship

It is unlikely that 'friendship' has always meant the same during its long history. Yet, even if we would agree not to call friendship everything Aristotle called *filía*, this agreement assumes that we know (a) what we mean, intuitively at least, by 'friendship', and (b) what Aristotle meant with '*filía*'. The question is, from the perspective of political philosophy, if and how notions developed by Aristotle or others can be invoked in present-day discussions in order to highlight important aspects of socio-political reality. It is clear that we are not living in Greek *poleis*, but it is also clear that we are living in *polities*; it is clear that, for us, warfare is not primarily a matter of moral education, but it is also clear that giving one's life for the military defense of the polity still is an important civic virtue – otherwise, the scene in Michael Moore's *Fahrenheit 9/11*, in which he asks congressmen whether they would send their sons to war in Iraq, would not have been so shocking.

I distinguish five notions of friendship, without any strong truth-claims. The difficulty to define friendship has to do with friendship's flexible and uncertain nature. These five notions, therefore, merely serve to distinguish five hypothetical core meanings of the concept of friendship, with gray zones of transition between them:

a. *True friendship* ('FA'), *exclusive* personal relation between a limited number of individuals (not necessarily two: 'The first two would be glad to find a third (Lewis 2002: 79)'.); the model is the *pair*, in extended form a *triangle* or *square*; keywords are stability, unconditionality and *exclusiveness*, and the friendship is an end in itself.

b. *Friendships* with *larger numbers* ('FB') of people (colleagues, neighbors or co-citizens) – not all can be your friends, but nobody is a priori excluded; model: the *bifurcating chain*, with the potential of becoming a *network of friends*; keywords are relative stability, conditionality and *selectivity*, and the friendship is an end in itself, but with admixtures of utility and pleasure.

FA and FB are what I call 'spontaneous' friendship, arising out of a free desire to become friends with particular people. The primary goal is the friendship itself, although use and pleasure play a role, too. They can be part of a 'good life', but are not necessary for life as such.

c. *Friendliness* ('FC'), maintaining friendly relations within *the whole* of a given group (colleagues, members of a team, etc.) in order to achieve such things as 'a good atmosphere' – it applies to any situation in which people are 'bound to get along', thus including the situation of 'citizens of a polity', and it is a background quality for other activities; the model is a *field*, keywords are superficiality, situational stability and *inclusiveness*, and it is a means to another end, but also a source of pleasure.

d. *Friendly networks* ('FD'), a practical instrument to achieve particular aims, in fact an economic activity (a form of applied labor force); the model here is that of a *network*, keywords are conditionality, selectivity and *expediency*, and it is instrumental.

FC and FD are socially conditioned forms of friendship that can imply being friendly to people that you do not like; in the case of FD personal (dis)likings can be counter-effective. They are, strictly speaking, not necessary, but they may be highly desirable.

e. *Alliance* ('FE'), a strategic or tactical joining-of-hands between individuals and/or groups for a specific (set of) goals, which can be political, military, economic, even private (for example in a vendetta); the model is that of the *block* (which can be composite, and usually opposes another block) or party, keywords are temporariness, necessity, and *opposition*, and it is a means to realize (a) specific goal(s).

In FE, personal feelings and kinship relations are accidental, potentially blurring the 'clear view' that is necessary to perceive who is one's best ally or who one, in extreme cases, may have to kill. Alliances can be inescapable in the sense that the alternative may be 'death' – physically, economically or socially.

A few remarks must be made. First of all, all these forms of friendship can be sincere or insincere: therefore, they are *ideal-types*, not 'realities'. They can be part of discourses that perform an ideological function, as 'friend' is a positive notion by definition. Secondly, none of these forms is limited to a particular sphere of society: they can come into being anywhere. In the third place they all presuppose individual freedom; consequently, it is part of what it means to be a (modern) individual to keep these five forms of friendship apart: the distinctions are not naturally there, but have to be practically and discursively reproduced. Fourthly, they are 'morally neutral': friendship within a religious community or a group of human rights activists is as true as that within 'a circle of criminals, cranks, or perverts' (Lewis 2002: 97). The point is not simply that 'friendship (as the ancients saw) can be a school of virtue; but also (as they did not see) a school of vice' (Lewis 2002: 97), but more seriously that we cannot pretend to know what is virtue, what vice. Finally, friendship is always about something.

How can this discussion of forms of friendship be linked to the topic of political friendship? To be sure, neither Schmittian ('PFS') nor Aristotelian political friendship ('PFA') fits easily into this scheme. The reason for this is, obviously, that although all the forms of friendship just distinguished can occur in polities, in established politics, and among politicians, none of them is per se *political*. The second step, therefore, must be a clarification of the concept of the political.

Politics and the Political

If 'friendship' is difficult to define, the same applies a fortiori to 'the political'. As Schmitt noted, 'one rarely finds a clear definition of the political' (Schmitt 1963: 20). In a series with the general title 'X & the Political' (X including Derrida, Heidegger, Irigaray and others), the editors, Keith Ansell-Pearson and Simon Critchley, state that the concept of 'the political' is 'essentially contestable' (Beardsworth 1996: inside front flap). Generally speaking, 'the political' is a general name for the feature that allows us to call something 'political'. This is why, as Schmitt noted, the political does not have an object field of its own: *anything* can be 'political', and this also is why anything can (but *must* not) lead to a division into friends and enemies with the ultimate possible consequence of physical death (Schmitt 1963: 38, 33) Two pitfalls must be avoided here: substantivization and reductionism. The first would mean to fall prey to the grammatical structure of language, and to turn 'the political' into something substantial or thing-like: 'the political' is *not* 'whatever is political' but 'that which makes something political political', its *'politicitas'*, as a medieval philosopher might have called it. The other pitfall is reductionism: the temptation to 'politicize' everything and reduce it to its 'politicalness'. If everything societal is always-also political, one should add that nothing is ever *only* or *purely* political: both the idea of some things being 'free from politics' *and* the idea of a realm of 'pure politics' are to be rejected. However, the fact that there is an element of pure decision in everything societal, including in the phrasing of a definition – in the field of theory, definitions arguably *are* the clearest example of decisions – does not force us to absolutize the moment of decision (decisionism).

But what *is* this feature that can be properly called 'political'? It is, to my mind, the very 'essential contestability' that Ansell-Pearson and Critchley ascribe to the concept, the possibility of a *real* conflict by virtue of the fact that there is an element of decision in everything human. If a decision is recognized as human, i.e. as *somebody's* decision (rather than as divine intervention or as belonging to the order of nature), the political that is dormant in it can (but *must* not) be articulated. A real conflict is one that cannot be solved by applying rules (including laws) or criteria that are accepted by all parties concerned (the notion of the political also highlights that these rules and criteria themselves are 'essentially contestable') – this understanding of the political draws upon Lyotard's distinction between *différend* and *litige*. This does not mean that insoluble conflicts *must* arise: very often, they do not, and the functioning of society and culture depends on this. Moreover, a situation in which nobody contests anything because all agree upon the rules to settle any conflict is, in theory, thinkable (even if it is not 'realistic' to assume it). It does mean, however, that *politics*, understood as a general term denoting all ways of dealing with the political (including the denial of this fact as well as the claim of certain fields of activity as being a-political), is something inevitable and that we, 'political animals', are also *politicians* by definition. As Slavoj Žižek has put it: 'every neutralization of some partial content as "non-political" is a political gesture *par excellence*' (Žižek 2000: 234). A prime example of this is the limitation, in established polities, of politics to a particular sphere, called 'politics' in the sense of political parties, government, legislation. There is nothing wrong with such attempts to pacify society by canalizing the political, but they cannot eradicate the political because they cannot annihilate the essential contestability, i.e. *political* nature, of the established order itself.

Throughout this essay, I thus use the notion of 'the political' (*'das Politische'*) to mean the ubiquitous possibility, in everything social, of real conflict. 'Politics' (*'die Politik'*) I define as the totality of ways of dealing with the fact of the political – this notion of politics covers 'politics of friendship' just as it covers 'identity politics' or 'politics of recognition', but it also covers 'politics' in the sense of the place within society where 'politics is done'. A *polity* – polis, empire, nation-state, IGO – is the institutionalized form of political order, often called 'the state'. *Political society*, finally, is that part of civil society where public discussion over political issues – including the discussion about what is and what is not to be considered 'political' – takes place.

What Kind of Friendship is *filía politikè*?

The classical notion of friendship, from Seneca down to Clive Staples Lewis, presupposes the idea of the 'person'. However, this is not obvious in the case of such classical authors as Plato or Aristotle. In Plato, the adjective *'filos'* appears to mean 'that to which one entertains a relation of friendship [*filía*]' and this applies mainly, but not exclusively, to human beings. Socrates asks, for example, whether 'health is a *'filon'* or not (Plato 2001: 219A).' It is opposed to *'ekhtros'* and *'to ekhthron'*, i.e. 'that which is inimical'. Friendship between inanimate objects is possible only in a very limited sense – e.g. the Empedoclean senses of *'filotès'* and *'neikos'* as the two opposed metaphysical forces.[2] It is not accidental, however, that both Aristotle and Cicero refer to this 'physical' notion of friendship as something to set their conception of true friendship off from (Aristotle 1994: VII, i, 6, 7; Cicero 2001: vii, 24). Plato sets off friendship in which 'the real friend is a friend for the sake of nothing else that is a friend' (Plato 2001: 220B), i.e. not a means to another *'filon'*, but an end in itself (FA and FB in my scheme), from the general relation of friendship, in which 'the friend is a friend of its friend for the sake of its friend and because of its foe' (Plato 2001: 219B). Aristotle, who focuses on friendship as an end in itself, first makes clear that the object of *filía* must be something 'lovable [*to filotèn*]', then excludes inanimate objects, and finally defines friendship as a relation between humans who wish each other's good, are aware of each other's goodwill, and found their goodwill in some lovable quality (Aristotle 1994: VIII, ii, 1; iii, 3–4). Something can be *filotèn* for three different reasons, viz. use, pleasure, and virtue – correspondingly, Aristotle distinguishes between three kinds of friendship: of utility, of pleasure and of virtue (Aristotle 1994: VIII, iii).

Is political friendship, then, a 'weaker' form of friendship of the virtuous, i.e. friendship 'between the good, and those that resemble each other in virtue' (Aristotle, 1994: VIII, iii, 6), or a generalized friendship of pleasure or of utility, or that form of *filía* that can be translated as friendliness, a virtue that holds the middle between the vices of obsequiousness and flattery on the one hand, quarrelsomeness and surliness on the other (Aristotle, 1994: II, vii, 13)? To begin at the end, the virtue of friendliness (FC) as generalizable within a given group, is clearly a civil and civic virtue. Often, we might equal it with civility or with 'good manners', and it certainly is a necessary condition for the 'good life' of society, including good politics. Friendship of utility and of pleasure, which I would rank under FB, are important, too, because they can incite people to do things together, and even to found a polity as a place for business and for collective activities such as sports. Aristotle, however, who suggests that *filía* is the drive behind social life (Aristotle 1990: III, v, 14), emphasizes the priority of political virtue (*'e politikè arête*): it is 'manifest that the same life must be the best both for each human being individually and for states and mankind collectively' (Aristotle 1990: VII, iii, 6), and 'the political fellowship must ... be deemed to exist for the sake of noble actions, not merely for living in common' (Aristotle 1990: III, v.14). Utility and pleasure are an effect of social life, not its cause or drive, and mere interest will never yield *more* than a common place for economic and cultural activity.

Aristotle's notion of PFA, as a form of friendship of virtue, articulates an ideal of a political community which is a far cry from present-day political realities. 'Friendship' seems to have lost all political applicability. One of today's leading social theorists, Zygmunt Bauman, wrote:

> Scared loners without a community will go on searching for a community without fears, and those in charge of the inhospitable public space will go on promising it. The snag is, though, that the only communities which the loners may hope to build and the managers of public space can seriously and responsibly offer are ones constructed of fear, suspicion and hate. Somewhere along the line, friendship and solidarity, once upon a time major community-building materials, became too flimsy, too rickety or too watery for the purpose. (Bauman 1999: 14).

Is this not mere nostalgia for a situation that may have never existed other than as an ideal to begin with? Are we not idealizing friensdhip in a way not unlike the idealization of the ancient *polis* with its *agora* and its *bios politikos* by Hannah Arendt and other 'civic humanists' (Rawls 1993: 206)? Friendship is a form of *positive* liberty, but a system that is based on free individuality puts a natural emphasis on *negative* liberty: citizens must be left free to act, they must be protected against each other and against the possible intrusion of the polity itself, in order to reach a position of maximum liberty. What they *do* with this liberty is, by and large, their own business – apparently, this has led to Bauman's 'inhospitable public place'.

There is a lot of nostalgia and idealization in political philosophy, and this affects the combined notions of politics and friendship, too. At the same time, however, I would like to suggest a link between that combination and the tradition of republicanism: we may well ask what the difficulty of the combination politics–friendship and the relatively weak position of republicanism have to do with each other. Simplifying, one could argue that the two predominant traditions in political thought, namely democratic liberalism on the one hand, and 'corporatism' in its many forms (including socialism, Christian utopianism, nationalism, fascism and communitarianism),[3] on the other, are both *essentially anti-political*: liberalism seeks to sublate societal antagonism through maximum liberty for the individual (limiting the political space, that is), and the solution of conflict by means of correct legal procedures, thus minimalizing the polity and marginalizing and criminalizing political conflict; corporatism, by contrast, replaces antagonism by solidarity and brotherhood, thus making the polity in the end superfluous and denying and exporting the political. *Neither* of them holds a *political* place for friendship: in liberalism it is replaced by friendly relations within the various spheres of society, while in corporatism it is replaced by *agapè*, the love of all with all, whether in this or in another, post-revolutionary or post-apocalyptic world.

The disappearance of the notion of friendship as an important bond between people in the public sphere is related to the increasing instrumentalization and functionalization of society (which 'threaten' friendship because it is not 'useful'). Its disappearance is also related to the rise of democracy (with which friendship, selective by nature, is potentially at odds). It also has to do with the predominant notions of societal bond within the Christian tradition. Lewis ends his analysis with a eulogy of God opening, through Friendship, our eyes to the beauties of other people, thus turning it into 'His instrument for creating as well as for revealing' (Lewis 2002: 108). Of course, from a Christian point of view, friendship, as part of God's creation, *must* have a purpose. But it is precisely friendship that is largely absent from the relation between the divine and the human: 'Finally, we must notice that Friendship is very rarely the image under which Scripture represents the love between God and Man. ... Affection is taken as the image when God is represented as our Father; Eros, when Christ is represented as the Bridegroom of the Church' (Lewis 2002: 94). And charity, love-agapè, is of course the primary model of interhuman relations. This means that, out of the 'four loves' distinguished by Lewis, it is precisely friendship that is missing.

Lewis rightly points to the 'distrust which Authorities tend to have of close Friendships among their subjects' (Lewis 2002: 94), and this holds not only for 'secular', but also for ecclesiastical authorities, who rightly suspect the development of monastic orders and other forms of sisterhood and brotherhood. This position of friendship in political theology requires further exploration, not least because 'the Ancients', for whom friendship *was* a political virtue, worshipped a divine world inhabited by gods who were like humans because for them, too, friendship among themselves and between them and humans was a relevant phenomenon, contrary to the 'lonely' and sovereign God of monotheism. In a post-Christian world, in which monotheistic political theology is dominant and republicanism a mere undercurrent, there seems to be no connection between friendship and the political.

The Nature of the Political – Carl Schmitt Amended

To some, however, friendship is a political category by definition. Carl Schmitt defines the political as that which divides groups of people into friends and enemies. The 'logic' of the political entails a 'radical' choice: *either* you are an enemy [*hostis*] *or* you are a friend [ally]. Schmitt has been a *persona non grata* in political theory for quite some time, but his insights have been gradually appropriated by the conservative right, and by leftist thinkers such as Chantal Mouffe, who invoke his notion of the political to oppose the depoliticizing tendencies of liberal-democratic polities and mainstream political philosophy (Mouffe 1993: 41–59, 135–154; Mouffe 1999).

An opposition of a political world of enmity and discord and a non-political world of love and harmony is not only less than helpful, it is even disastrous, since it is a major source of both quietist escapism and revolutionary utopianism, with a strong Leviathan as the only alternative. One way to develop a theoretical alternative, in which a *positive* connection of politics and the political with the notions of friendship and love becomes possible, is to take a closer look at the notion of the political itself. Departing from Schmitt's 'harsh' formulation, and using comments on his position by Mouffe, I suggest four steps to arrive at a conception that does greater justice to the 'fact of the political'.

A first step is to *acknowledge* the political as a *ubiquitous feature* of all societal relations: everything human, even the most personal, *is* always also political, i.e. potentially engaged in a real conflict, but nothing is ever *purely* political. Further, the political should not be understood as the *reality* of a friend–enemy division, but as its *possibility*. For Schmitt, the possibility of 'war' is what ultimately defines the political, but it is more adequate, I believe, to relate the political primarily to the *possibility* of real conflict, which, at a second stage, entails the possibility of physical death, i.e. 'war'. This amendment allows for a distinction between *war* (*Krieg*) and *struggle* (*Kampf*), not made by Schmitt: struggle is what gives antagonism a place without necessarily leading to physical violence. Also, it makes it possible to assess the polemical and *political* nature of Schmitt's own theoretical intervention: his own attempt to revive the *limitation* of politics to the *polity* involves a profoundly political decision which establishes what is and what is not 'political'.

A second step is to question Schmitt's understanding of friend and enemy as *groups*. For Schmitt, friend and enemy are not individuals, but *groups*: a people, a party, a partisan movement, etc. This implies that the ones that I am with *within* a given unit, i.e. my co-nationals, the other members of my party, my comrades, are *not* my political friends, but part of the 'we' that shapes my identity: 'Feind ist nur eine wenigstens eventuell, d.h. der realen Möglichkeit nach *kämpfende* Gesamtheit von Menschen, die einer ebensolchen Gesamtheit gegenübersteht' (Schmitt 1963: 29; Schmitt 2002: 20).[4] These identities must be unambiguous and closed (or: they become unambiguous and closed as the political intensifies). Further, there is no connection, for Schmitt, between a private enemy-inimicus and a public enemy-hostis, nor can there be, consequently, any other than accidental connection between *personal* and *political* friends: to the extent to which 'the political' divides radically and exhaustively, *every* personal friend and enemy must, ultimately, also be part of either my own group or of my political friend – another group – or, finally, of my political enemy. While this may create a lot of practical problems, since it implies both that I may have to be comrades with people whom I hate and that I may have to kill somebody who is my friend (my Bosnian neighbor, my Jewish teacher) because she or he belongs to the hostile group, it does not present a theoretical problem, at least not for Schmittians.

But we do not have to follow Schmitt on this point: his double assumption that (a) *political* units are collective by definition and that (b) private and public are separated can be *politically* contested and *philosophically* questioned. The first is absurd, if only because it would imply that those who stand alone in their struggle, such as Lenin in 1916, would stop being *political* actors by virtue of their loneliness (the last of the Mohicans – or the last Islamist terrorist – would not be a political actor, whereas the last two would). Of course this can be countered by the assumption that it is never a political actor's *intention* to be alone, so that the political loner would be a limit-case, but even so it would exclude the possibility of ascribing *political* significance to movements begun by a single individual. As for the second, the assumption of a private-public distinction as founding a distinction between *inimicus* and *hostis*, presented as a *fact* by Schmitt, conceals the *political* character of that distinction. For Schmitt, the absence of the distinction of public and private enemy in German and other modern languages is a source of 'misunderstandings and distortions' (Schmitt: 1963: 29), but this can only be a matter of *mis*understanding if the distinction is naturally or necessarily given. If the distinction is not *given*, but *made*, then the alleged 'misunderstanding' can be a corrective move or a protest, articulated in natural language, against a political decision, materialized in law. To declare the personal or the private to be *political* is a political decision by individuals, with which one may agree or disagree, but it is not a misunderstanding of an objective reality: politicization is possible because everything is 'politicizable', as conflicts about skin color, the wearing of spectacles, the number of fingers raised when crossing oneself, or circumcision testify. It is its character of *distinction*, finally, which explains why, in case of conflict between personal friendship and public hostility, the conflict is solved publicly – if I don't shoot my friend, I will be shot myself (and my comrade will shoot my friend) – while personally it remains and can take the shape of lifelong remorse. The fact that the same deeds can be validated as acts of cowardice or as cases of heroic courage, does not negate the political, i.e. essentially contestable and potentially conflictual nature of either the deed or the validation.

Indeed, many languages do not distinguish between the private *inimicus* and the public *hostis* (Schmitt 1963: 29). The question is why this distinction has 'got lost', and whether this is (only) a loss and not (also) a gain. Two explanations suggest themselves: one is that, in modern vernaculars, rising with the nation-state, this distinction is blurred, offering an ideological legitimization for personal hatred with respect to one's public *hostis*; perhaps, this was a better way of motivating soldiers fighting in a national army based on conscription, because the enemy was not the *hostis* of the soldiers, but of their king or government, and was thus better presented as an *inimicus* of the nation. The other explanation is that, in 'reality', the distinction is less clear than Schmitt suggests. What, after all, is 'reality' in this context? Schmitt presents a description of an objective state of affairs, using forms of 'to be' to indicate what 'enemy' means, and he explicitly denies any normativity: 'Hier handelt es sich nicht um Fiktionen und Normativitäten, sondern um die seinsmäßige Wirklichkeit und die reale Möglichkeit dieser Unterscheidung' (Schmitt 1963: 28f). But what if the political reality that we are talking about is shaped by the conceptual decisions that we make, and what if Schmitt himself was trying to shape reality? What if, like Plato in the *Politeia*, Schmitt is not doing empirical political science, but is waging a battle on the never politically neutral field of political theory? Schmitt's primary aim, like Plato's, is the depoliticization of the inner life of the polity.

A third step is to replace the opposition of friend and enemy by that of 'the amicable' and 'the inimical' (reflecting '*to filon*' and '*to ekhtron*' in Plato). Inimical can be considered the equivalent of *ekhtros*, which Plato uses as general term in his *Politeia* (Plato 1999: V, 470). When he makes a distinction between Barbarians, who are enemies by nature (*fusei*), i.e. *polemioi*, and against whom war (*polemos*) can be waged, and Greeks, friends (*filoi*) by nature, but who can become enemies when they are the cause of unnatural faction (*stasis*), he uses *ekhtroi* for the latter as well (Plato 1999: V, 471-A), which, *pace* Schmitt, shows that *ekhtros* is a general term for *inimicus* and *hostis* alike (Schmitt 1963: 29, n.5). Equally, *polemos* and *stasis* appear as two forms of enmity (*ekhtra*). Amicable and inimical, as qualities of something, are less harsh than their identification with entities: the ultimate consequence of identifying something as inimical is that it must disappear; consequently, to identify the inimical with an enemy implies that this enemy must be destroyed. In Schmitt's analysis, the other 'dividing principles' – the moral, the aesthetic, the economic – also divide into adjectival notions: good and evil, beautiful and ugly, useful and harmful (Schmitt 1963: 27). The meaning of the political is *adjectival*, not substantive, and to identify something amicable or inimical with its 'bearer' – an institution, a human, a country, a terrorist network – is possible (it is what happens in 'war'), but not necessary. A principle of 'dissociation' is the condition of dealing with conflict in a *civilized* way, just as a dissociation of person and opinion is what makes it possible to disagree with a friend while remaining friends.

A fourth step, finally, is to *replace* the binary opposition of amicable vs inimical by a tripartition through the introduction of a 'neutral' third element. Just as, from an economic perspective, that which is not useful does not have to be harmful, but can also be 'economically indifferent', in politics that which is not amicable does not have to be inimical: it can also be 'politically neutral', or be 'politically left alone', and it is this *indifference* that makes the difference between the deadly logic of dichotomy and the freedom generated by a tripartition. To be sure, the political does entail the possibility of forcing a neutral third into the friend–enemy dichotomy, a force which can only be countered by becoming the enemy of this dichotomy. A *neutral* third escapes from the 'dichotomous logic' generated by a binary opposition of friend and enemy, which forces one to turn all one's non-enemies into friends (allies) *or* to relegate all personal friendship to a non-political realm.

These steps, the radicalization of the concept of the political, the 'decollectivization' of the categories of friend and enemy, the replacement of friend–enemy by amicable-inimical, and the introduction of a third, 'neutral' category of 'the indifferent', create a place for a positive appreciation of political friendship.

Squaring the Circle: The Fundamental Problem of Political Friendship

Among Modern political philosophers, enmity occupies a much more important place than friendship. Since the rise of Modern political philosophy, with Niccoló Machiavelli and Thomas Hobbes, emphasis is on the essentially conflictual nature of social relations and on the potential hostility of every human being towards every other human being. Hobbes's idea of man being the natural enemy of every other man in particular has both inspired and 'haunted' Western political thinking. Consequently, the political and politics are connected with conflict and *discord*, and the aim of political order as such is the pacification of society and the avoidance of civil war. Devised to end man's 'nasty, poor, solitary, brutish and short' life in the pre-political natural state, this political philosophy has the grim face of a sovereign power which may employ every possible means to secure its position.

Today's dominant line of political thinking, the Lockean–Rawlsian–Habermasian line of liberal democracy, is more optimistic, but also more 'ideological': it not only assumes that human beings are reasonable enough to understand that their safety and property are better protected if they organize themselves in a polity, but also that they are free and equal and, therefore, must retain, within such a polity, their right to engage in politics. This line of thought is based upon an anthropology in which human beings are, first of all, individuals, who have a clear view of their own interests, and organize their behavior in such a way as their power of reason tells them will best serve their interests. Despite the differences between comprehensive Lockean and political Rawlsian liberalism, the two set in motion the same interplay of basically self-centered free individuals with rational capacities. On the whole, this is how modern Western liberal-democratic societies, i.e. the kind of society that Locke wanted to substantiate and that Rawls set out to write the political philosophy for (Rawls 1993: 3–10), work (or are believed to work): democracy is organized around the individual citizen casting a free vote or running for office, a market economy resting upon the idea of individual free 'enterprise', and a civil society based upon the notion of voluntary association between free individuals. We thus arrive at a pacified *society* (*Gesellschaft*) in which conflict obtains the 'positive' forms of plurality (in political society), competition (in economic society), and voluntary association (in civil society) (Schmitt 1963: 28, 70).

This model appears to contrast, but in fact matches perfectly with another line of thought, in which the opposite of *discord*: *concord*, is applied to society at large. This can be the idea of a *community* (*Gemeinschaft*), a typical variant whereof is the idea of *sobornost'* elaborated by Russian Orthodox thinkers, perceived as an *expansion* of ecclesiastical community (this expansion is called *otserkovlenie* – 'churchification') (van der Zweerde 2001), but a communitarian position does not have to be 'conservative', as the example of Elizabeth Bounds shows (Bounds 1997). An alternative is to situate a harmonious and a-political society outside the present world in a near or distant future (an example is Marxism) or in a version of the Kingdom of God. This line of thought runs from Augustine to the contemporary work of Michael Hardt and Antonio Negri (*Empire* and *Multitude*).

While the core of the first line of thought is formed by the notions of interest and self-love, the core of the second line is formed by the notion of love-of-other or *agapè*. The problem with the idea that one ought to love not only one's neighbor, but even one's enemy, is not only that it turns into a too-hard-to-achieve task (for 'saints' only), but also that it becomes *abstract-universal* and fails to do justice to concrete feelings of love and sympathy. Friendship then becomes something of the private sphere. Within the dominant tradition of political philosophy friendship is not a political category, which is reflected by the absence of the very notion (Kymlicka 1999; Barry 1990; Rawls 1978, 1993, 2002; Sartori 1987).

However, friendship does have a public aspect: friendship and its effects can be visible to others, and, as Hannah Arendt observed, such public display does not harm the friendship (Arendt 1989: 51). The public display of friendship can be politically effective, and a group of friends is often the best qualified actor to solve a practical (or theoretical, for that matter) problem: division of tasks is smooth, critical feedback is constructive, the idea of working together a stimulus. As C.S. Lewis observed, friendship, contrary to love, is not focused on the persons involved, but is *about* something: friends typically are 'absorbed in some common interest' (Lewis 2002: 73, 80). This 'common interest' *can* be the good life of the polity as a whole, which is why the idea of a group of friends 'running' the polity and taking care of the common good is not absurd, provided that their visions of the common good must be the same or compatible, which is the case if the common good *is* the 'running of the *res publica* in a good (virtuous) way' (this explains the proximity with republicanism). The idea of an 'amigocracy', however, faces two problems, one fundamental, the other factual: it only works if *all* are friends, and it only seems to work on a relatively small scale.

With respect to the first problem, 'amigocracy' understood as 'rule by friends' is, when the group of friends does not coincide with the *dèmos*, a form of aristocracy. Any form of aristocracy is fundamentally anti-democratic, not so much because it is government by an elite –that in itself can be the outcome of democratic procedure – but because the question *who decides* who is an aristocrat is answered by the *aristoi* themselves: aristocracy is a form of self-appointed government, and this is what any *dèmos* rightly fears when it perceives friendly relations between those in power.

With respect to the second, it is not accidental that friendship was regarded as an important political concept within the context of relatively small city-states like Athens or the Roman republic, and, later, Italian and other city-republics. Amigocracy and democracy are compatible only if the group of friends *is* the *dèmos*. If friendship is 'an affair of the few', it is understandable that 'some forms of democratic sentiment are naturally hostile to it' (Lewis 2002: 72). Nothing is harder to beat that an old boys' network, and since the old boys started out like college or business friends, it is impossible to *become* an old boy. If, in large democratic polities, friendship is looked upon with hostility by the *dèmos*, in authoritarian polities it is looked upon with suspicion by those in power, because a group of friends can be the beginning of a conspiracy or rebellion, 'a pocket of potential resistance' (Lewis 2002: 96). This is why both democratic and authoritarian regimes make friendship, like love, a private, not a public affair. Friendship then *becomes* political when it crosses the border between the private and the public spheres.

There is also an obvious tension between the idea of networks-of-friends and the formal character of the modern polity. Networks of friends are essentially anti-democratic and anti-juridical, yet crucial for a working economic and political society under liberal-democratic conditions. Moreover, if politics takes place, first and foremost, in the spheres of 'politics' and political society, then it is clear that both offer opportunities for individuals to develop relations of friendship (and of love, hatred, etc.). At the same time, a relation of friendship (just as one of love, hatred, etc.) is at odds with a professional and neutral approach. Only if *all* people involved would be friends, things would go smoothly and, perhaps, optimally. And the problem with friendship –contrary to love-agapè that can be universal, and love-eros that is exclusive- is that it is selective, but not necessarily exclusive, and that the coincidence of *dèmos* and *filoi* is not impossible. While love-agapè is a political dream which, if realized, would not hurt anybody, and love-eros a fact of life which can be given a place within the private sphere, friendship is open by definition.

From a democratic point of view, friendship is a *risk* to politics, because it potentially generates inequality. Hence part of the 'meta-politics' of a democratic polity is the *privatization* of friendship. Friendship between elected politicians is fine, as long as it does not interfere with the political process itself – the trouble, however, is that it does. In an era of globalization and of the development of forms of supraterritoriality (Scholte, 2000: 41–61), friendship no longer presupposes a shared place, and it is easy to see how the inhabitants of, to quote Bauman, 'the first world – the increasingly cosmopolitan, extraterritorial world of global businessmen, global culture managers or global academics' (Bauman 2000: 89) can form extraterritorial networks-of-friends [**FB**] just as easily as global friendly networks [**FD**].

The Truth in Aristotle's Notion of Political Friendship

The notion of 'true friendship' appears unfit for playing any public role, and there is a tendency to make it so special as to be completely distant from anything public or political. Manifest in Cicero and Montaigne is a *normative* opposition of the extremely rare *amicitia vera et perfecta* on the one hand, and the numerous *amitiés ordinaires et coutumières* on the other (Montaigne 2001: 294; Cicero 2001: XXI, 76). One suspects, in this idealization of true friendship, a depoliticization of friendship. But *is* political friendship friendship of the truly virtuous? Aristotle states that 'such of course are rare, because such men are rare' (Aristotle 1994: VIII, iii, 8, 25f). So rare indeed that Cicero refers to Laelius as having hoped that the friendship between Scipio and himself might be added as a *fifth* case to the existing three or four known pairs of friends throughout history (Cicero 2001: iv, 15). We may add Michel de Montaigne and Étienne de la Boétie, or Hannah Arendt and Mary McCarthy, but it is clear that *this* kind of friendship is an insufficient basis to keep the polity together.

Aristotle, however, at this point as on many others, is much more realistic and pragmatic than his later followers. Not only, as Derrida has shown, Montaigne's famous 'Ô mes amis, il n'y a nul ami', which suggests that even having *one* friend is nearly impossible, but also – with a dative instead of a vocation – Diogenes Laertius' 'he who has friends, has no friend [*ō' filoi, oudeis filos*]' (Diogenes Laertius 1972: V, 21), is an exaggeration with respect to the actual Aristotelian position that one can entertain relations of true friendship only with a *few*, not many, while at the same time one can be friends with a great number of fellow-citizens: 'Persons of many friendships ... are thought to be real friends of nobody (other than as political friends); ... one may be friendly with many fellow-citizens and not be obsequious, but a model of excellence' (Aristotle 1994: IX, x, 6; also EE VII, xii, 17). In the case of 'friendship of the virtuous', the quality of friendship quickly decreases with an increasing number. However, the same does not necessarily hold for political friendship, i.e. friendship with the other members of the polity (Derrida 1994: 240).

In Aristotle, we find two statements which, together, articulate the basic paradox of political friendship, namely that 'friendship appears to keep the polities together as well', and that 'there is no need for justice among friends' (Aristotle 1994: VIII, i, 4, 23f and 27f.). If all citizens (of the same polis) are friends, then running the polis in full *concord* becomes a real possibility, and justice, i.e. taking just decisions in case of conflict between citizens, becomes superfluous. Among the truly virtuous, there is no need for politics, since the full realization of virtue implies the disappearance of *discord*. The *problem* with the idea of full concord, is that it may be practically impossible, but that it is not an impossibility of principle: the possibility of discord (the political) is metaphysically inevitable, but the actuality of discord is not; hence, although the absence of the *possibility* of discord is impossible, the actual absence of discord is *not*.

From Aristotle's analysis of the nature of the polis we can retain the idea that what keeps the polis together is a kind of friendship – the question is *which* kind of friendship. Both the liberal form, the generalized friendship of utility, and the authoritarian form, the total unity that ensues from the logic of the political in the interpretation of Carl Schmitt, do keep the polis together, but at the expense of it being political. The question is, therefore, which kind of political friendship is capable of *both* keeping the polis *together* and keeping it *political*. Aristotle makes it clear that it is not friendship of utility: although the polis is very useful, it is not use that is the motive force behind the 'living together' (*suzèn*) that is the necessary precondition for the good life (*eu zèn*), which is the goal of the *polis* (Aristotle 1990: 1258b). Similarly, pleasure, like use, may be an effect of *suzèn*, but it is not its motivation. Hence it must be a form of friendship of virtue, but not friendship of virtuous men, of which there are so few examples that a polis will be lucky to house one. Therefore, *filía politikè* must be a *weakened* and *generalizable* form of friendship of virtue: it must include *all* citizens, i.e. all participating members of the polity, and it must have an orientation on virtue.

Plato, Aristotle and Cicero base their argument on an unproblematized distinction between men who are good (virtuous), bad (vicious), or neither good nor bad (Plato 2001: 216B; Aristotle 1994: VIII, iv, 2, 16–20; Cicero 2001: XII, 42). Although we make this distinction in the private sphere, and also within the sphere of civil society, it is at odds with the democratic principle on which a liberal-democratic polity is based. The difficulty is that, contrary to Aristotle or Cicero, we no longer to claim to know what or who is virtuous. Or do we? Are present-day citizens not repeating the logic of virtue and vice at a meta-level when they recognize the legitimate existence of a plurality of 'visions of the good life' *and claim that this plurality has to be accepted*? The virtuous citizen then is the citizen who is capable of living with difference, including radical difference. The question is not so much whether this capacity is a virtue, but rather whether it can be realistically demanded from the vast majority of citizens (there is a strongly *elitist* strain in discussion of pluralism and citizenship at this precise point).

Four further questions present themselves here. First, how does political friendship relate to the *size* of the polity: was Aristotle right there is a limit, or can it be expanded endlessly, including all members of a cosmopolity? Second, how does it relate to the *number* of the polity: was Schmitt right that a political pluriverse (Schmitt 1963: 54) is necessary, or can it, again in principle, be the basis of a political universe, i.e. a single global polity? Third, how can a form of friendship that must be a bond between equals – all citizens must *equally* be my political friends – be compatible with the actual inequality of citizens in terms of wealth, intelligence, virtue, and eagerness to engage in politics, and still be *political* friendship. Fourth, how can any form of political friendship be a goal for lawgivers (Aristotle 1994: 1155a 23f), i.e. an objective of the polity itself, if the objectives of the polity are to come out of the politically active citizenry?

The Truth of Schmitt's Notion of the Political

An 'orthodox Schmittian' has no difficulty with these questions. It is the political itself which forces citizens, i.e. members of a politically organized people, together. The (possible) existence of an external enemy suffices to create this bond and makes friendship-as-political-objective impossible, irrespective of the size of the polity, but presupposes a plurality of polities, and the question as to which form of friendship can exist *inside* the polity does not present itself, because it is not friendship at all.

The challenge of Carl Schmitt to liberal democracy as a system and democratic liberalism as a theory has not been met yet, because he points at its *intrinsic* weakness. If, along with Mouffe, we understand agonistic politics as 'confrontations among adversaries' and pluralism as 'legitimate dissent among friends' – an understanding that brings us close to Arendt – and if we also follow her in her diagnosis that both liberal democracy and Carl Schmitt end up with a negation of the political *within* the polity, the first by reducing it the possibility of antagonism, i.e. of real conflict, to the logic of negotiable conflicts of interest or the model of rational deliberation, the second by 'exporting' antagonism to the outside of the polity, then we must conclude that Schmitt forces us to address a problem at the heart of liberal democracy, viz. the difficulty it has to devise 'ways in which *antagonism* can be transformed into *agonism*' (Mouffe 1999: 5).

The idea of agonistic politics, which I define as a *recognition* of fundamental difference of opinion – a *différend* – in combination with a *refusal* to let this difference result in a friend–enemy opposition, invokes the notion of political friendship. Liberalism ends up with negotiation of interests and rational deliberation, the logic of the political pushes it in the direction of criminalizing and marginalizing the adversaries (including, in Rawlsian terms, the adherents of all those comprehensive doctrines that do not fit into the overlapping consensus, but also including all those who make radical redistributive claims) into an inimical group of anarchists, chaotics, anti-globalist or terrorists (plus their 'friends' in the Schmittian sense, i.e. fundamentalist regimes and rogue states, functionally replacing the communist regimes of the past). The Schmittian solution solves this problem, but at the cost of killing politics inside the polity.

The possibility of political friendship as the basis of agonistic politics depends on the ability to find a way between complacent and depoliticizing liberalism on the one hand, and belligerent and 'extra-politicizing' authoritarianism on the other. This position is a priori antagonistic with respect to both the existing order *and* the 'authoritarianism' and 'fundamentalism' (or, of course, 'chaos') which that order construes as its only, undesirable alternative, and it is political in the sense of turning liberal democracy and authoritarianism into Schmittian 'friends'. (To put it in different terms: the political theology of the adherents of agonistic politics is a 'polytheistic' theology which will, ultimately, come under attack from both the side of the 'protestant' political theology of liberalism *and* from the 'catholic' political theology of authoritarianism.)

Conclusion

Plato ends his *Lysis* with the statement that he has not made clear what friendship 'is' (Plato 2001: 223B). The traditional answer to this embarrassment is that we have thus far *failed* to grasp the essence of friendship due to our own insufficiency, or that we will *necessarily* fail to do so, or, finally, that the point is in the striving for an answer, rather than in the grasping of it. The reaction to these answers can be summarized in anti-essentialist terms: there is no such thing as 'friendship per se', but there is a word which we use to designate any number of things that display, to our mind, a sufficient degree of similarity. While the anti-essentialist position is generally sound, we risk missing the important point that, contrary to many other phenomena, the indefinability of friendship might be part of its 'essence'. It is neither accidental, nor our 'failure' that we 'circle around' the precise nature of friendship – on the contrary, this is inevitable, since friendship itself is about 'circling around'.

Still, we can state two conclusions. First of all, PFA and PFS appear to be two different options for a foundation of the polity that goes beyond the generalized interest group lying at the basis of the liberal model. However, although their nature is different, and even opposed (individual vs collective, open vs closed, free vs forced), they can coexist, and complement each other within the same polity, perhaps even within the same individual, but not without tension. Effective PFA makes PFS superfluous, total PFS makes PFA impossible. This tension is insuperable and non-sublatable, as well as constitutive, i.e. it is part of the dynamics of political life without ever reaching a final synthesis. PFA is a realistic, i.e. non-utopian ideal, while PFS is a non-ideal reality. At this point, Aristotle can be considered a friend of good politics, but one should equally take the lesson from Schmitt that the very idea of PFA cannot but be political, i.e. essentially contestable and polemically dividing into friends and enemies: the idea of political friendship is not only an issue for *bios theoretikos*, but is also at stake in *bios politikos*, and can be an important force in the struggle for a pluralistic polity in which the political is articulated instead of being denied or exported.

But there is another, more fundamental conclusion. Derrida has distinguished two ways in which 'true friendship' is inachievable (Derrida 1994: 249f). One is that it is a goal which is clearly conceived but never achieved, an unfulfilled desire, with the result that the way is more important than the goal. The other is that the goal itself is inconceivable because it is self-contradictory: it implies deification, but gods do not need friends. Following Mouffe's interpretation, I think this is applicable to political friendship as well (Mouffe 2000: 136f). Fully achieved all-inclusive political friendship among perfectly virtuous citizens leads to total unity of opinions and objectives and thus to the end of politics, i.e. to that for which it was designed as a means in the first place. As Cicero makes clear, there is no place for politics in true friendship between public figures: 'cum emendati mores amicorum sint, tum sit inter eos omnium rerum consiliorum voluntatum sine ulla exceptione communitas' (Cicero 2001: XVII, 61). Derrida's statement that 'Montaigne semble continuer de rêver un apolitisme ou un transpolitisme de fond' (Derrida: 1994: 211), should be taken at heart in the sense that a *dream* is precisely what this should remain. But PFA should remain as a project: *achieved* political friendship is a major danger for a pluralistic polity in which the political is to find a place, but *striving* political friendship is crucial for the agonistic articulation of the political: 'This is why it [democracy, EvdZ, but the same applies to PFA] should be conceived as a good that exists as good only as long as it cannot be reached' (Mouffe 2000: 137).

Finally, if Schmitt is right that *nothing* can escape the logic of the political (Schmitt 1963: 38), and that even my truest friend can become my public enemy whom I may have to kill, then we have an even more pressing conflict: true friendship is not transpolitical, but becomes political itself. It is a *political* stance to claim that true friendship is eternal and unbreakable and, therefore, must be exempted from the logic of the political, *because* it can be broken by it. Friendship, personal as well as political, is all-important yet fragile, and for *that* reason must be protected against the logic of the political, and this *also* is a political stance. Arguably, political philosophy is, and should be, a place of never-ending oscillation between *amor amicitiae* and *horror amicitiae*.

Notes

1. Throughout this essay, I use the classical distinction of friendship- *filía*/amicitia from love-eros/amor and love-agapè/caritas, as well as from affection-storgè/affectio (Lewis 2002).
2. Empedocles, fragments D.B. 17, 7f and 19f, and D.B. 35, 3–6 in particular.
3. I take this opposition from Lenn Goodman, who ranks fascism, Marxism and communitarianism under the general heading of corporatism; I use it merely to suggest a spectrum of anti-liberal positions in political philosophy (Goodman 1988: 68–71).
4. See also the paper by Gabriella Slomp in this volume.

References

Arendt, H. (1989 [1958]) *The Human Condition* (Chicago, IL & London: Chicago University Press).
Aristotle (1996) *Eudemian Ethics*. Loeb Classical Library 285 (Cambridge, MA & London: Harvard University Press).
Aristotle (1994) *Nicomachean Ethics*. Loeb Classical Library 73] (Cambridge, MA & London: Harvard University Press).
Aristotle (1990) *Politics*. Loeb Classical Library 264 (Cambridge, MA & London: Harvard University Press).
Bacon, F. (1985 [1957]) *Essays* (London: Penguin).
Barry, Brian (1990) *Political Argument* (New York: Harvester Wheatsheaf).
Bauman, Z. (1999) *In Search of Politics* (Cambridge: Polity Press).
Bauman, Z. (2000) *Globalization; the Human Consequences* (Cambridge: Polity Press).
Beardsworth, R. (1996) *Derrida & the Political* (London & New York: Routledge).
Bounds, E. (1997) *Coming Together/Coming Apart; Religion, Community, and Modernity* (New York & London: Routledge).
Cicero (2001) Laelius de amicitia, in: Cicero, *De senectute, De amicitia, De divinatione*, Loeb Classical Library 154, pp. 108–211 (Cambridge, MA & London: Harvard University Press),
Derrida, J. (1994) *Politiques de l'amitié* (Paris: Galilée)
Diogenes Laertius (1972) Lives *of Eminent Philosophers*. Loeb Classical Library 184 (Cambridge, MA & London: Harvard University Press).
Goodman, L. (1988) Political Philosophy in: O. Leaman (Ed.), *The Future of Philosophy Towards the 21st Century*, pp. 62–76 (London & New York: Routledge).
Kharkhordin, O. (1998) Civil Society and Orthodox Christianity, *Europe–Asia Studies*, 50, pp. 949–968.
Kymlicka, W. (1999) *Contemporary Political Philosophy* (Oxford: Clarendon Press).
Lewis, C.S. (2002 [1960]) *The Four Loves* (London: Harper Collins).
Montaigne, M. de (2001 [1595]) *Les Essais* (Paris: Livre de Poche).
Mouffe, C. (1993) *The Return of the Political* (London & New York: Verso).
Mouffe, C. (Ed.) (1999) *The Challenge of Carl Schmitt* (London & New York: Verso).
Mouffe, C. (2000) *The Democratic Paradox* (London: Verso).
Plato (2001) Lysis, in: Plato, *Lysis, Symposium, Gorgias*, Loeb Classical Library 166 (Cambridge, MA & London: Harvard University Press).
Plato (1999) *The Republic, Books I–V*. Loeb Classical Library 237 (Cambridge, MA & London: Harvard University Press).
Rawls, J. (1978) *A Theory of Justice* (Oxford: Oxford University Press).
Rawls, J. (1993) *Political Liberalism* (New York: Columbia University Press).
Rawls, J. (2002) *Law of Peoples* (Cambridge, MA & London: Harvard University Press).
Sartori, G. (1987) *The Theory of Democracy Revisited* (Chatham, NJ: Chatham House Publishers).
Schmitt, C. (1963 [1932]) *Der Begriff des Politischen* (Berlin: Duncker & Humblot).
Schmitt, C. (2002 [1963]) *Theorie des Partisanen* (Berlin: Duncker & Humblot).
Scholte, J.A. (2000) *Globalization: A Critical Introduction* (Houndsmills & New York: Palgrave).
Seneca, L.A. (2002) *Epistles*. Loeb Classical Library 75 (Cambridge, MA & London: Harvard University Press).
van der Zweerde, E. (2001)'Sobornost' als Gesellschaftideal bei Vladimir Solov'ev und Pavel Florenskij', in: N. Franz, M. Hagemeister, F. Haney (Eds), *Pavel Florenskij – Tradition und Moderne*, pp. 225–246 (Frankfurt am Main: Peter Lang).
Walzer, M. (1983) *Spheres of Justice* (New York: Basic Books, 1983).
Žižek, S. (2000) Da Capo senza Fine, in: J. Butler et al. (Eds), *Contingency, Hegemony, Universality*, pp. 213–262 (London: Verso).

Friendship as a Reason for Equality

DANIEL SCHWARTZ
Aston University, Birmingham, UK

Introduction

According to some political philosophers equality is valuable because it enables members of society to relate to each other in a way that is, or resembles, friendship.[1] One arguably unwelcome consequence of social inequality is that it impedes friendships between persons of unequal status. The central aim of this essay is to identify the circumstances in which the pursuit of friendship gives people of high status reason to reduce inequality in society. I wish, in other words, to answer the question: 'when should people placed high in a status hierarchy regard it as a bad thing that they cannot cultivate friendship with those who are placed below in a status hierarchy?'

Broadly following Aristotle's account of friendship, as well as contemporary social research, I argue that one of the forms of equality that friendship requires is equality of status. Too much inequality of status would undermine that similarity required for two people to cultivate companion friendship.

It follows that if one wants to be a friend of someone of lower status, one should make his/her status equal first. But this raises two queries: (a) would the cultivation of friendship between members of upper and lower status groups reduce inequality in that two-class society?; (b) when do upper-status people have reason to seek to cultivate friendship with modest-status people? The discussion will be assisted by examination of some of John Stuart Mill's views about friendship between spouses. According to Mill, one reason to reduce inequality between the sexes is that this would enable us to benefit from the good of marital friendship.

Having shown that friendship does not generally give reason to introduce greater social equality, I close by arguing that the opposite is true: equality gives reason to encourage friendship as a replacement for less egalitarian forms of relationship. Egalitarians who want to see democratic constitutions in as many political units as possible, should also want to see companion friendships in as many social units as possible. Friendship, in this broadly Aristotelian view, is not merely supervening on some sort of equality, but a type of equality in itself.

Equality as a Requirement of Friendship

Aristotle's classic account comprises a list of the features of companion friendship.[2] The inventory includes the separateness of the friends, their shared social arena, their similarity, their roughly symmetric power relations, their capability for reciprocity and for shared activities, pursuits and projects.

Many of these features are inconsistent with large inequality between the friends. My aim here is to assess the impact of one specific sort of inequality – inequality of status – on one of the listed features of friendship, namely, on similarity.

A person's status will be understood here as the position she occupies in a hierarchy in which positions are determined by how much of a given good or a combination thereof each person has. Different choices of good(s) generate different hierarchies. The ascriptions and comparisons between people's status to be made in this essay are open about the choice of hierarchy-constituting good(s).[3] Therefore, the conclusions to be arrived will apply for any choice of hierarchy-constituting good(s). Status, in the sense discussed here, should not therefore be confused with socio-economic position or social esteem as these reflect a *de facto* choice of hierarchy-constituting good(s).

For reasons I will give below, Aristotle and others believe that inequality of status or worth (*axia*) impedes friendship.[4] Friendship need not, however, merely reflect pre-existing status. The pursuit of friendship can be a creative activity through which the position of persons within a hierarchy can be altered. It is important, therefore, to distinguish between that friendship made possible thanks to *recognition* of already existing equality of status, and friendship the pursuit of which either directly or indirectly *introduces* equality of status.

The pursuit of a not-yet-existing friendship does involve some recognition. The superior who wants to be a friend of someone of inferior status must regard the prospective friend as at least capable of inhabiting his superior status. The prospective friend's lowly position must be seen as ungrounded in his nature, but rather a result of alterable circumstance and contingence. Persons regarded eligible for friendship are considered as naturally capable of equality of status.

Let me provide one illustration taken from a classic topic in Christian theology. For centuries Christian theologians were exercised by the challenge of making friendship compatible with initial radical inequality. This is so, because they had to show that friendship with God is a feasible ideal. The solution they proposed relied on the idea of grace. Grace is normally understood as a gift freely bestowed by God that allows us to participate in some of His attributes and so to become His friends. Trees and stones are not eligible for grace, only rational beings are. While friendship with God is status-affecting in that it lifts a rational being over her natural condition, it does not go as far as providing her equality of status with God.

How, according to this, does the pursuit of friendship propagate, to use Cupit's term, 'status-affecting attributes'? The superior wants to make friends with the inferior, that is, he wants the inferior to have those qualities that would allow the inferior to share his status. The motivation for this is not equality itself, but rather the desire to make a friend out of someone who is eligible for friendship. The value of friendship gives the superior reasons to propagate status-affecting attributes: if a superior wants to be a friend of the inferior, he will have to make the inferior alike to him in a certain ways, and then, in that respect, an equal.

The superior will sometimes be unable to generate the conditions that propitiate friendship. Status-affecting attributes divide into those that we can make (directly or indirectly) available to others, and those that cannot. Friendship can equalize status only when status is determined by status-affecting attributes that are capable of propagation. Even when propagation is possible, it has a cost (think about education as propagation of knowledge). It may be the case that friendship with someone may not be worth paying the price of attribute propagation.

It is important to mention another sense in which friendship equalizes. The good of friendship does not just give us reason to propagate status-affecting attributes, it itself can be a status-affecting attribute.

Think of a three-rank hierarchy composed by: friends of the king, those who are neither friends nor enemies of the king, and enemies of the king. In this hierarchy, friendship is status making not by virtue of involving propagation of something other than friendship, but directly by making the person a friend. This is one of the reasons why sometimes people deny to those of inferior standing certain ways of relating to them. Perhaps it is because of this that aristocrats often avoid friendship with their servants and do not allow their children to make friends with servant's children (in their eyes they would be loosing status in so doing).

Let me then close this section by restating its main thesis: the desire to cultivate friendship with someone of inferior status is a productive desire. That is to say, acting on the desire to cultivate friendship introduces changes in the world, such as the propagation of status-affecting attributes which amount to the creation of an equal.

Status Inequality and Similarity

This section assesses the impact of status inequality on the prospects of friendship by appraising its effect on the friends' similarity.

Similarity has always played a central role in philosophical accounts of friendship. Aristotle (*NE* 1155 a 32–35, *EE* 1235a5–30) raises the question, already discussed in Plato's *Lysis* (214–215), whether similar loves similar or contrary loves contrary. He argues that natural scientists tend to approach this question in terms too general to benefit the ethical theoretician. He then goes on to explain that it is in fact similars that love similars, and that many of the cases of *philia* between dissimilars either involve some aspired and not yet present similarity or fall under utility friendship (a non-paradigmatic type of friendship).

Sociologists have termed the tendency of people to engage socially with their perceived similars as 'homophily' (Lazarsfeld and Merton 1954: 23). A considerable body of experimental sociological literature has elevated homophily from social phenomena to social principle (McPherson et al. 2001: 416). Sociologists claim to have shown that there is 'a bias that leads similar people to associate more often than they would be expected to, given their relative numbers in the opportunity pool' (McPherson et al. 2001: 416).

A significant part of homophily research concerns friendship: friends tend to be similar. The similarities that bring people together have been shown to go beyond those based on socio-demographic qualities such as location, socio-economic background, age, race and religion. They also comprise 'values, attitudes, beliefs and aspirations', including character traits (McPherson et al. 2001: 428 based, among others, on Huston and Levinger (1978) and Almack (1922)).

It would be impossible to offer here an explanation of *why* similars like similars. Two complementary reasons that philosophers, like Thomas Aquinas (*ST* I–II q. 27 a 3c.), provided are: (a) we love the similar diffusively: inasmuch as we love ourselves, and we find in others the same attributes that we find in ourselves, our love propagates to those who are like us; (b) we love similarity extensionally: inasmuch as we find in another lovable attributes that we lack and would like to possess we seek to be similar to them.

How does status inequality affect dissimilarity? If there is just one factor that affects status (say, intelligence) then any increase in status inequality will also involve an increase in dissimilarity. Nonetheless, the same seems not to be strictly true when status is determined by two or more mutually independent factors (say intelligence+generosity). When status is determined by two or more independent factors there can be a reduction of inequality accompanied by an increase of dissimilarity, and alternatively an increase of inequality with a reduction of dissimilarity.[5] It would follow that, as far as concern for similarity goes, status equality is not required for friendship. Perhaps, then the only reason why friends need to be of equal status is because this makes possible just reciprocity between them, a point profusely elaborated by Aristotle (*NE* 1162b–1163a).

That last conclusion is, however, unrequired. While it is true that reducing inequality does not necessarily increases similarity, it is also true that (a) so long as there is status inequality, there remains a degree of similarity that cannot be achieved except by further reducing inequality; and (b) more importantly, the maximal dissimilarity tolerated by friendship imposes a limit to the degree of inequality that friendship can tolerate. The lower we set maximal tolerated dissimilarity, the lower will be the maximal admissible inequality.[6]

Hence, if we agree with the view that similarity is a requirement of friendship, optimization of the conditions for friendship requires as much equality of status as possible. Optimal friendship would be weakened by the adverse effect of any increase in inequality of status on similarity.

It is important to note that, in any case, the status-affecting attributes that affect companion friendship, are seldom independent from one another. This, at least, is Aristotle's view with respect to virtues of character: they grow together and decay together (*NE* 1144b33–1145a2, Telfer 1989–90). Companion friendship is friendship based on shared character traits.[7] Hence, the independent behavior of status-affecting attributes would not, in this view, be of relevance for companion friendship.

Does Friendship Give Reason for Equalizing Status?

On the assumption that establishing companion friendship with someone of lower status requires status equalization, it would follow that the good of friendship gives us reason to equalize. Francis Bacon says of friendship that

> princes, in regard of the distance of their fortune, from that of their subjects and servants, cannot gather this *fruit* [i.e. friendship]; except (to make themselves capable thereof) they raise some persons, to be as it were companions, and almost equals to themselves, which many times sorteth to inconvenience. (Bacon 1905: 767)

The value of friendship provides Bacon's prince reason to uplift some of his inferiors. The same thought seems to be present in Mill's exhortation to equality between the sexes: such equality, he says, would conduce to the good of marital friendship (1869: 333). Nonetheless, I argue in this section, the circumstances in which friendship provides reasons to reduce inequality are exceptional. According to my argument this holds for *any* inequality that obstructs friendship. So, even if inequality of status were not, as claimed above, an impediment to friendship, as long as there is *an* inequality that impedes friendship, the view that friendship does not generally give reason to equalize is still correct.

In the fourth chapter of his *Subjection of Women*, Mill acquaints the readers with the various benefits, other than justice itself, that would follow from introducing greater equality between the sexes. One such benefit, he tells us, is marital friendship. Inequality between the sexes deprives the spouses of the fruits and benefits of friendship:

> There is another very injurious aspect in which the effect, not of women's disabilities directly, but of the broad line of difference which those disabilities create between the education and character of a woman and that of a man,

requires to be considered. Nothing can be more unfavourable to that union of thoughts and inclinations which is the ideal of married life. Intimate society between people radically dissimilar to one another, is an idle dream ... Unlikeness may attract, but it is likeness which retains. (Mill 1984: 333)

Mill describes friendship very much along Aristotelian lines: friends share tastes, wills and opinions. He puts a great deal of emphasis on the importance of similarity, affinity and common tastes, wishes and wills for the development of a long-lasting friendship. Differential education for boys and girls undermines the similarity or affinity needed for friendship. Such artificialy induced heterogeneity makes impossible the ideal sort of marriage between man and woman, a partnership resembling or constituting friendship. Inequality between the sexes outside marriage conspires against the realization of the ideal type of association between man and woman. Criticizing the marital institution of his time Mill says:

> when each of two persons, instead of being a nothing, is a something; when they are attached to one another, and are not too much unlike to begin with; the constant partaking in the same things, assisted by their sympathy, draws out the latent capacities of each for being interested in the things which were at first interesting only to the other; and works a gradual assimilation of the tastes and characters to one another ... This often happens between two friends of the same sex, who are much associated in their daily life: and it would be a common, if not the commonest, case in marriage, did not the totally different bringing up of the two sexes make it next to an impossibility to form a really well-assorted union. (Mill 1984: 334)

Unequal treatment in society not only prevents the flourishing of marital friendship by making the spouses dissimilar: it also creates inequality within the marriage. The opposite of friendship in the case of marriage is not mere indifference, but normally servitude and domination (although, according to Mill (1984: 335), this is less so among the affluent: there rather than domination, we find tedium and personal stagnation).

The inequality that inhabits most marriages is, for Mill, inequality of status. According to Mill (1984: 334), friendships makes the difference between 'being something and nothing, between being an upper servant, a nurse, a mistress or a partner'.

Mill seems to make two separate claims, which, in generalized form, would look like this: (a) within any group composed of individuals of unequal status (such as the family of Mill's time) lifting up modest status individuals for the purpose of cultivating friendship with them would increase equality within that group; (b) the good of friendship provides reasons to effect such equalization.

I will argue that for any of these claims to be true many conditions must be met. The conditions needed for (b) to be true, in particular, are too exceptional for (b) to be generally correct.

Let me consider claim (a) first, namely the claim that the inequality in a group would be reduced when those of superior status (leaving open what makes them such) lift up those of inferior status with a view of cultivating friendship with them. I will now assess the force of two objections to this claim: (i) if the number of persons of superior status vastly outnumbers the number of persons of modest status, then even if all former maximize their capacity to make friends, this may leave modest-status persons 'unlifted' by friendship, (ii) inasmuch as friendship is exclusionary, it *requires* the exclusion of most people from the privileged relationship in which it consists. Consider the case of Bacon's prince choosing to cultivate companion friendship with a commoner. It is no just that he is unable to extend friendship to everyone, but that he must exclude from friendship most of them in order to be friends with the others.

Mill can escape both objections, but he can do so, I will argue, only because of peculiarities of marital friendship that are not generalizable to friendships in general.

Let me start from this last objection. (ii) argues that friendship necessarily leaves someone out, so that its advent will mean greater inequality for the left outs. The writer C.S. Lewis (1993: 41) says 'Friendship arises out of mere Companionship when two or more of the companions discovers that they have in common some insight or interest or even taste that the *others do not share*'; 'every sort of friendship is a sort of secession, even a rebellion' (1961: 45) and that it involves 'the innocent and necessary act of excluding' (1961: 47).

As regards equality, the advent of friendship may make the situation of the excluded persons relatively worse.[8] Consider a three-person setting in which Anne is positioned above Bobby and Benny who share the same status. Anne elevates Bobby to her rank to make him a friend. Now Benny is worse off than he was before. For one thing there is a new available good – friendship with Anne – of which he is being deprived. We can easily resolve the problem by positing the existence of Andrea, who shares Anne's status. It is enough that Andrea cultivates friendship with a Benny for everyone to benefit from the equalizing motivated by friendship and in keeping with friendship's presumed exclusionary nature.

This reply suggests that the reason why Mill escapes objection (ii) is that he is discussing friendship between groups of roughly equal size. If, as objection (i) argues, you had a society in which the ratio between the size of the groups is 1:20, then, for everyone to be equalized, each uplifter would have to establish friendship with 20 members placed below in the status ranking. But it is impossible to have that many friends. Even if it was possible to have 20 friends, upper-status persons may not be wealthy enough to be able to uplift to their own status 20 persons each. Once every upper-status person establishes as many friendships as he can, there would still be a remnant of modest status persons, who would lack any upper-status class 'lifters'. Being left out of the upgrading process and finding themselves with more people above them and less in their own rank, the left-outs will see their conditions worsen from the point of view of equality.

The defender of the equalizing nature of friendship could argue that initial size difference does not block equalization, it just slows it down. If some upper-status people lift lower-status people, the new upper-status people would again seek to cultivate friendship with lower-status people so that *over time* everyone would be absorbed into the upper-status class.

The conclusion that follows from discussion of these two objections is that *if* upper-status people seek to cultivate friendship then there would be a decrease in the number of modest-status people. The extent and pace of the decrease is dictated by (1) the initial relative size of the groups, (2) the cost of uplifting, relative to the means of the people of upper status, (3) the number of friends that upper-status people wish to have from among the ranks of the lower-status people. If the groups are of unequal size and the number of friendships cultivated by each upper-status people is one (as in the case of monogamous marital friendship) then the equalization process would never reach everyone.

Whether a decrease in the numbers of modest-status people means less inequality in society depends on our choice of criteria for evaluating inequality. Even if we were to side with the view that any reduction in the size the number of modest-status people amounts to a reduction of inequality, we still have to show that friendship gives reason to people high in the status hierarchy to uplift those place below. To this claim I turn next.

Claim (b) holds that 'the good of friendship provides reason to lift up those of lower status'. Indeed, if God or Bacon's prince wants to have friends they have no alternative but to elevate persons closer to their rank, i.e. to make them in some respect equal. Mill, however, cannot say the same of men. If a man wishes to benefit from friendship he need not create an equal, for he already has equals around: other men. Mill does not discuss the pertinent, if unfashionable, question that his account prompts: Why does the good of friendship give men reason to lift women to equality, when they can cultivate friendship with each other? Mill is particularly open to attack in this front, as he emphasizes that marital friendship should resemble as much as possible same-sex friendship. Why should then men go for it, given that same-sex friendship already exists?

Various arguments are available to defend the view that marital friendship should be sought even when men can cultivate companion friendship with other men. Here I provide a non-exhaustive list of some them. Before going into the list it is important to recall that marital friendship is of interest here as a case of that friendship that allegedly creates reasons to lift up the initially unequal. In Mill's time and society spouses had two additional characteristics: they were invariably of different sex (this is still mostly the case), and they normally perceived each other as initially unequal. Hence, many of the plausible reasons for marital friendship are not strictly reasons for friendship with the initially unequal, but rather, either reasons for heterosexual friendship, or for friendship between the spouses. These reasons can *accidentally* function as reasons for friendship with the initially unequal, namely, when it so happens the spouse or the person of a different-sex, are also of unequal status.

We may start from the view (not argued by Mill) that there is a qualitative difference between same-sex friendship and different-sex friendship. Different-sex friendship contains a valuable component not to be found in same-sex friendship. Hence different-sex friendship is irreplaceable by same-sex friendship.

This view seems indeed plausible. (An account of the nature of the valuable component unique to different-sex friendship cannot be provided here.) If correct, the view indeed shows that upper-status members have reason to cultivate friendship with the initially unequal of different sex (that is, whenever sex and status go together). The correctness of the view does not, however, give reason to cultivate friendship with the initially unequal as such, only when the initially unequal monopolize an attractive quality not to be found among upper-status people. A Greek master has no reason to believe that friendship the person who is now his slave would be any different from the friendship he already has with free men.

Another possible reason for cultivating friendship within marriage is that some pursuits are more efficiently carried out when the partner is also a friend. If the kind of work to be done involves extended daily contact with a person, then, often, you better become a friend. A woman and a man who decide to undertake the task of procreation and bringing up, or perhaps just the sharing of a home and domestic work, would do well becoming friends.

This proposal is not very persuasive. First, strictly from the view point of efficiency, it may be sometimes better to enslave or otherwise dominate the person of lower status rather than become a friend. Employers, for instance, often avoid social closeness to employees, feeling this would jeopardize discipline and obedience. Second, even if we grant that friendship enhances efficiency, this would fail to give us reason to cultivate friendship with those lower-status people with whom we *do not* share activities.

More persuasively, one could say that sharing time and place, in the absence of friendship, is generally an awkward and unbearable situation. So, when one finds oneself in such a position, one has reason to cultivate friendship and so to equalize the other party's status if it is not already equal. What matters here is not satisfying the need for sociality or escaping solitude. When you are stuck with someone in an elevator, the reason to chat is not to substitute your friends outside, but rather to make the waiting bearable and fruitful.

While the argument holds for spouses (at least those who spend a lot of time together) it does not give reasons to cultivate friendship with those of unequal status with whom we are *not* stuck together.

A further reason that might be offered in favour of marital friendship is that sexual physical stimulation and intercourse is the sort of thing that should be done only between persons who have intimacy, trust and affection.

Assuming that sex is indeed to be conducted only between friends, in what circumstances does the value of sex provide reasons for effecting the equalization needed for the cultivation friendship? The answer is: 'when all potential sex partners of upper-status people have modest status'. If men and women are ascribed unequal status and the sort of sex to be practised is heterosexual, then men do have a reason to uplift women to their status. It is difficult however to see how this argument about friendship between the sexes could be expanded so as to provide a general reason for friendship with the initially unequal when sex and status no longer coincide. In more formal terms, there would be reason for friendship when the initially unequal when they monopolize a capacity needed for performance of some only-between-friends activity.

It might be argued that upper-status people have reason to enlarge the pool of potential friends by opening the ranks to outsiders, inasmuch as doing this increases their social options. Yet it seems that the incentive for inclusive policies depends on the number of upper-status people: the greater their number, the lower the value of each incorporation of a new member taken from the modest-status group.[9]

Suppose you believe that for each of us there is just one matching soul that complements you, and it is somewhere out there (*Symposium* 192–193). Each individual, irrespective of status, has the same probability of being this person. So, in this view, we have equal reason to put each individual in a position in which he is suited for friendship.

This is true, but assuming one cannot screen the groups so as to know their composition, then the smaller the numbers of lower-status people relative to the numbers of people of upper status, the smaller the probability that your matching soul is there.[10] Therefore, the smaller the relative number of modest-status people, the lesser the reason to equalize all members of society at once.

This non-exhaustive survey suggests that friendship provides reasons to equalize status only in uncommon circumstances: namely when (i) lower-status people monopolize a desired quality, (ii) the two potential friends are stuck together, (iii) there are no alternative equals with whom the superior can perform attractive 'only-between-friends' activities, (iv) if the number of people of upper status is relatively small, and so there is significant incentive to enlarge the pool of potential friends, (v) if one believes in matching souls and attaches to incommensurable value to forging a relationship with them.

It does not seem that valuing friendship gives upper-status people a *general* reason to uplift those placed below, it gives them reason only when the aforementioned circumstances are in place (or provided one has specific beliefs about matching souls). This conclusion should not surprise us. After all, many societies renowned for having praised the ideal of companion friendship, such as Greek *poleis*, where also highly inegalitarian, and saw no need to extend companion friendship to women, let alone to slaves.

Should Egalitarians Promote Friendship between Unequals?

So far I have focused on whether friendship provides reasons to those who have high social rank to lift up those placed below when it is in their power to do so. It has been argued only seldom does friendship provide such reasons.

In this section I want to approach the connection between equality and friendship from a different angle. Should someone who values equality have any special interest in the promotion of friendship?

On the face of it, as far as status equality goes, friendship is superfluous: what matters is that the members of the group have equal status. Once this goal is achieved, why should the egalitarian be concerned about the type of relationship or association that they form, if they form one at all?

I will temper this assertion by arguing that friendship, rather than being a sort of addition to equality, is itself a certain type of equality. In developing this argument I will draw from points invited by Aristotle's parallel between types of *philia* and types of constitutions.

According to Aristotle, types of political constitution (*politeia*) resemble types of *philia*: monarchy resembles paternal *philia*, aristocracy resembles marital *philia*, and timocracy and democracy resemble fraternal friendship, i.e. friendship of those of equal status. So, we could say that the *polis* is large-scale *philia*, or, alternatively, that the *philia* is a mini-*polis* (*NE* 1161 a23–b15).

Aristotle's parallel invites two different points. First, just as the political power egalitarian should prefer a democratic constitution to aristocratic and monarchic ones, so in the mini-*polis* of social relationships she should prefer companion friendship over paternal and aristocratic-style marital *philia*.

Second, for Aristotle the constitution is not something separate from the social order that it constitutes, the constitution *is* the social order (*Pol.* 1253a37–39). A democratic constitution is that configuration in which the citizens are on an equal footing. The configuration does not make possible the constitution, nor is the constitution an efficient cause of the configuration. The constitution *is* the configuration. It is this same sense then we could perhaps say that friendship is not something separate that is made possible by equality, but rather is a sort of equality.

What sort of equality is friendship? According to Aristotle's parallel, companion-friendship seems to be a sort of equal power-sharing resembling that power-sharing found in democracies. This equal power sharing in which companion friendship consists is, in Aristotle's mind, dependent on worth or status. It is worth that grants legitimacy to claims to shares of power. Equal worth as found between companions determines that the right government should be a sort of power-sharing in which none dominates the other (or at least they take turns to do so).

At this point one could object that in social relationships, as opposed to *poleis*, there is no power to be shared. The example of the family, however, tells otherwise. Families decide how to administer burdens, and also where to live, where to go on holidays, how to divide labor. Perhaps this is true also of friends. Friends, inasmuch as they cooperate and have joint pursuits and activities also will face decisions about what is to be done and by whom.

From Aristotle's parallel it follows that she who wants equality of status has no reason to want friendship as such, but she who believes that power should be equally shared should want friendship *as such* (that is, not as something made possible by some sort of equality). In other words, in some circumstances, valuing this sort of equality of power seems to commit oneself to the promotion of companion friendship.

Why 'in some circumstances'? A move in the direction of companion friendship can take place in two ways: from no relationship to friendship, or from some sort of relationship other than friendship to friendship. Between two mutually disaffected individuals there seems to be no power to be shared. Someone whose concern is restricted to the equal sharing of whatever is had in common should not see any reason to promote friendship between so far unrelated individuals. However, *if* there *is* power (that is, action in potency), as it is in all cases of *philia*, then she who values equality should want to see friendship. She should probably want that as many relationships as possible make the transition from non friendship to friendship (whenever the conditions for this transition are found).

An Aristotelian should want to see friendship only whenever two persons of equal status engage in a relationship. Unlike Aristotle, most of us think that sex is not worth-affecting, and therefore that, all other things between equal, men are women have equal worth. Hence we should seek to see friendship rather than aristocratic style government within the family. In order to believe this we need not, however, disagree with Aristotle's view that there is *some type of worth* that makes power claims legitimate.

To summarize: while those interested in the good of friendship have seldom non egalitarian reasons to want to cultivate friendship with the initially unequal, those interested in equality have reason to want to promote friendship as a replacement of less egalitarian forms of relationship. Evaluation of the impact of an increase in the number of friendships on the level of inequality depends on the criteria that one chooses to measure inequality. It is not self-evident than an increase in the number of egalitarian relationships in society (with a consequent reduction of the number of people who find themselves dominated within their relationships) amounts to an overall reduction of inequality.

Acknowledgements

I would like to thank Nir Eyal, Shlomi Segall and Joseph Shaw, who read and commented upon an early draft of this essay. Thanks are also due for their comments to the participants of the Granada 2005 ECPR workshop on 'Politics of Friendship', and specially to Preston King and Oleg Kharkhordin, who organized the workshop and to Graham M. Smith who, with Preston King, have edited the present volume. I am grateful for the help and support provided by the Truman Institute for the Advancement of Peace at the Hebrew University of Jerusalem.

Notes

1. As noted by Harry Frankfurt (1987: 24), who seems to be alluding to David Miller's argument labelled 'equality as a foundation of fraternity' (Miller 1982: 84), according to which one noxious effect of inequality is that it restricts fraternal relationships within classes while it eliminates inter-class solidarity. For a revised version of this position see Miller (1990: 240–241). Earlier arguments on the salutary social effects of equality (such as solidarity and a sense of community) can be found in Baker (1987: 35, 39), R.H. Tawney (1931: 31–32) and J. S. Mill (1869: 334).
2. Throughout this essay I reserve the term 'friendship' for 'companion friendship' and will call other types of *philia* 'relationships'. Friendship between companions corresponds to what Aristotle calls

hetayrike philia. 'For the friendship of companions is not found in groups of many people, and the friendships celebrated in songs are always between two people' (*NE* 1171a13–16). As Gauthier and Jolif (1970: 763) point out, Aristotle probably has in mind famous friendships such as those between Achilles and Patroclus, Orestes and Pylades, Theseus and Peirithous.
3. This approach to status is inspired by Geoffrey Cupit (1996: 5).
4. Aristotle's proposes a twofold criteria to classify types of *philia*: heterogeneous/homogenous and between equals/between unequals. This yields four types of friendship, between: unequal similars, equal similars, equal dissimilars, unequal dissimilars. See *NE* 1162 a3–b2 and Gauthier and Jolif (1970: 688). Companion and fraternal friends are regarded as cases of friendship between equals and similars. *NE* 1161 a 25–27, 1161b 30–37, 1162a 10–13.
5. Assume status (S) results from the sum of intelligence (i) and generosity (g). For persons a and b, status inequality=$Sa-Sb$ and dissimilarity=$|(ia-ib)|+|(ga-gb)|$ (i.e. the sum of the absolute value of the differences). Assume that a's intelligence is valued at 9 and his generosity at 3, while for b the values are 3 and 9 respectively. An example of increase of inequality and decrease of dissimilarity for a and b respective values [annotated {(ia, ga), (ib, gb)}] is {(9,3),(3,9)}→{(9,3),(5, 9)} (inequality goes up from 0 to 2, dissimilarity goes down from 12 to 10). An example of decrease of inequality and increase of dissimilarity is {(9,3),(5, 9)}→{(9,3),(3,9)}.
6. This conclusion follows from examining the following graph:

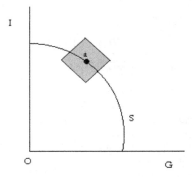

Assume person a to have status S, when S=$f(i,g)$ (i=intelligence, g=generosity). All people placed on the S curve share a's status. All people placed on the perimeter of the square-shaped diamond with the centre in a are dissimilar to the same extent with respect to a (see formula of dissimilarity given in the previous note). The diamond perimeter drawn in the graph indicates maximal dissimilarity consistent with friendship with a. (In other words, if we want b to be a's companion we should place him within the diamond.) As it transpires from the graph, the diamond also sets limits to the degree of maximal inequality consistent with friendship: this degree corresponds to the gap between the S-curves touching the most outer and inner points of the diamond. Different zones in the map correspond to the different sorts of relationships that a and b would have if b was placed in those zones. These sorts of relationship are: (i) between heterogeneous equals (b placed on S, close to the axes), (ii) between heterogeneous unequals (b placed close to the axes, but removed from S), (iii) between homogeneous equals (b placed on S, close to a), (iv) between homogeneous unequals (b placed on the radius (O, a), but far from S). A relationship is homogeneous when each person values the same thing(s) in the other (say virtue). A relationship is heterogeneous when each values different things in each other: say, one person is valued because she is rich and the other is valued because she is beautiful.
7. It might be argued that similarities based on shared non-status-affecting attributes are not disrupted by status inequality no matter how large they be. Nonetheless, one may suppose that the shared characteristics that bring persons together are always status-affecting, i.e. that in their eyes make a person

better or worse. While similarity based on the non-status-affecting attributes (such as having the same name) are left unperturbed by status inequality, this similarity is not important to us because it does not yield friendship.
8. According to Larry Temkin (1993: 29–30), one of our powerful egalitarian intuitions is that the smaller the number of people placed in a position of inferiority the greater the force of their complaint against the inequality thereby present. The lonelier one is in the modest-status rank, the worst one's situation from the point of view of inequality.
9. The increase of the membership of the Aristocratic Club (assuming it to exhaust all suitable potential friends) from two to three members, has much more weight from the point of view of the members' chances to find a good friend, than a change from ten thousand to ten thousand and one.
10. If, however, a person has just *one* matching soul, and assigns incommensurable value to establishing a relationship with her, then this person would consider any exclusion from the circle of possible friends a great loss no matter how low the probability that the excluded person be her matching soul.

References

Almack, J.C. (1922) The influence of intelligence on the selection of associates, *School and Society,* 16, pp. 529–530.

Aquinas, T. (1980) *Summa Theologica.* Fathers of the English Dominican Province (trans.) (Westminster, MD: Christian Classics). (*ST* I–II = first part of second part, q. = question, a. = article, c.=corpus).

Aristotle (1995) *Eudemian Ethics,* in: Barnes, J. (Ed.), *The Complete Works of Aristotle* (Princeton, NJ: Princeton University Press). (*EE*).

Aristotle (1985) *Nicomachean Ethics,* Ed. and Trans. T.H. Irwin (Indianapolis, IN and Cambridge: Hackett) (*NE*).

Aristotle (1996) *The Politics and the Constitution of Athens,* Ed. S. Everson (Cambridge: Cambridge University Press) (*Pol.*).

Bacon, F. (1905) On friendship, in: *The Philosophical Works of Francis Bacon* (London: Routledge).

Baker, J. (1987) *Arguments for Equality* (Verso: London and New York).

Cupit, G. (1996) *Justice as Fittingness* (Oxford: Clarendon Press).

Frankfurt, H. (1987) Equality as a moral ideal, *Ethics,* 98(1), pp. 21–43.

Gauthier, R.-A. & Jolif, J.-Y. (1970) *Aristote, l'éthique à Nicomaque,* vol. 2(2) (Louvain: Publications Universitaires, Paris: Beatrice-Nauwelaerts).

Huston, T.L. & Levinger, G. (1978) Interpersonal attraction and relationships, *Annual Review of Psychology,* 29, pp. 115–156.

Lazarsfeld, P.F. & Merton, R.K. (1954) Friendship as a social process: a substantive and methodological analysis, in: Berger, M., Abel, T. and Page, C.H. (Eds), *Freedom and Control in Modern Society,* pp. 18–66 (New York: Van Nostrand).

Lewis, C.S. (1993 [1961]) Friendship – The least necessary love, in: Kapur Badhwar, N. (Ed.), *Friendship: A Philosophical Reader* (Ithaca, NY and London: Cornell University Press).

McPherson, M., Smith-Lovin, L. &. Cook, J.M. (2001) Birds of a feather: homophily in social networks, *Annual Review of Sociology,* 27, pp. 415–444.

Mill, J S. (1984 [1869]) The subjection of women, in: Robson, J.M. (Ed.), *Collected Works of John Stuart Mill,* XXI (London and Toronto: Routledge & University of Toronto Press).

Miller, D. (1982) Arguments for equality, *Midwest Studies in Philosophy,* 7, pp. 73–87.

Miller, D. (1999) *Principles of Social Justice* (Cambridge, MA: Harvard University Press).

Plato (1961) *Lysis,* in: Hamilton, E. & Cairns, H. (Eds), *The Collected Dialogues of Plato, Including the Letters* (Princeton, NJ: Princeton University Press).

Plato (1967) *Symposium,* Trans. W. Hamilton (London: Penguin).

Tawney, R.H. (1931), *Equality* (London: Pickering).

Telfer, E. (1989–90) The unity of moral virtues in Aristotle's Nichomachean Ethics, *Proceedings of the Aristotelian Society,* 90(1), pp. 35–48.

Temkin, L. (1993) *Inequality* (New York & Oxford: Oxford University Press).

Kierkegaard: Responsibility to the Other

GRAHAM M. SMITH
Department of Politics and International Relations, Lancaster University, UK

Introduction

Of all the thinkers to have emerged from Europe in the nineteenth century, Søren Kierkegaard (1813–55) is both one of the most influential and distinctive. Kierkegaard is influential not only because of the impact in inheritance of his thought and work in the twentieth century (first through existentialism, and subsequently through various streams of postmodernism),[1] but also because of the sheer breadth of his concerns, which explore themes in philosophy, theology, literary criticism, psychology and politics. Kierkegaard is distinctive not simply because of his use of the Danish language and his perspective on the questions of Europe from Copenhagen, but also because

Kierkegaard's literature uses the strategy of pseudonyms, and is also designed to bring the reader to the consideration and resolution of one central problem: *what does it mean to be and act as a human being?* (Jansen 1990: 2–3; Outka 1982: 172). For Kierkegaard there was only one possible solution to this problem: being human is to recognise oneself and others as spiritual equals constituted by God: it is to *choose* to live as Christians.[2]

However, despite his acclaimed focus on the existential aspects of human life, it has sometimes been thought that Kierkegaard has little to say about ethical existence as such – and even less about questions of sociality and the political.[3] Fortunately, contemporary scholars are beginning to redress this imbalance and (although Kierkegaard cannot be considered a political theorist), his social and political thought is now receiving the attention it deserves.[4] Thus, whilst Kierkegaard might have written for 'that Single Individual' (Kierkegaard 1993: 4–5), he was by no means an individualist. Whilst Kierkegaard was clearly interested in commenting on *what* it means to be a human being, he was also (and necessarily) concerned with the dynamics of society which disguise, confuse and thwart the task of understanding and becoming a human being. In this respect, Kierkegaard is continuously concerned to work out, or perhaps more correctly 'play out', the logic and dynamics of a whole host of human relationships. This is clear in both his 'signed' authorship, and in the authorship of the pseudonyms.[5] His concern is to illustrate the inadequacies and ultimate bankruptcy of alternatives to a correctly constituted Christian life.[6] It is in this light that Kierkegaard turns his attention to an analysis of friendship.

Kierkegaard's most sustained analysis of friendship is set out in *Works of Love* (1847) (Kierkegaard 1995; henceforth simply *Works*).[7] Although this is a Christian polemic it is much more than this. What the writings of this period are especially concerned with is the individual's relations with others in a socio-political setting.[8] What Kierkegaard attempts in *Works* is to show how Christian relations *should* be constituted. It is important to note that Kierkegaard links the external relations that an individual forms with others directly to the inward relationship between the individual and God. For Kierkegaard, human beings have the *potential* to recognise themselves as spiritual selves. As such they should be properly related to God (as their creator and the source of their being), as well as to all others who are to be recognised and treated first and foremost as spiritual equals. Such a relationship Kierkegaard describes as the relationship of the *neighbour* (Müller 1993: 25). Failure to recognise ourselves and others as spiritual equals who should be correctly constituted with our spiritual relationship to God is the misrelation of *despair*.

This account of spiritual selfhood is crucial to understanding Kierkegaard's writings as a whole, and it could even be described as the ontological fact of Kierkegaard's thought. However, whilst it is Kierkegaard's intention to promote the 'neighbour' as the ideal response to the other, he does not simply assume that his reader will understand what this means – even if they believe themselves to be a Christian reading a Christian polemic. As with the strategy of Kierkegaard's authorship as a whole, Kierkegaard does not simply present his case, instead he entertains and undermines the strongest alternative to his own case. In *Works* the strongest alternative to neighbourliness (as a response to others) is an understanding of 'love' considered through the relationships of 'romantic love' and 'ethical friendship'. Thus, what is particularly interesting about Kierkegaard's account of friendship is not just that he finds this form of sociality deficient from his Christian perspective: what is interesting is that, unlike many of his contemporaries, he takes this phenomenon or ideal seriously as a forum for an authentic response to, and responsibility for, the Other. Moreover, that Kierkegaard finds difficulties with friendship raises serious problems for those who have advocated friendship as an ethical and political ideal, and those who would seek to understand and utilise the relationship in contemporary times.

Having made these initial comments, we can now turn our attention to a reconstruction of the account of friendship that Kierkegaard offers in *Works*. As has been indicated, initially we will concentrate on his account of secular or non-Christian friendship. However, ultimately we will see how we must return to his spiritual account of the self to complete Kierkegaard's examination of friendship and relations with others. Although Kierkegaard's account of friendship is infused with his own Christian concerns, it is possible to draw out three main features or aspects of friendship which structure his account as a whole: (1) friendship is characterised by preference or partiality; (2) friendship is characterised by drives and inclinations; (3) friendship is dependent upon reciprocity, and is ultimately selfish.

Preference and Partiality

Early in his account of friendship Kierkegaard claims that one of the defining features of friendship is that it is *preferential* (Kierkegaard 1995: 19, 44–46, 52–69). It is this feature that allows Kierkegaard to make another initial move: associating friendship with erotic love. Kierkegaard writes that:

> The same holds true of friendship as erotic love, inasmuch as this, too, is based on preference: to love this one person above all others, to love him in contrast to all others. Therefore the object of both erotic love and friendship has preference's name, 'the beloved', 'the friend', who is loved in contrast to the whole world. (Kierkegaard 1995: 19)

By highlighting this feature of friendship, Kierkegaard is able to portray the relationship as one that has its potential for extension and inclusiveness severely limited. For Kierkegaard this is necessarily the case, because the preferential nature of friendship involves the individual contrasting his friend 'to all others', and even loving him in 'contrast to the whole world'.[9] Additionally, the friend is 'chosen' as the friend from all possible persons whom one might correspond with in this relationship. As such Kierkegaard's claims concerning preference do not entail the exclusion of the world. However, they do point to the logic of preference *if* a person was confronted with such a choice. Thus, it is important to note that preference in and of itself does not exclude an authentic response to the other; Indeed, it might even create *special* responsibilities to that other.

So, Kierkegaard's initial claim that friendship is *preferential* is not one that would raise particular controversy in itself, at least not if we assume that whilst friendship might create a special responsibility towards the other, it need not also over-ride or devalue responsibilities to all others (at least not *prima facie*). However, the particular direction in which Kierkegaard develops his account of this feature is less than uncontroversial.[10] Kierkegaard claims that the 'preference' of friendship does in fact develop to the *exclusion* of others. What is more, the 'preference' of friendship is actually a preference for the *human aspects* of the friend (Kierkegaard 1995: 52, 56–57). In short, it is not the other person understood as a self that is admired, but a particular set of features of that self. In saying this, we must bear in mind that Kierkegaard has a specific understanding of the self as a spiritual equal before God. In addition, the friend does not simply admire the other's self as such (or aspects of that self) but they are concerned that their friend will admire and relate to them. In short, the preference of friendship must be reciprocal (Kierkegaard 1995: 34, 54–55). Without active reciprocity the friendship will perish.[11] This is particularly problematic not only because it is exclusionary, but also because it is subject to change. Kierkegaard points out that the poet seeks to 'join' the friends in their relationship, and that friendship is praised precisely because the friends promise to remain true to each other in eternity (Kierkegaard 1995: 30–31, 168–170). This adds a new dimension to Kierkegaard's early observation that the friends prefer each other in contrast to the whole world. From Kierkegaard's point of view, the focus of the friend's relationship dooms the relationship as the friends cannot secure themselves against change, and so the ideal of remaining *true* to the friend cannot be achieved. The friends cannot secure themselves against change not only because they are a part of the temporal sphere where change is inevitable, but because what they really admire about each other is not the other person as such, but some specific and particular human features of the other person.[12]

Drives and Inclination

The second feature of Kierkegaard's account of friendship is that it is based upon 'drives and inclinations' (Kierkegaard 1995: 44, 45, 49, 52). As with 'preference' this second feature of friendship is held in common with romantic love. Kierkegaard's claim here is that both relationships are sourced not in choice (rational or otherwise) or in ethical direction and decision, but are founded upon forces within the emotional life of the individual.[13] The individual therefore exercises little (if any) control over the appearance or evaporation of emotion.[14] As such, the individual cannot manipulate or direct the intensity or development of the sentiment. Indeed, the individual is *subject* to the purely human emotion. Thus, for Kierkegaard three areas of concern arise form this feature of friendship: (1) that the friendship contains no moral task (Kierkegaard 1995: 50-1); (2) that friendship is prone to instability (Kierkegaard 1995: 32, 34, 36-40); and that (3) the passion involved in friendship is rooted in selfishness (Kierkegaard 1995: 55). We shall deal with the first two of these claims in this section. The third claim will lead us into our next section, 'selfishness and reciprocity'.

Kierkegaard's first concern is that friendship's feature of 'drives and inclinations' betrays friendship as simply a stroke of luck or good fortune. As Kierkegaard writes:

> Erotic love and friendship, as the poet understand them, contain no moral task. Erotic love and friendship are good fortune. In the poetic sense, it is a stroke of good fortune ... to find this one and only friend. At most, then, the task is to be properly grateful for one's good fortune. But the task can never be to *be obliged* to find the beloved or to find this friend. (Kierkegaard 1995: 50–51).

Kierkegaard's point here is that it is certainly desirable to find a friend, but that friendship itself is little more than simply 'desirable'. It is true that friendship places ethical demands upon us, but it *is not* an ethical demand to seek friendship.[15] Friendship is removed from the sphere of ethical activity *not* because it involves drives and inclinations as such, but because those drives and inclinations do not and cannot constitute an ethical task. It cannot be the case that we should seek the friend as we cannot be obligated to foster and demonstrate emotions over which we have no control. Conversely, even if it were possible that we could be asked to seek and choose our friends, it does not follow that there *is* a friend to actually seek and choose. From this point of view, then, friendship is simply a beneficial coincidence.

The second area of concern is Kierkegaard's claim that because friendship is based on 'inclination' it is subject to instability (Kierkegaard 1995: 32, 34, 36–40). For example, Kierkegaard claims that 'spontaneously love can be changed *from itself*, it can be changed over the years, and is frequently enough seen. The love loses its ardour, its joy, its desire, its originality, its freshness' (Kierkegaard 1995: 36).

For Kierkegaard, any sociality or response to others, which is based *purely* upon drives and inclinations, is subject to change and dissolution. The passion which animates the friendship might wane; indeed, it might even turn into hate. If these events were to occur then the friendship would close. This observation is one which is familiar to us, and a part of everyday experience. Friendships form and dissolve, sometimes acrimoniously, but more often imperceptibly. However, Kierkegaard's account goes deeper than these commonplace considerations. It is Kierkegaard's claim that this feature of friendship not only has the potential to lead to instability, but that it actually makes the relationship *inherently* volatile and unstable. This is because both friends fear this change and cannot be sure that it will not occur despite assurances that they both might give to the contrary (Kierkegaard 1995: 3).[16] The true test of the love in friendship can only be eternity. This makes true friendship a riddle as this is precisely the test that the friends wish for, but cannot wish for; it is this test that the friends seek to apply, but cannot ever wish to apply. As Kierkegaard comments, the desire to test the friendship betrays the fact that the friends are uncertain in their relationship; Yet without such a test the friends cannot be secure (Kierkegaard 1995: 33).

Here we might challenge Kierkegaard's account of this feature of friendship in two distinct ways. The first is to draw out some of the logical possibilities of what Kierkegaard claims; possibilities that he does not seem to entertain himself. The second is to compare Kierkegaard's account of friendship to that of the Classical philosophers, and especially the paradigmatic model set up by Aristotle.[17] By doing so we will be able to get a clearer picture of the two varieties of friendship (poetic and philosophical) that Kierkegaard treats under the banner of friendship. However, we will also see that whilst these variations of friendship appear to have distinct features from each other, from Kierkegaard's perspective they are, in essence, the same.

Kierkegaard's account of the emotional aspects of friendship might initially appeal to our intuitions on the topic. However, whilst Kierkegaard's criticisms appear to have some initial value, it is important to recognise the limitations to the scope of this account. It might be conceded that friendship involves an element of emotional inclination; but it might also be argued that Kierkegaard has overplayed his hand here. If we think of some of the logical possibilities that drives and inclinations might play in friendship, the picture might not be as clear-cut as Kierkegaard presents it. First, if we were to accept that *some* friendships *are* formed on the basis of drives and inclinations, it does not follow that (a) *all* friendships are formed in this way (which can include those which might *later* display these qualities); nor does it follow that (b) those friendships which are initially formed in this way *continue* to be maintained by, and dependent upon, this feature (this can still be the case *even if* the inclination remains present).

What might be involved if we consider the line of enquiry opened by option (a) that not all friendships find their genesis in inclination? Here two people could form a friendship *not* through an (initial) inclination towards each other, but through a common circumstance, experience, or even a shared set of values. Here it is possible to conceive of a particular activity (such a mutual interest in a sport, a love of music, or the requirement that the individuals work together) forming the basis of the association, and possibly the friendship. Of course, it should be said that the friends must be 'inclined' to each other in the sense that they are civil to each other. However, the main focus of this friendship, and indeed the source of their association, is something other than the *feelings* that they have for each other which might only develop later. This bases friendship not on a sentiment alone, but a shared commonality which is not dependent on the emotional life of the individuals involved.[18]

Equally we might pursue the possibilities of option (b): that friendships which *are* formed on drives and inclination need not be dependent upon emotions or maintained in this way. Indeed, this is a clear possibility that is open in Kierkegaard's account precisely because he claims that drives and inclinations *can* change. Possibility (b) could be said to be the inverse of (a). Here two people might be drawn to each other through affection or emotion, and (initially) form a friendship on this basis. However, the shared thoughts, experiences and activities of that friendship might lead to a new bond of commonality. Although the initial excitement of the new affinity might very well wane, it could be replaced by a deeper and more fulfilling bond or even by a mutual 'tie' in an external activity, or set of beliefs. This could be enriching for both the individuals involved and even act to secure the friendship.

Despite the plausibility of the relationships described in both (a) and (b), these accounts of friendship appear to be far less intense than the relationship that Kierkegaard has in mind. His conception appears to be a much more passionate and enclosing relationship than the one that we would commonly recognise on any standard account of friendship. Indeed, the kind of friendship to which Kierkegaard refers is described variously by him as being both 'poetic' and capable of association with the features of 'erotic-love'. It is the intensity of the feelings involved in this poetic friendship that enable Kierkegaard to point to its volatility. So, whilst Kierkegaard's critique of friendship is pertinent, we might be tempted to conclude that it appears to apply only to a specific form of close and passionate relationship. It is conceivable that there could be a spectrum of relationships which might fall under the general rubric of friendship, relationships which do not include the defects that Kierkegaard identifies. Therefore, these would stand as candidates to offer the potential for a meaningful sociality, and an authentic response to others.

However, Kierkegaard has one more line of attack which he employs in conjunction with his previous two: that friendship is essentially *selfish*. Using this notion Kierkegaard's account not only bolsters the criticisms that he has made thus far, but actually shows how his account of friendship embraces all possible candidates for a model or basis for sociality and response to others. It is not simply an account of a high or intense form of friendship, it is a *decisive* account of friendship. If it falls, all forms of friendship fall with it. However, before we can turn to this final feature of friendship in Kierkegaard's account we need to say a word or two about Kierkegaard's parallel claim that friendship contains no 'moral task'. This extends Kierkegaard's account of friendship beyond the poetical forms of friendship explicitly referred to thus far, and allows Kierkegaard's critique to be applied to the kinds of 'philosophical' friendships that are described and analysed in the Classical tradition. These friendships are of importance as, being based upon virtue or the love of the Good, they offer the possibility of a basis for a social bond through either the love of virtue, or a form of love extended from the specific relationship to a face-to-face, or perhaps even a more abstract humanity.[19]

We will recall that Kierkegaard's position concerning the lack of 'moral task' in friendship was that it cannot be the ethical obligation of an individual to seek their friend, as friendship is based upon preference directed by passionate inclination. The 'ethical task' of friendship is reminiscent of Aristotle, and is used by Judge William to bolster his account of friendship in *Either/Or* (Kierkegaard 1987: 322).[20] Indeed, Judge William's position is explicitly opposed to that of Kierkegaard in *Works*. The judge views friendship as a moral corrective between good persons: 'The person who views friendship ethically sees it, then, as a duty. Therefore, I could say that it is every person's duty to have a friend' (Kierkegaard 1987: 322).

However, if Kierkegaard's position is tenable, then (*contra* both Aristotle and Judge William), it cannot be the ethical obligation of an individual to *seek* a friend, as friendship is based upon a preference directed by passionate inclination. As is well known, Aristotle's account of friendship divides the relationship into three distinct categories, each characterised by the good at which they aim. The lower two forms of friendship aims for usefulness and pleasure (Aristotle 1985: 210–212). The aim of the highest form of friendship (and the model which the other two emulate) is virtue (Aristotle 1985: 212ff.). Here the friends aim at discovering, contemplating and cultivating the Good: They love each other as lovers of the Good. In this way the friendship becomes much more than an exercise in goodwill (Aristotle 1985: 209ff), or an association with a particular (limited) end such as usefulness or pleasure (Aristotle 1985: 215–216). Virtue-friendship achieves stability because it is focused upon the mutual love of the Good itself. This is one of the reasons why Aristotle claims that bad men cannot be friends: they fail to understand or apprehend the Good, their 'associations' are therefore inherently unstable, and they could not form friendships with good men (Aristotle 1985: 243–244, 246–247). However, for Aristotle (as for Plato), friendship *is* an ethical task insofar as not only is it the site of ethical activity both in terms of demonstrating virtue and contemplating the Good, it is also a requirement of the good life itself. The ethical life was incomplete unless it included the virtue and relationship of friendship.[21]

How might Kierkegaard respond to this model, which stands in contrast to his own? Specifically, how might Kierkegaard respond to the claim that there is an ethical dimension to friendship? There are two major differences between the structure of the accounts of friendship offered by Kierkegaard and Aristotle. These differences relate to the wider structure of their thought. However, the differences not only provide points of contrast between their accounts, they also render their accounts irreconcilable. The first difference relates to what we might term *telos*. The second (discussed more fully under 'selfishness' the third feature of Kierkegaard's account of friendship) is the notion of the self and selfhood itself.

What might be meant by invoking the notion of *telos*? The term points to what we might call the end cause of an action, event, phenomenon or entity. In Aristotle's philosophy and account of social life, human beings seek *eudemonia* or the fulfilment of the Good Life. As we have also noted, the *telos* of the highest form of friendship (virtue-friendship) is the Good itself. That is to say, friendship forms a part of the general good life, and it also contemplates the Good as a part of the Good life. It is true that the friends receive lower goods from the relationship (such as material benefits, assistance and pleasure) but what unites the friends is the mutual apprehension, appreciation and love of the Good in, and through, each other. For Kierkegaard this attempt at founding a sociality on a human ethics is fundamentally misguided. In Kierkegaard's account the only possible *telos* of human life is not 'the Good' but God. That is to say, the primary relationship that must be formed is that of the individual's God-relationship. It is this relationship that (existential and based on a variety of command-ethic) motivates and guides the individual's life. This is true for all individuals, and the requirements (although based on a personal response to God) are the same for all individuals. The ethical life cannot be achieved through human action or contemplation alone. The desire to do so reflects a misplaced understanding of the ethical, and an attitude of 'despair' (a misrelation of the self).

Therefore, if we place the accounts of Aristotle and Kierkegaard side-by-side, what we see are fundamentally opposed concepts of friendship. Aristotle bases his ethical account of friendship on the notion that human beings can appreciate the Good through reason, and that human flourishing can follow from this appreciation. Kierkegaard bases his account (and criticisms) of friendship on the importance of the individual's relationship to God, and the need to overcome and transcend the *purely* human. In Aristotle's account friendship presupposes and leads to the Good and *eudemonia*; in Kierkegaard's account friendship is an earthly and potentially misguided snare that drives the individual away from their true human *telos* of becoming a self before God, and further into the misrelation of the self which is despair. It is clear then that these two accounts do not, and cannot, speak to each other as they fail to recognise the starting-points of the other's account to be legitimate.

Thus we are brought to the recognition that what truly separates Aristotle's and Kierkegaard's accounts of friendship (and thus the non-Christian and Christian accounts of friendship) is not the logic or dynamics of friendship as such, but their underlying accounts of the self. Kierkegaard cannot accept Aristotle's ethical notion and understanding of the self. As Kierkegaard writes in a *Journal* entry:

> Aristotle has not understood the self deeply enough, for only in the aesthetic sense does contemplative thought have an entelechy, and the felicity of the gods does not reside in contemplation but in eternal communication. – Aristotle has not perceived the specification of spirit. (Kierkegaard 1995: 397)

It is this distinction between contemplating the self as a temporal being, and that of apprehending the self as a spiritual being, which helps us to understand the third and final set of claims that Kierkegaard makes concerning friendship: that it is 'selfish'. It is to this claim that we will now turn.

Reciprocity and Selfishness

Thus far we have explored Kierkegaard's claims that friendship is both 'partial' and based upon 'drives and inclinations'. However, to fully appreciate Kierkegaard's criticisms of friendship it is important to understand how it is possible for Kierkegaard to claim that friendship is selfish. It is noteworthy that, despite his criticisms of friendship, Kierkegaard does not reject friendship completely. He rejects it as a despairing existence only if not underpinned by spiritual selfhood. It can form a component of a Christian existence *if* the individual underpins and transforms the relationship by recognising others as spiritual equals or neighbours. To see why this is the case (and to consider the nuances in Kierkegaard's position) let us turn first to Kierkegaard's claim that friendship is selfish.

Unlike Kierkegaard's previous claims concerning the features of friendship, to claim that friendship is selfish appears to militate against our intuitions. It would not be at all controversial to claim that our common understanding of friendship conjures up a relationship of mutual concern, sharing, support and even (in possibly the most 'ideal' type) selflessness or self-sacrifice. Indeed, in friendship it could be supposed that the focus was on the other person rather than on ourselves. The only modification we might wish to make to such a statement is that the reciprocal qualities of friendships might invite us to claim that the friendship is *mutually* other-orientated. Therefore, it is perhaps even more surprising to us when we read that this is *also* a picture of genuine friendship that Kierkegaard recognises as being common, and even accepts as an account of friendship. Despite this, Kierkegaard still maintains that the relationship is selfish.

Kierkegaard's claim that friendship is selfish challenges our assumptions concerning the place of the self in friendship in three ways. The first of these is to claim that the preferential and emotional aspects of friendship make the relationship 'selfish' insofar as they are focused upon the 'self' of the other person (Kierkegaard 1995: 53–60, 266–267). This would be a clever but somewhat disappointing move if Kierkegaard took this no further and left his criticism in the realm of semantics; he does not. As we shall see, this semantic 'clarification' has more to it than meets the eye. In fact, it is employed as the taskmaster for a good deal of philosophical labour. Having pointed out the focus of friendship, Kierkegaard's second move is to argue that the concentration on the self is coupled with the importance that the friends place on reciprocity. Here the concern with reciprocating the fidelity of the friend is *not* a test of the friend's love (although it might take this form and it might appear to do this). It is actually a concern with the friend's own self. To be concerned with reciprocity and especially with reciprocating fidelity and love is for the questioner to pose the question not, *Do I love the other?* but instead, *Does the other really love me?* The third and most significant claim of Kierkegaard's in relation to the selfish nature of friendship is that the friendship focuses on the human self and does so in purely temporal terms. This brings us back to Kierkegaard's understanding of the spiritual self and despair. Purely temporal friendship is actually a misrelation as the individual fails to relate primarily to God. As such it fails to provide the grounds for genuine selfhood. As a relationship of despair, friendship is doomed to failure and actually represents a triple-misrelation: to God, to self, and to the other.

Kierkegaard's initial move, then, is to draw attention to the focus of friendship through the semantic device of claiming that friendship is selfish as it focuses on the 'self'. In itself this observation appears obvious, perhaps even trivial. However, in making this observation explicit, Kierkegaard actually forces his readers to look afresh at what is implicit in friendship. In doing so he not merely exposes this feature, but forces his reader to confront it as a fundamental choice. In this way Kierkegaard's semantic device achieves much more than a simple change in the structure of description. It also forces a change in the structure of the world-view of the reader.[22]

Having refocused our attention on the object of friendship (the self) it is now possible for us to pursue Kierkegaard's criticisms. We have seen that the selfish element of friendship is that it is not an expression of love for the other, but for a particular self (or aspects thereof). However, Kierkegaard's criticisms extend beyond this observation to focus on one of the other features of friendship, that it is reciprocal or has a reciprocal element (Kierkegaard 1995: 18–19, 54–55, 236–238, 367, 349–351). This attack would appear somewhat peculiar (and perhaps even misguided) if we do not bear in mind that Kierkegaard's attack on the reciprocity of friendship is not an attack on reciprocity *per se*. His point, rather, is that the reciprocal aspect of friendship reveals the misguided nature of the love involved in friendship. This is how Kierkegaard describes the relation in *Works*: 'To admire another person is certainly not self-love, but to be the one and only friend of this one and only admired person – would not this relation turn back in an alarming way into the I from which we proceeded?' (Kierkegaard 1995: 54–55).

Kierkegaard claims that it is perfectly possible to admire the qualities of another person, but that in friendship there is a degree of exclusivity and intensity that takes the friends beyond simple admiration and into the desire to claim or possess the other. The fidelity of the friendship, which is manifested in a partial love and admiration, must be reciprocated if the friendship is to survive. Indeed, the very notion of friendship entails a reciprocal relationship: the basic unit of friendship is the pair.

Here Kierkegaard is able to link the preferential and emotional elements of friendship to the most thoroughgoing notion of selfishness. As the friendship is a reciprocal focusing on the self, Kierkegaard is able to stress that the partiality and passion of friendship lead to both exclusivity (Kierkegaard 1995: 52) and the jealousy which he claims is 'always fundamentally present in erotic love and friendship' (Kierkegaard 1995: 55). Indeed, friendship leads the friends away from a sociality with others, as the friends isolate themselves from the world. As Kierkegaard claims: 'The more securely one I and another I join to become one I, the more this untied I selfishly cuts itself off from everyone else' (Kierkegaard 1995: 56). Whilst under the illusion that they share a self, the friends actually focus on themselves (Kierkegaard 1995: 266–269).[23] Far from encouraging or laying the foundations for a wider sociality, the reciprocity in friendship prevents a selfless or other-orientated approach as the friendship becomes a calculation and exchange of benefits (Kierkegaard 1995: 273, 267) and/or an exchange of assurances and admiration (Kierkegaard 1995: 155–156, 237, 267). Friendship can only exist where there is reciprocity, or the hope and expectation thereof (Kierkegaard 1995: 351). This last claim of Kierkegaard's is extremely hard to avoid, as it is difficult to see how reciprocity could not be a feature of friendship. This is betrayed in both ordinary and philosophical talk of friendship, where we speak of the friends supporting and caring for each other, and even the friends' choosing of each other. The reciprocal feature of friendship is also essential if we are to distinguish it form other relationships and attitudes such as civility, goodwill or well-wishing.

Having focused our attention on the reciprocal dimension of friendship, it is now possible to see how Kierkegaard's account of friendship extends beyond what at first appear to be the fairly narrow confines of an especially intimate and intense relationship. It is true that Kierkegaard's main focus is on what we might term the 'highest' form of friendship, but it is important that Kierkegaard can discount this form of friendship as it is the most promising form of authentic response to the other. Whilst other social relationships have merits, it is only in friendship that they combine to create the potential for a fulfilling and ethical human sociality. In this way, far from attacking a remote, rare, and perhaps even irrelevant model of sociality, Kierkegaard is playing his hand against 'paganism's' best player in the surroundings of its choosing. What Kierkegaard concludes from his examination of the reciprocal dimension of friendship is that even this most ideal of relationships is laced with selfishness, exclusivity and jealousy. Moreover, Kierkegaard attempts to show not only that this is often the case, or even potentially the case, but that this is a necessary feature of the relationship itself. Reciprocity is one of friendship's defining features and one of its most celebrated merits: Kierkegaard's analysis attempts to expose it as also being one of friendship's deepest flaws.

Response and Responsibility

It is now possible to draw together the strands of Kierkegaard's analysis of friendship, and to reconsider his reasons for rejecting it as a response to the other, and a ground for an extensive and stable sociality. Kierkegaard's account is one which draws out three key features of friendship. Indeed, these features appear to be intrinsic to the relationship both in the history of the idea, and also recognisable by those who are engaged in friendships. As we have seen, Kierkegaard identifies preference and partiality, drives and inclinations, and reciprocity and a focus on the self as being characteristic of friendship. This account of friendship is no 'straw man'. The features that Kierkegaard identifies and explores are also the features which are celebrated and contemplated by the poets and philosophers of friendship. However, whilst others have found these features ethically praiseworthy, Kierkegaard develops them in such as way as to show that they are either not subject to ethical evaluation, or even (in some cases) unethical. Kierkegaard does this not only from the perspective of his own conception of 'neighbourliness', but also from *within* the terms of an ethical understanding of friendship itself. Thus, the preferential and affective aspects in friendship are found, by Kierkegaard, to lie outside the realms of the ethical, and even damaging to the ethical status of friendship. Similarly, Kierkegaard finds the elements of reciprocity and focus on the self troubling. Whilst reciprocity would appear to be open to conscious ethical direction, the dependency of friendship upon this feature betrays a demand on the other. The line is blurred between (1) genuine care for the other, and (2) a significant dependency upon the other. At best, the other becomes a willing, *but conditional*, participant in the friend's conception of well-being and self-worth; at worst, the other is the instrument of the friend's own self-concern, and the unrecognised and devalued victim of selfishness.

Kierkegaard's sociality is that of the neighbour. This relationship is built on a normative conception of a spiritual selfhood in relation to God. The relationship of the neighbour presupposes and acts on the most radical form of spiritual equality. Additionally, there can be no confusion as to who the neighbour is – the neighbour is unconditionally everyone (Kierkegaard 1995: 21). There can be no question of preference, inclination or reciprocity in the neighbour relation. For all persons are spiritual equals, and the command to love the neighbour remains in force regardless of any anticipated or actual response from the neighbour. Thus friendship is a despairing relationship in two main senses. First, friendship fails, philosophically and poetically, to recognise the centrality of spirit in the formation of self. Friendship can recognise the spiritual aspects of persons, but fails to build upon the full implications of this. Indeed, it cannot recognise spirituality *qua* friendship. In Kierkegaard's account, friendship ignores or displaces the God-relationship and focuses on the purely human aspects of self, or transforms spirit into a human category. Second, this misconception concerning spirit not only fails to place God at the centre of the relationality, but deifies the human. The loyalty, fidelity and love shown towards the friend is not only a secret reflection of selfishness, but is also an impossible foundation for human sociality. As Kierkegaard has claimed, friendship is made into the highest good, or finds its place in a plurality of equal goods. This results in either the worldly ethical being placed as the highest good, or the human self becoming deified. From Kierkegaard's point of view this is a manifestation of despair (or a misrelation of the self).

Thus, in the final analysis, Kierkegaard presents us with two contrasting accounts of our response to the other. It is possible to argue that from Kierkegaard's perspective friendship is a dangerous self-deception that, in responding to the other, also deceives the friends about their true responsibilities. It is possible to characterise Kierkegaard's account of friendship as one which espouses a self-deception as for Kierkegaard there is a double-movement in the relationship. Whilst (overtly) friendship appears to be other-orientated, and thus not primarily about the self, in fact (argues Kierkegaard), the reciprocity needed for the maintenance of the relationship points us straight back to a concern with the self. However, the second movement shows that we are deceived about our 'selves'. That is to say, the self which we (secretly) seek to maintain and foster in friendship is a limited, temporal self. The enclosing dynamics of friendship elevate this self and far from creating a forum for truly self-less and other-orientated activity, friendship reinforces and entrenches the limited temporal self which is mired in despair. Friendship is certainly one response to the other, but it is far from a relationship in which responsibility for the other is exercised. Again, there are two movements to this. The first is that the friend is not taking unconditional responsibility for the other. Moreover, the friend is not truly concerned with the other, but with their temporal self. The second movement is that, even though the 'responsibility' to the other betrays the selfish concern of the friend, ultimately the friend is not even acting responsibly towards self. This conception of self is based on temporal dependency, and does not engage with true responsibility towards the spiritual foundations of the self. In Kierkegaard's view, if an individual is to act responsibly (religiously-ethically) towards others, s/he must do so in relation to self. Until an individual has performed the one essential task (establishing a relationship with God), no responsibility can be taken for others. No individual can act in a truly ethical way without founding such behaviour in a self. The individual who is subject to the moulding and influence of others cannot take responsibility for self.

In conclusion, whilst we might not care for nor feel able to endorse Kierkegaard's demanding religious conception of a spiritual self, it remains that his criticisms of friendship are powerful and troubling. The problems that Kierkegaard outlines are problems that have to be traversed by anyone proposing an account of friendship – especially if it is claimed that the account lays the framework for a genuine response towards the other, and is a truly ethical manifestation of responsibility. Although Kierkegaard rejects friendship as a basis for sociality, he does identity what is important about friendship, and what makes it a strong candidate for such sociality: reciprocity and a concern for the self. Thus, in his treatment of friendship (albeit a critical one) Kierkegaard raises again what may be considered a key question of the political: what is the ontological status of the self and other. Insofar as Kierkegaard investigates the possibilities for an ethical response to the other, and the possibilities of responsibility towards self and others *in relation*, Kierkegaard returns friendship to the discourse of politics and modernity.

Notes

1. For a discussion of this see Best and Kellner 1990; Poole 1998; Macquarrie 1973: 13–33, 53–55.
2. As Bruce H. Kirmmse writes, 'Kierkegaard was fundamentally and radically *Christian*. No reasonable sense can be made of him by ignoring or toning down his Christianity.' (Kirmmse 1998: 188–189).
3. For two examples of such literature consult Mackey 1972, who doubts Kierkegaard's ability to generate an ethics of human community from his thought; and Zuidema 1960, who considers Kierkegaard to be sceptical of human fellowship and to have an attitude of rejection.
4. For examples of such scholarship consult the following: Perkins 1984; Westphal 1987; Pattison and Shakespeare 1998; Perkins 1990; Connell and Evans 1992; Plekon 1982 (which draws out the implications of Kierkegaard's thought along social lines) and Smith 2005 (where I draw out Kierkegaard's thought along political lines connecting politics with Kierkegaard's notion of 'despair').
5. For a full discussion of the relationship between Kierkegaard and his pseudonyms consult Crites 1970; Taylor 1975.
6. The 'problem' of bringing his reader to the point of accepting Christianity and choosing to become a Christian was a complex one for Kierkegaard, and involved a battle on two fronts. Initially he had to show how non-Christian forms of life were ultimately bankrupt, from both a Christian and non-Christian point of view. However, Kierkegaard also had to battle against the established and bourgeois Christianity of his own Denmark. Indeed, the problem was one of making those who assumed themselves to already be Christians to come to a point of actually thinking and acting as Christians. As Kierkegaard himself writes: 'The situation (becoming a Christian in Christendom, where consequently one is a Christian) – the situation, which, as every dialectician sees, casts everything into reflection, also makes an indirect method necessary, because the task here must be to take measures against the illusion: calling oneself a Christian, perhaps deluding oneself into thinking one is without being that' (Kierkegaard 1998: 8n2). For an account of Kierkegaard's relationship with *established* Christianity and the role of the state Church consult Kirmmse 1998.
7. There are two general commentaries on this book which are worth special note. The first is that of Paul Müller who writes that *Works* helps to distinguish Kierkegaard's position from that of the pseudonyms, but it also shows some continuity with them (Müller 1993: viii). The second (Ferreira

2001) discusses *Works* in relation to the thought of Levinas. Additionally, Bruce H. Krimmse also gives an account of *Works* (Kirmmse 1990).
8. Crucial to this development are the books *Two Ages* (1846), *Works of Love* (1847) and *The Sickness Unto Death* (1849). Cf. also Kirmmse 1992: 167; and Cady 1982: 240.
9. Whilst we might consider Kierkegaard's account to be slightly dramatic in its expression here, it also seems to ring true. It is not difficult to accept the notion that in friendship the friends show partiality towards each other in contrast to those who are not involved in the friendship. Of course, this does not mean that the friends necessarily or deliberately seek to undermine the claims and rights of others, or even act in an uncivil or uncaring way towards others. It merely means that the friends choose to act in an especially caring way towards each other.
10. As we have seen, Kierkegaard associates friendship with erotic love on account of the preference that both display. It is this preference that makes both relationships the subject of the poet's admiration (Kierkegaard 1995: 19, 46). It is important to stress here that although friendship and erotic love are associated and share many features in Kierkegaard's account, he does not claim that they are *actually* the same on account of this. They remain as distinct relationships even though they are both placed under the general category of 'poetic love'. However, it is the *partiality* of friendship (that the poets celebrate) that becomes the focus of Kierkegaard's attack.
11. A feature which was clearly recognised by Aristotle, cf. Aristotle 1985: 210, 234–235; a feature which is also endorsed and discussed by Cocking and Kennett 1998: 519ff; and is also identified by Richard White, who connects it to 'recognition' (White 1999: 29).
12. The focus on the specificity of the other person opens space for Kierkegaard's second line of attack which we will explore presently. To anticipate, Kierkegaard moves from the specific focus on the other person to claim that this focus betrays friendship as being *selfish*. Kierkegaard attaches various degrees of 'depth' to this claim. For Kierkegaard the preference in reflecting love of some feature of the other ultimately leads back to the love of the human self. Friends relate only to the other as *specific human* selves. They do so by making the friendship the highest good, but can do so only at the expense of a correct formulation of their own self. That the friends do this is brought to our attention by Kierkegaard's reminder that philosophers call the friend the 'other self' or 'other I' (Kierkegaard 1995: 53).
13. This account of the emotional life of individuals is both fairly intuitive and perhaps widely accepted. It is not difficult to recognise the force and intensity of emotions, even if we also wish to claim that their demands and affects can and should be balanced or diminished when we judge and act. We can also agree that in our common understanding of friendship we assume that the friends have some form of emotional attachment to each other. Indeed, the terms 'friendly', 'liking' and 'affection' are closely related and (in some contexts) even synonymous with each other. Indeed, it is either comic or tragic to utter the phrases that 'we do not like our friends' or that 'our friends bring us no pleasure'.
14. (Cf. Barrett 1984: 66–67), who points out that in *Either/Or* Judge William expresses concern that the constancy of immediate love is illusionary, and that it is dependent on feelings over which the individual has no control. This is also continuous with Kierkegaard's own comments (Kierkegaard 1993: 35).
15. Something with which Kant would agree (Kant 1947: 72).
16. Indeed, fear of change and betrayal in friendship is a common theme in the history of the idea itself. Aristotle raises it (Aristotle 1985: 243–244); it is clearly a concern of Plutarch in his 'How One May Distinguish between Flatterer and Friend'; it is reflected in Bacon's somewhat instrumental account of friendship in his 'Of Friendship'; and Nietzsche is overtly aware of this problem in passages such as *Daybreak*, section 287.
17. Aristotle's principle account of friendship appears in his *Nicomachean Ethics*. It would be difficult to over-state the influence of Aristotle's account of friendship on subsequent thinkers – indeed, it is hard to break away from Aristotle's shadow. As might be expected, there is a large literature commenting on Aristotle in relation to friendship. For a brief selection, see Cooper 1977; Sherman 1987; Stern-Gillet 1995.
18. Clearly this is akin to the idea of friendship that Aristotle develops insofar as he asks what is the 'good' aimed for in friendship, and is especially true of his 'partial' friendships based around utility and pleasure.

19. This is what Kant appears to have in mind in his unfinished 'Lecture on Friendship' (Pakaluk 1991: 210–217).
20. Whilst Kierkegaard was undoubtedly aware of Aristotle's account, and we might expect any substantial deliberation on the theme of friendship to at least make reference to Aristotle's account due to its undoubted influence in this area of thought, there are certain features of Kierkegaard's account which militate against this direct engagement. The most significant of these is that Kierkegaard's account is often directed at 'poetic love', which (as we have seen) is both preferential and passionate. The relationship of friendship as Aristotle describes it does not appear to fall under this rubric. Indeed, for Aristotle virtue-friendship is formed around contemplation and not passion. Kierkegaard does not deal in depth with Aristotle's account of friendship, but not because he fails to appreciate it as an account of friendship. On the contrary, it is precisely because it is an account of friendship, rather than simply friendly relations, that enables Kierkegaard to 'deal' with Aristotle's (and others') accounts of a more philosophical friendship under the same banner as he deals with poetic friendship. Both of these accounts have the same root: that the relationships are constructed in human rather than spiritual terms. It is this root which Kierkegaard attacks.
21. The focus of friendship as a site of ethical activity and the love of the Good is echoed and endorsed throughout the Classical literature. For example in his *De Amicitia* Cicero has Laelius claim that friendship results not from any 'inadequacy' found in the individual, but from a love of virtue (Cicero in Pakaluk 1991; Seneca claims that friendships are formed so as our 'noble qualities may not lie dormant' (Seneca 1917: 120); and finally in 'How One May Distinguish between Flatterer and Friend', Plutarch counsels that we should 'realise and remember always that our soul has two sides: on the one side are truthfulness, love for what is honourable, and power to reason, and on the other side irrationality, love of falsehood, and the emotional element; the friend is always found on the better side as counsel and advocate, trying, after the manner of a physician, to foster the growth of what is sound to preserve it' (Blosser and Bradley 1997: 111).
22. This device is powerful for (if the reader accepts Kierkegaard's argument) then it is simply impossible to 'return' to the world and friendship as if nothing had happened. To return to friendship after understanding Kierkegaard's account is to live in a category of conscious despair. Indeed, it is to choose despair as the individual realises that friendship is a despairing relationship, but chooses the relationship.
23. Montaigne's essay is perhaps one of the best expressions of this 'sharing' of a self in friendship.

References

Aristotle (1985) *Nicomachean Ethics* (Indianapolis, IN: Hackett).

Barrett, L. (1984) Kierkegaard's *Two Ages*: an immediate stage on the way to religious life, in: Perkins, R.L. (Ed.), *International Kierkegaard Commentary Volume 14*, pp. 53–71 (Macon, GA: Mercer University Press).

Best, S. & Kellner, D. (1990)Modernity, mass society, and the media: reflections on the *Corsair* affair, in: Perkins, R.L. (Ed.), *International Kierkegaard Commentary: The Corsair Affair*, pp.21–61 (Macon, GA: Mercer University Press).

Blosser, P. & Bradley, M.C. (1997) *Friendship: Philosophic Reflections on a Perennial Concern* (Lanham, MD: University Press of America).

Cady, L.E. (1982) Alternative interpretations of love in Kierkegaard and Royce, *The Journal of Religious Ethics*, 10(2), pp. 238–263.

Cocking, D. & Kennett, J. (1998) Friendship and the self, *Ethics*, 18(3), pp. 502–527.

Connell, G. & Evans, C.S. (1992) *Foundations of Kierkegaard's Vision of Community: Religion, Ethics, and Politics in Kierkegaard* (Atlantic Highlands, NJ & London: Humanities Press International).

Cooper, J.M. (1977) Friendship and the good in Aristotle, *The Philosophical Review*, 86(3), pp. 290–315.

Crites, S.D. (1970) The Author and the authorship: recent Kierkegaard literature, *Journal of the Academy of Religion*, 38(1), pp.290–315.

Ferreira, M.J. (2001) *Love's Grateful Striving: A Commentary on Kierkegaard's Works of Love* (New York & Oxford: Oxford University Press).
Jansen, N. (1990) The individual verses the public: a key to Kierkegaard's views of the daily press, in: Perkins, R.L. (Ed.), *International Kierkegaard Commentary: The Corsair Affair,* pp.1–21 (Macon, GA: Mercer University Press).
Kant, I. (1947) *The Moral Law: Or, Kant's Groundwork of the Metaphysic of Morals* (London: Hutchinson University Library).
Kierkegaard, S. (1987) *Either/or Part II* (Princeton, NJ Princeton University Press).
Kierkegaard, S. (1993) *Upbuilding Discourses in Various Spirits* (Princeton, NJ: Princeton University Press).
Kierkegaard, S. (1995) *Works of Love* (Princeton, NJ: Princeton University Press).
Kierkegaard, S. (1998) *The Point of View: On My Work as an Author* (Princeton, NJ & Chichester: Princeton University Press).
Kirmmse, B.H. (1998) 'But I Am almost never understood...' or, who killed Soren Kierkegaard?, in: Pattison, G. & Shakespeare, S. (Eds), *Kierkegaard: The Self in Society,* pp.173–195 (Basingstoke: Macmillan).
Kirmmse, B.H. (1990) *Kierkegaard in Golden Age Denmark* (Bloomington, IN: Indiana University Press).
Kirmmse, B.H. (1992) Call me Ishmael – call everybody Ishmael: Kierkegaard on the coming-of-age crisis of modern times, in: Connell, G. & Evans, C.S. (Eds), *Foundations of Kierkegaard's Vision of Community: Religion, Ethics, and Politics in Kierkegaard,* pp.161–182 (Atlantic Highlands, NJ & London: Humanities Press International).
Müller, P. (1993) *Kierkegaard's 'Works of Love', Christian Ethics and the Maieutic Ideal* (Copenhagen: C.A. Reitzel).
Mackey, L. (1972) The loss of the work in Kierkegaard's ethics, in: Thompson, J. (Ed.), *Kierkegaard: A Collection of Critical Essays,* pp. 268–282 (Garden City, NJ: Anchor Books).
Macquarrie, J. (1973) *Existentialism* (London & New York: Penguin Books).
Outka, G. (1982) Equality and individuality: thoughts on two themes in Kierkegaard, *The Journal of Religious Ethics,* 10(2), pp.171–203.
Pakaluk, M. (1991) *Other Selves: Philosophers on Friendship* (Indianapolis, IN: Hackett).
Pattison, G. & Shakespeare, S. (1998) *Kierkegaard: The Self in Society* (Basingstoke: Macmillan).
Perkins, R.L. (1984) *International Kierkegaard Commentary: Two Ages* (Macon, GA: Mercer University Press).
Perkins, R.L. (1990) *International Kierkegaard Commentary: The Corsair Affair* (Macon, GA: Mercer University Press).
Plekon, M. (1982) Moral accounting: Kierkegaard's *Social Theory and Criticism, Kierkegaardiana,* 12, pp. 69–82.
Poole, R. (1998) The unknown Kierkegaard: twentieth-century receptions, in: Hannay, A. & Marino, G.D. (Eds), *The Cambridge Companion to Kierkegaard,* pp. 48–75 (Cambridge & New York: Cambridge University Press).
Seneca (1917) *Ad Lucilium Epiestulae Morals* (Cambridge, MA: Harvard University Press).
Sherman, N. (1987) Aristotle on friendship and the shared life, *Philosophy and Phenomenological Research,* 47(4), pp. 589–613.
Smith, G.M. (2005) Kierkegaard from the point of view of the political. *History of European Ideas,* 31(1), pp. 35–60.
Stern-Gillet, S. (1995) *Aristotle's Philosophy of Friendship* (Albany, NY: State University of New York Press).
Taylor, M.C. (1975) *Kierkegaard's Pseudonymous Authorship: A Study of Time and the Self* (Princeton, NJ: Princeton University Press).
Westphal, M. (1987) *Kierkegaard's Critique of Reason and Society* (Macon, GA: Mercer University Press).
White, R. (1999) Friendship: ancient and modern, *International Philosophy Quarterly,* 19(1), pp. 19–34.
Zuidema, S. (1960) *Kierkegaard* (Philadelphia, PA: Presbyterian and Reformed Publishing Company).

Carl Schmitt on Friendship: Polemics and Diagnostics

GABRIELLA SLOMP
School of International Relations, University of St Andrews, Scotland

Introduction

Until very recently a major concern of the Anglo-American literature on Carl Schmitt has been to establish his ideological identity.[1] Writers such as Gopal Balakrishnan (2002) who try not to engage with the long-standing debate on Schmitt's affiliations with the Nazi regime have been challenged by those who claim that the spectre of Nazism and the Holocaust should, in the words of Jef Huysmans, 'always haunt any invoking of Schmitt or Schmittean understandings of the political'. Huysmans goes on to argue that 'normative questions about the ethico-political project his concept of the political incorporates' ought to be 'the kernel of any working with or on Schmitt's ideas' (Huysmans 1997: 323). Huysmans also warns against the history-of-ideas approach to Schmitt claiming that 'introducing Schmitt's work by means of a history of ideas shaped around an epistemological puzzle considerably limits the possibility of incorporating the shadow of the Holocaust and Nazism in the story' (Huysmans 1997: 324).

By contrast, the European literature on Schmitt, and particularly the Italian and French Left,[2] has shown a much stronger interest than its Anglo-American counterpart in establishing the validity of some of Schmitt's analytical claims about the political in the twentieth century. Indeed, the presence of incisive political analysis and intelligent diagnosis in Schmitt's writings is acknowledged by writers as diverse as Jurgen Habermas, Mario Tronti and Jacques Derrida (see also Borradori 2003). For example, Derrida writes in the *Politics of Friendship*:

> In certain respects, we believe it [the *Concept of the Political*] offers a pure and rigorous conceptual theory of the political, of the specific region of that which is properly and without polemical rhetoric called the political, the politicity of the political. Within this region, in the enclosure proper to a theoretical discourse all examples, all facts, all historical contents should thus issue in knowledge; indeed, in those forms of disinterested theoretical reports called diagnostics. (Derrida 1997: 117, but see also Dallmayr 2000: 105–130)

Diagnostics and polemics are intertwined aspects of Schmitt's thought, a fact of which he was well aware. On the one hand, he portrayed himself as someone offering a diagnosis of the crisis of the state, the crisis of *jus publicum europaeum*, the crisis of the notion of *Justus hostis*, etc. On the other hand, sometimes in the very same works, Schmitt claims that 'all political concepts, images and terms have a polemical meaning' (Schmitt 1996a: 30), thereby attracting attention to the 'polemicization' inherent to his own interpretation of the political and to his discussion of liberalism, democracy, just war, enmity and so forth (see Arditi & Valentine 1999: esp. 36–43).

The aim of this essay is to consider both Schmitt's polemical and his analytical claims in dealing with a concept which is central to his theory and yet strangely overlooked by the secondary literature: the concept of friendship. I will argue that, for Schmitt, friendship is an inherently political concept whose meaning and role cannot be decided abstractly. Indeed, its definition depends upon the ideological bent and historical context of the person who attempts to define it and, for Schmitt, a concept such as friendship becomes a misleading and misguided abstraction when reference to real conflicts is lost.[3]

The essay proceeds in three steps; as a first step, it makes some textual claims about the meaning and role of friendship in Schmitt's writings; secondly it puts forward an interpretation of the significance of friendship in Schmitt's political thought; and finally it tries to disentangle polemics from diagnostics in Schmitt's discourse and draws some tentative conclusions.

Textual Analysis of Schmitt's Friends and Enemies

The best starting point for an analysis of Schmitt's understanding of friendship is an examination of his 1962 *Theorie des Partisanen* and his 1963 Foreword to the German edition of the *Concept of the Political*. In these writings, one can find textual evidence to support the four separate interpretative claims that I am going to make in this section. At this stage, the four claims will seem largely independent; but their interconnectedness and relevance will hopefully appear more clearly in subsequent sections.

Friends and Allies

Two types of friend populate the world of *Theorie des Partisanen*: on the one hand there is the friend who is external to one's own group or party, whom we can call the ally, and on the other hand there is the friend who belongs to one's own group or party. This type of friend is mentioned only once in *Theorie des Partisanen*, but it features in an important passage where the key characteristics of the partisan are discussed. The bond between the partisan and members of his group or party is described by Schmitt as total (*die totale Erfassung*), altogether different from any allegiance existing among individuals under normal circumstances in a liberal democracy (Schmitt 2002b: 21). For Schmitt, the relationship between the partisan and his *compagno* or *camerata*[4] is intensely political in so far as they are both prepared to die and kill for each other and for their shared way of life. The friend as member of the same group or party is a defining element of the partisan's identity: it helps establish who the partisan is to a far greater extent than other associations or characteristics such as his family or church or class, or even race and gender. While the friend-as-*compagno* or *camerata* is part of the partisan's identity, the external friend, the ally, is the source of recognition of the partisan's identity. When Schmitt refers to friends in *Theorie des Partisanen*, he does not usually mean one's fellow fighters, with whom one has 'a total political bond', but the external and *public* friends or allies of one's own group and cause. In Schmitt's account of twentieth-century partisan guerrillas, 'friends' or allies tend to be nation-states. The function attributed by Schmitt to the public friend is twofold: on the one hand, it provides the partisan with arms and supplies, and on the other it gives political recognition to the partisan – recognition that is crucial to the partisan's political status. Without an external ally, Schmitt maintains that the activities of the partisan cease to be political and instead become merely criminal.

To recap, Schmitt refers to two types of friend in his writings. There are the public friends or allies (be they a state, a party or some other group) of one's own political unit with whom Schmitt insists there exists a symbiotic yet *utilitarian* relationship,[5] and there are also friends with whom one has a shared way of life and who are members of the same group or party. With regard to the second form of friendship, Schmitt claims that its basis lies in an *existential bond*.

The Importance of Having a Friend

We may recall that Schmitt often points out that the essence of the political is not enmity as such, but the possibility of distinguishing between one's friend and one's enemy; therefore the presupposition of both friend and enemy are essential to politics. Indeed, even if Schmitt concentrates primarily on the nature of enmity, he is keen to point out that this by no means implies that the concept of friendship is somehow secondary or less important in his understanding of the political.

In the existing literature, one can find a thorough examination of Schmitt's claim that there is no politics if there is no enmity, and yet there is an inexplicable absence of analysis focused on Schmitt's assertion that the reverse is equally true, that there is no real politics if there is no friendship. There is textual evidence to support the view that both friends and allies are essential to Schmitt's understanding of the political. Schmitt insists that without the relationship with a public friend, politics becomes 'just a cover up of a never ending state of hostility' (Schmitt 1996a: 12). In my opinion, the best way to appreciate what Schmitt meant by this claim is to concentrate on a most illuminating anecdote in *Theorie des Partisanen*: the story of Raoul Salan.

In 1958, Schmitt tells us, General Salan was made commander-in-chief of French armed forces in Algeria. Although initially a supporter of General de Gaulle, Salan became increasingly hostile to the French president as he was disillusioned by de Gaulle's shaky commitment to the defence of French sovereignty over Algerian soil. As a reaction, Salan founded the OAS (Organisation d'Armee Secret) in 1961, a secret organization that started to plan terrorist attacks against both the Algerian 'enemy' and French nationals on Algerian territory. In 1962 Salan was arrested and tried. In discussing the Salan case, Schmitt makes a point that, I would argue, is of critical importance for a correct reading of his concept of the political, and of his concept of friend and enemy. Schmitt stresses the fact that Salan initially had one enemy (the Algerians), then two enemies (the Algerians *and* the French) and finally a universal enemy (the whole anti-colonial world): in this way his enmity became absolute, abstract and universal. As a result, in the *mare magnum* of world politics, Schmitt tells us, Salan was unable to find any agency or third party that supported his cause, and, on the contrary, he clashed head on with the compact front of anti-colonialism. *Salan had only enemies and thus, says Schmitt, his enterprise was no longer political.* Such a remark seems to me all important in correctly understanding Schmitt's concept of the political, and I will come back to it later on in this essay.

Schmitt believed that real politics could not take place in a world which was divided in two. The presence of external allies is as important to Schmitt as the existence of enemies. The absence of allies removed the political dimension of Salan's enterprise, and Salan emerges from Schmitt's story as the Don Quixote of politics.

Carl Schmitt's Typology of Enmity

Schmitt's typology of enmity, discussed in *Theorie des Partisanen*, is worth considering because it offers three main insights which can be further explored in order to gain a fuller understanding of Schmitt's concept of friendship. First, for Schmitt, the meaning of enmity is not fixed and unchanging, but it rather mutates and evolves in order to adapt to different historical circumstances. Secondly, Schmitt makes the point that the definition of enmity of an age is dependent upon a number of different yet inextricably linked factors. Taking these two observations into account, Schmitt makes a third point in which he asserts that three different notions of enmity co-existed in the international sphere at his time of writing. Moreover, he showed great political acumen in realising that one notion of enmity in particular was becoming more and more prominent.

The friendship–enmity dualism in Schmitt's writing creates a number of parallels between these seeming opposites. In the next section, I will argue that, just as there are three types of enemy, one can also extrapolate to characterise three different types of friend. Moreover, I will argue that the same set of factors affecting the nature of enmity also control the meaning of friendship.

One type of enmity that Schmitt takes for granted and never defines in any great detail is *conventional enmity*; conventional enmity is limited and regulated – it materialises in the defined arena of an inter-state war. The protagonist of this type of enmity is the sovereign state, its limitations and regulations come from *jus publicum europæum,* namely the system of law which regulated European inter-state relations from the Treaty of Westphalia to the First World War. This system of law enforced distinctions between war and peace, between criminal and enemy, between civilian and combatant.

Another type of enmity that appears repeatedly in Schmitt's writings is *'real enmity'*. Schmitt links this form of enmity to the birth of the partisan during the Spanish Wars against Napoleon. Real enmity is subversive of, and unbounded by, the distinctions and regulations of *jus publicum europæum*. Schmitt explains that this type of enmity was first seen in civil and colonial wars and was essentially defensive. The enemy is seen by the partisan as an oppressor, an invader to be fought with all available means (Schmitt 2002b: 17).

Schmitt is keen to point out that real enmity is unbound by legislation and yet is not completely unbridled in so far as the 'telluric' characteristic of the partisan (his bond to a particular land) imposes spatial and temporal limits upon his hostility and prevents him from making claims of absolute justice. Real enmity is, as Schmitt points out, relative and not absolute, defensive and not aggressive (Schmitt 2002b: 93).

The third type of enmity that one can find in Schmitt's writings is *absolute enmity*. Schmitt ascribes this type of enmity to the global revolutionary, or terrorist. What sets the revolutionary apart from the autochthonous or telluric partisan is the lack of a special bond to a particular land. Whereas, for the autochthonous partisan, the enemy is located in time and space, the revolutionary sees his enemy as a universal enemy, a class or a racial enemy. Schmitt points out that the enmity of the revolutionary is totally unbridled: 'the war of total and absolute enmity knows no limitations', neither the limitations of *jus publicum europæum* (that constrains conventional enmity), nor the limitations of time and space (that confine real enmity).

Factors Affecting the Meaning of Enmity and Friendship

Although the notion of enmity goes back to biblical times and the story of Cain and Abel, Schmitt stresses the fact that the specific meanings of 'friend' and 'enemy' emerge from the interaction of a large number of factors in each epoch. These factors include the structure of the international political system, the ideology of the political agent, the level of technological advancement in weaponry and communications, the stage of economic development, changes in jurisprudence and the prevailing culture (discussed in Slomp 2005: 502–519). Not only can these factors not be isolated from one another, but the relation of cause and effect between each of these factors and the prevailing notion of enmity (and friendship) is also far from clear.

Of all the factors influencing the meaning of enmity and friendship in a given age, Schmitt seems to pay particular attention to two: ideology and technology. As a first step, let us consider briefly the role given by Schmitt to ideology in the definition of enmity.

Schmitt does not discuss the ideology that inspires conventional enmity in *Theorie des Partisanen* (see instead Schmitt 1950b), but he does devote a large section to the elucidation of the ideological sources of real and absolute enmity. Whereas Schmitt associates Clausewitz with real enmity, he links absolute enmity to Lenin.

For Schmitt, Leninism is just an example (admittedly a crucial example at the time of writing *Theorie des Partisanen*) of an ideology promoting absolute enmity, an enmity which divides the world into two camps. In *Theorie des Partisanen*, Schmitt mentions other ideological views which undermine the classical notion of enmity, views that are also touched upon in *The Concept of the Political,* namely, the notion of the 'last war of humanity', coined after the First World War (Schmitt 1996a: 36), and the 'just war' tradition. By trying to find a moral justification for war and killing, the 'just war' tradition is, according to Schmitt, compelled to portray the enemy as an evil to be eliminated, thereby embracing the notion of absolute enmity.

There is no doubt that in today's world, Schmitt would see religious fundamentalism and global terrorism as well as the 'war on terror' as unambiguous examples of ideologies endorsing absolute enmity.

For Schmitt, the notion of enmity in the twentieth century has not only been affected by changing ideologies; other factors such as technological developments and global interdependence have also changed its nature. Schmitt argues there is a relationship between the advancement of weapons technology and the underlying notion of enmity. He offers the powerful example of the nuclear bomb and claims that in order to justify the production and the possession of nuclear weapons, not to mention their use, one must convince oneself that the enemy is worthless. Schmitt argues that weapons of mass destruction presume the notion of absolute, limitless enmity.

In Schmitt's account, the two factors that undermine the conventional notion of enmity, ideology and technology, were at work in the partisan wars of the twentieth century and were also influencing factors in another phenomenon that followed the Second World War – the Cold War. Writing in 1963, Schmitt states:

> Also in the other type of today's wars, the so-called Cold War, the whole conceptual framework that has so far supported the traditional system of defining and regulating war breaks down. The cold war mocks all the classical distinctions between war, peace and neutrality, between politics and economics,

between the military and the civilian, between combatant and non-combatant, and maintains only the distinction between friend and enemy, on which it grounds its very origin and essence. (Schmitt 2002a: 18)

In *Theorie des Partisanen*, Schmitt does not commit himself to suggesting that either factor, ideology or technology, is more important in defining the notion of enmity of an age. In other parts of his opus, however, there is the suggestion that ideology without the help of technology could not promote a truly absolute form of enmity. For example, in *Ex Captivitate Salus* Schmitt argues that in the Middle Ages 'theologians' held an 'absolute' concept of enmity; yet he stresses that these wars, though bloody, were essentially different from the partisan wars of the twentieth century primarily because of the differences in weapons technology. In Schmitt's opinion, the twentieth century's crisis of conventional or limited enmity is a direct result of advances in weapon technology; Schmitt points out that such a crisis is as unlikely to be halted or reversed as technological development.

The Meaning and Significance of Friendship from a Schmittean Perspective

The aim of this section is two-fold: first, I will propose a typology of friendship which mirrors Schmitt's typology of enmity. Such an interpretation suggests that, from a Schmittean perspective at least, the meaning of friendship is largely dependent upon one's own ideology as well as the level of technological development of an age. Secondly, I will reconstruct a typology of the political and argue that, for Schmitt, friendship acquires a special political significance for those who understand politics as a pragmatic search for identity, whereas friendship plays a far less important role for ideologies that regard the identity of political actors as given, as is the case in Liberalism, or unproblematic, as in Leninism or religious fundamentalism.

Although the major claims of this section are speculative and open to debate, my contention is that they are consistent with the spirit of Schmitt's philosophy and with the textual evidence introduced in section II.

A Typology of Friendship

Nowhere in his works does Schmitt define the meaning of friendship in any great detail. This may seem to support the claim that Schmitt was primarily concerned with the concept of enmity rather than friendship. In his Foreword to the 1963 German edition of *The Concept of the Political*, however, Schmitt defends himself by saying that the construction of a juridical concept always proceeds from its negation and that this method does not imply the primacy of the negated concept. He refers to criminal law and observes that it would be absurd to contend that criminal law gives special value to criminality over law-abidance. Schmitt claims that it is similarly absurd to consider enmity as more important than friendship in his concept of the political.

Just as one's definition of enmity *largely* depends upon ideology in Schmitt's understanding, it would appear to follow that an individual's definition of friendship is similarly dependent upon one's underlying ideological perspective; hence there are as many different meanings of friendship as there are different ideologies.

As Schmitt gave us a typology of enmity inspired, among other things, by three different ideologies, so we may attempt to speculate about what a Schmittean typology of friendship would look like, a typology that reflects each of the three different definitions of the enemy. I suggest that conventional enmity (namely an enmity which is controlled, limited, regulated and, in Schmitt's own words, game-like) has an equivalent sort of friendship that is similarly contained and restrained. This friendship is neither dramatic nor intense, but more akin to the relationship found between players. Such a form of *game-like friendship* is the lukewarm bond that, in Schmitt's view, individuals form in liberal democracies.

In a similar vein, it can be argued that the friendship corresponding to real enmity is much deeper, much more fundamental, and much more dramatic than its game-like counterpart. For a telluric partisan or for a nationalist terrorist, the commitment to the group is total; he[6] is willing to endure imprisonment, torture, and even death to defend his fellow fighters. He is willing to kill civilians and even children to protect his group. He would risk everything for his friends: his safety, his liberty, his reputation, his honour, and even his own family. In Schmitt's philosophy, the ultimate source of this *existential* or *true friendship* is a common bond to the land (*Heimat*): a partisan's friend is located in time and space.

Finally, the third type of enmity, absolute enmity, is related to a more abstract form of friendship. Although the global revolutionary or global terrorist may have physical contacts with some friends, he is equally committed to friends whom he may have never physically met or even seen. This type of person is willing to kill and die for abstractions, be they ideals or people. For Schmitt, ideologies such as Leninism or religious fundamentalism have to some extent contributed to the development of absolute enmity and its counterpart: abstract friendship.

But, as in the case of enmity, ideology is not the only important factor that affects the meaning of friendship. We may recall that Schmitt gave special status to technology and suggested that advancement in communications and weaponry was crucial for the advent of absolute enmity and the gradual but unstoppable crisis of both conventional and real enmity. As globalisation has affected the notion of enmity of the age and has fostered absolute enmity, so too has it affected the destiny of the concept of friendship: globalisation has led to a shift towards 'abstract' friendship.

To sum up, there is no explicit typology of friendship in Schmitt's works but one can nevertheless extrapolate and hence differentiate between three types of friendship (game-like, existential, and abstract) which are mirror images of Schmitt's own typology of conventional, real, and absolute enmity. The first type of friendship derives from an individualistic ideology in so far as friendship is a game only for someone who can claim to have an identity independent from his association to a group or party. The second type of friendship, true or existential friendship, can never be just a game; it is an existential bond between agents struggling to establish their political identity. The third type of friendship, abstract friendship, is inspired by 'dogmatic' ideologies. The global terrorist or fundamentalist does not need to find identity through a process of interaction; his own identity, or rather the identity of his group, is already known to him; all he needs to do is to protect and safeguard it against the enemy.

A Typology of the Political and the Issue of Identity[7]

From Schmitt's typology of enmity, I would argue that one can reconstruct not only a typology of friendship but also a typology of the political. A starting point for such an investigation can be found in the case of Salan. When relating the general's story, Schmitt points out that Salan had many enemies. How it is possible, Schmitt asks, to have more than one real enemy? His reply (that echoes Däuber) is worth recalling:

> '*Der Feind ist unsre eigne Frage als Gestalt*'.[8] If our own Gestalt is unambiguous how can this duality of our enemy come about? The enemy is not something that we can do away with for some reason or another or that we can destroy for its complete worthlessness. The enemy places himself on my own level. For this reason, I must engage with him, in order to establish the very measure of myself, of my own boundaries, of my own Gestalt. (Schmitt 2002b: 42)

As in logic, there cannot be two distinct negations of a given statement. Schmitt argues that in politics, too, there cannot be two enemies (negations) of the same entity. The enemy is not just 'another', but is the very negation of the self. For Schmitt, the enemy does not simply put in question our role, actions, values and interests, but in fact challenges our very being. The result of any confrontation with the enemy is a verdict on our own identity. This view of enmity that Schmitt sometimes referred to as 'existential' is an enmity that comes from the soul and not from abstract ideals or principles, an enmity that has a concrete target, that is relative and bounded exactly because the enemy is concrete.

For Schmitt, one cannot have more than one real enemy any more than one can have more than one real identity. Therefore, in the case of Salan we find the story of a man who, according to Schmitt, lost his political identity.

Schmitt's opposition to a world divided into two camps ('us and them') arose from his belief that the identity of a political unit is neither given nor fixed – one's identity instead undergoes a constant process of change and development. Friends, allies and enemies are not important because they are mere terms of comparison: we measure ourselves against our enemies; our friends are an integral part of our identity; our allies are our witnesses and our helpers. Allies and enemies serve a further crucial function: present allies can become our future enemies just as our present enemies can become our future friends. Bendersky is certainly correct when he claims that, in Schmitt's view, 'no nation is the natural or permanent enemy of any nation or group' (Bendersky 1983: 89).

Schmitt's own concept of the political and his insistence that we need allies as much as enemies is predicated on the assumption that our identity is not given *a priori* or fixed. For Schmitt, real politics is an Orwellian, never-ending series of shifting alliances and changing identities. Friends and allies, as well as enemies, are all equally important for this process to take place. Real politics is dynamic for Schmitt and he believed that if the world were to be split into two opposing sides, this dynamic element would vanish and politics would become futile.

This belief led Schmitt to reject the polarised view of the world that was predicated by Leninism, supporters of humanitarian intervention and of just war theory, because it was incompatible with his understanding of *identity as a process*. This emphasis on the importance of the friend explains why drawing too close an analogy between the friend–enemy *principle* and the self–other *dichotomy* can be seriously misleading. Unlike the self–other duality, there are not two, but three elements that make up Schmitt's concept of the political, namely, the self, the friend and the enemy. Real politics is about ourselves, our friends and our allies engaging with our enemy and with the enemy's friends and allies.

In a world with no friends but only enemies (or, to use Schmitt's terminology, a 'universal enemy') politics becomes a mere façade, a cover-up for a never-ending state of hostility which culminates with the victory of one side over the other, a result which brings about the end of politics and the pretence of politics. Schmitt saw the Cold War, with its attending division of the world in two opposing camps, as an example of 'futile politics'. Alternatively, in a world with only allies and no real enemies, as in a liberal democracy, Schmitt claims that one does not even find the pretence of politics. For Schmitt, however, the political does not disappear in a liberal democracy but merely becomes invisible; the search for identity eventually leads one group or another to break free from the secret and hidden underworld of civil society, bringing the challenge of real politics to the fore[9].

To recap, it is possible to reconstruct a typology of the political from Schmitt's writings. Schmitt suggests that when there are only enemies and no external allies or friends, when the world is divided in two groups, 'us and them', 'Good versus Evil', politics becomes *futile,* as was the case during the Cold War. Secondly, when there are no enemies but only game-like friends as in liberal democracies, the political becomes *invisible* and thrives underground. It is only when we have not just enemies but also friends (in the form of those who belong to the same group as well as external allies) that *real* politics takes place. From a Schmittean perspective, futile and invisible politics go hand in hand with ideologies that see political identity as unproblematic; real politics instead is inspired by the pragmatic search for identity.

The reconstruction of a typology of the political from Schmitt's writings seems to have the additional benefit of enabling the reader to appreciate the ideological distance between Hitler and Carl Schmitt. Hitler's proclamation that 'with the conception of race, National Socialism will carry its revolution abroad and recast the world' (cited in Montagu 1997: 81) is an endorsement of what Schmitt regarded as absolute enmity and futile politics; in this respect, I believe that Schmitt was correct in saying that he was a nationalist but not of Hitler's kind[10].

Polemics and Diagnostics

At the Nuremberg trial, Schmitt protested that he had offered diagnostics of problems, not recommendations, in the speeches for which he was being tried (Bendersky 1987: 98–101). It is difficult to accept Schmitt's line of defence with respect to those speeches. Having said this, however, one finds that there is more than mere nationalistic propaganda in his writings. Although Richard Bellamy is right to highlight the inadequacy of Schmitt's critique of liberalism (Bellamy 2000; but see also Hirst 1990, McCormick 1997a, Cristi 1998), Schmitt was highly perceptive of the changes which had taken place in the twentieth century with regard to the international political system, jurisprudence and the general attitude towards enmity and war. Keen to come across as a political analyst rather than an ideologist, Schmitt's own views about enmity and friendship are often unclear and ambiguous: it is up to the reader to disentangle analysis from polemics, insight from rhetoric. For example, what was his favourite notion of enmity? Real, conventional or absolute? When he wrote in *Ex Captivitate Salus* that he was the last supporter of *jus publicum europaeum* to which he had given 'a new existential basis', he must have been aware that his qualification rendered this statement ambiguous. Although Schmitt favoured the state as a political agent and dreaded civil and revolutionary wars, his claim that politics contains enmity and the potential for war went against both classical political theory and *jus publicum europaeum*, which was predicated on the stark separation of war and peace. As Hobbes had used natural law theory subversively, so Schmitt sabotaged classical European jurisprudence. By claiming throughout his life that politics contains enmity and the looming threat of war, Schmitt provided recognition and a theoretical underpinning to the claim made by partisan fighters of the nineteenth and twentieth centuries who felt that their irregular fighting and their engagement in colonial and civil wars was not criminal but political, not legal but legitimate.

While in his works Schmitt is ambiguous when commenting on real and conventional enmity, he speaks of absolute enmity only in a very derogatory way. He never fails to point out disapprovingly that absolute enmity dehumanises the enemy; it depicts him as a monster; it urges us to fight aggressive and punitive wars against him; it convinces us that we have the right not simply to contain, but also to annihilate the enemy on the ground of some supposedly objective criteria decided *in abstracto*.

Interpreters have responded differently to Schmitt's open condemnations of absolute enmity. Sympathetic readers have highlighted this aspect of Schmitt's thought in order to support their claim that there is some ideological distance between Nazism and Carl Schmitt. More cynical readers have remained unconvinced by Schmitt's disapproval of absolute enmity and have argued that it is inconsistent with his other claims (see, for example, Stirk 1999: 363–364). According to Derrida, Schmitt feels that the closer a group comes to the extremity and purity of the friend/enemy antithesis, the more political it is; Derrida goes on to point out that absolute enmity is the most political form of enmity and therefore the most consistent with Schmitt's philosophy.

Although Derrida puts across his point of view forcefully, my contention is that the rejection of absolute enmity is implied by, and consistent with, the notion of real politics that I have discussed in this essay. Absolute enmity implies the duality of Good and Evil, which in turn prevents the formation of new alliances and the dissolution of old ones, hinders pragmatic politics and frustrates the redefinition of political identities.

There is no doubt in my mind that Schmitt genuinely preferred real enmity to its absolute alternative because he saw the former as being located in time and space and linked to a Heimat. For Schmitt, real enmity is the basis of real, vibrant politics with a dynamic political landscape whereas absolute enmity leads us into a world of futility and stagnation where the future is an echo of the past. As, in my opinion, Schmitt was committed to real politics and real enmity, so he preferred what I call true or existential friendship.

Schmitt was captivated by the total bond that the partisan has with his group and saw in that bond the foundation of a truly political unit. He was fascinated by the telluric partisan's commitment to his friends, by his complete dedication to his political cause and by his unshakeable willingness to kill and be killed in order to defend and protect the members of his group and their political purpose. In my opinion, 'true' or 'existential' friendship would be endorsed by Schmitt for a number of reasons. First, this sort of friendship assumes a non-individualistic definition of a person. It assumes that one's identity above all depends on 'belonging' to a group or another – in this understanding of friendship a friend is not simply external, a friend is crucial in the formation of one's identity. Secondly, 'true' friendship assumes that identity is not given *a priori* but is engaged in a constant process of 'becoming'; it is a search whose outcome cannot be known in advance: as the future friend is unknown, so is our identity.

For Schmitt, true friendship is the bond that leads us to kill and die for a friend. Friendship is a tragic, intense and extreme experience that goes hand in hand with what Schmitt regards as real politics, the experience of dying and killing for the defence of a way of life.

It is worth comparing the Schmittean, tragic view of friendship with Michael Oakeshott's dramatic definition of friendship; Oakeshott writes:

> [In the case of friendship] attachment springs from an intimation of familiarity and subsists in a mutual sharing of personalities. ... To discard friends because they do not behave as we expected and refuse to be educated to our requirements is the conduct of a man who has altogether mistaken the character of friendship. Friends are not concerned with what might be made of one another, but only with the enjoyment of one another; and the condition of this enjoyment is a ready acceptance of what is and the absence of any desire to change or to improve. A friend is not somebody one trusts to behave in a certain manner, who supplies certain wants, who has certain useful abilities, who possesses certain merely agreeable qualities, or who holds certain acceptable opinions; he is somebody who engages the imagination, who excites

contemplation, who provokes interest, sympathy, delight and loyalty simply on account of the relationship entered into. One friend cannot replace another ... *The relationship of friend to friend is dramatic, not utilitarian; the tie is one of familiarity, not usefulness; the disposition engaged is conservative, not 'progressive'.* (Oakeshott 1962, emphasis added)

Oakeshott's conservative man is deeply, dramatically attached to his friend but the issue of dying and killing for him does not arise. Oakeshott's friends go fishing together and settle their differences over a glass of wine; they spend their time engaged in idle conversation or debating the meaning of life. They share simple experiences together. Oakeshott's friends have no common plan of action, no agenda, no project, and this is what distinguishes them from Schmitt's friends. For Schmitt, there is no true or real friend without a project, and no real project that is worth pursuing that does not require us to die and kill. This exaggerated tragic element is the core of Schmitt's friendship, Schmitt's 'true' friendship takes place in emergencies, it is a friendship which arises and thrives in a case of exception.

But Schmitt goes further than simply describing this bond which forms in a state of emergency; he recommends it as the ideal type of friendship, he says that one could not claim to have a true friend unless one is willing to kill and die for him. Herein lies Schmitt's polemics, i.e. that the friendship of crisis is the best friendship, that the case of exception ought to be the ultimate aim of normality[11].

To conclude, Schmitt on friendship (as on everything else) is both polemical and diagnostic. Polemical in suggesting that true friendship ought to be about dying and killing and that any other form of friendship is inferior. But Schmitt is also diagnostic in noticing that the dominant notion of friendship in a society is an indicator of the status of the political in that society, that the meaning of friendship varies with ideologies, that the significance attached to friendship by each ideology depends on its understanding of political identity, that various factors affect the notion of friendship in an age, including the development of communications and other technological developments, that although the category of friendship does not coincide with any of its historical forms, nevertheless friendship gains its concrete content only when it does so.

Notes

1. Schmitt's ideology raises strong emotions today as it did 20 years ago when Joseph W. Bendersky and Stephen Holmes famously voiced opposite assessments of Schmitt's affiliation with the Nazi regime (see Bendersky 1983 and Holmes 1983: 1066–1067). Important contributors to the debate on Schmitt's ideology include, for example, Duncan Kelly (Kelly 2002: 458–496), Renato Cristi (Cristi 1993: 281–300), William E. Scheuerman (in Scheuerman 1993: 265–280; 1996: 571–590), Ellen Kennedy (Kennedy 2004); Heinrich Meier (Meier 1995; 1998). A powerful and uncompromising condemnation of Schmitt's ideology and racism was argued by Tomaz Mastnak at the recent ECPR conference in Budapest, Writing Leviathan in Behemoth's Shadow: Schmitt's Hobbes, September 2005.
2. Jan-Werner Muller discusses the influence of Schmitt's thought on the European Left (Muller 2003). See also Bolsinger (2001).

96 Friendship in Politics

3. 'They [political concepts] are focused on a specific conflict and are bound to a concrete situation whose ultimate consequence is a friend-enemy grouping ... Words such as state, republic, society, class, as well as sovereignty, constitutional state, absolutism, dictatorship, economic planning, neutral or total state, and so on, are incomprehensible if one does not know exactly who is to be affected, combated, refuted or negated by such a term' (Schmitt 1996a: 30–31).
4. I use the terms *compagno* and *camerata* to indicate the friend in a communist or fascist group or party respectively.
5. Self-interest, Schmitt stresses, is what motivates the ally or 'third party' (*der interessierte Dritte*) to help terrorist groups throughout the world; the influence and power that the third party has on the terrorist group enhances its own standing on the international stage. Conversely, the terrorist group has an interest in establishing a relationship of trust with an established state because in return it receives not only weapons and money, but also political recognition (Schmitt 2002b: 77–78).
6. Here I follow Derrida, who argues rather convincingly that the Schmittean political agent is male.
7. Important discussion of the political in Schmitt can be found in Sartori 1989; O'Sullivan 1997; Galli 1996; Gottfried 1990.
8. We may notice that the quotation from Däuber ('Der Feind ist unsre eigne Frage als Gestalt') can be found also in *Ex Captivitate Salus*, in the section entitled *Wisdom of the Cell*, where Schmitt reflects on the meaning of enmity for him personally, (Schmitt 1950a: 90).
9. Interesting views on this can be found in Mouffe (1999, 1993).
10. Having said this, it is difficult to believe Schmitt's sincerity in *Ex Captivitate Salus*, where he says that fear for personal safety prevented intellectuals such as himself from speaking out during the Hitler years and points out that there is a limit to the courage, sacrifice and martyrdom that one can expect from a theorist. Unfortunately, we know that Schmitt did not simply fail to speak out against Hitler; Schmitt spoke for Hitler, on more than one occasion. Even if, as I suggested above, Schmitt's strand of nationalism was far less abstract than Hitler's, the fact remains that for one reason or another Schmitt supported Hitler's policies. As argued forcibly by Tomaz Mastnak, in 1938 Schmitt found the way to blame nothing but the Jews for any shortcoming of Hobbes's theory (see Schmitt 1996a).
11. On the role of the 'case of exception' in Schmitt see, for example, John McCormick (1997b), William Scheuermann (1993, 1994), George Schwab (1970) and, last but not least, Giorgio Agamben (2004).

References

Agamben, G. (2004) *State of Exception* (Chicago, IL and London: University of Chicago Press).
Arditi, B. & Valentine, J. (1999) *Polemicization: The Contingency of the Commonplace* (Edinburgh: Edinburgh University Press).
Balakrishnan, G. (2000) *The Enemy. An Intellectual Portrait of Carl Schmitt* (London and New York: Verso).
Bellamy, R. (2000) *Rethinking Liberalism* (London and New York: Pinter).
Bendersky, J. (1983) *Carl Schmitt: Theorist for the Reich* (Princeton, NJ: Princeton University Press).
Bendersky, J. (1987) Carl Schmitt at Nuremberg, *Telos,* 72, pp. 91–107.
Bolsinger, E. (2001) *The Autonomy of the Political. Carl Schmitt's and Lenin's Political Realism* (London: Westport).
Borradori, G. (2003) *Philosophy in a Time of Terror, Dialogues with Jurgen Habermas and Jacques Derrida* (Chicago, IL and London: University of Chicago Press).
Cristi, R. (1993) Carl Schmitt on liberalism, democracy and Catholicism, *History of Political Thought,* 14, pp. 281–300.
Cristi, R. (1998) *Carl Schmitt and Authoritarian Liberalism, Strong State, Free Economy* (Cardiff: University of Wales Press).
Dallmayr, F. (2000) Derrida and friendship, in King, P. & Devere, H. (Eds), *The Challenge to Friendship in Modernity,* pp. 105–130 (London: Frank Cass).
Derrida, J. (1997) *Politics of Friendship* (London: Verso).

Galli, C. (1996) *Genealogia della Politica: Carl Schmitt e la Crisi del Pensiero Politico Moderno* (Bologna: Il Mulino).
Gottfried, P. (1990) *Carl Schmitt: Politics and Theory* (Westport, CT: Greenwood Press).
Hirst, P. (1990) *Representative Democracy and its Limits* (Cambridge: Polity).
Holmes, S. (1983) Book Review of Joseph W. Bendersky, *Carl Schmitt: Theorist for the Reich, American Political Science Review*, 77, pp. 1066–1067.
Huysmans, J. (1997) Know your Schmitt: a godfather of truth and the spectre of Nazism, *Review of International Studies*, 25, pp. 323–328.
Kelly, D. (2002) Rethinking Franz Neumann's route to Behemoth, *History of Political Thought*, 23, pp. 458–496.
Kennedy, E. (2004) *Constitutional Failure: Carl Schmitt in Weimar* (Durham, NC & London: Duke University Press).
McCormick, J. (1997a) *Carl Schmitt's Critique of Liberalism* (Cambridge: Cambridge University Press).
McCormick, J. (1997b) The dilemmas of dictatorship: Carl Schmitt and constitutional emergency powers, *Canadian Journal of Law and Jurisprudence*, 10, pp. 163–188.
Meier, H. (1995) *Carl Schmitt and Leo Strauss: The Hidden Dialogue* (Chicago, IL and London: University of Chicago Press).
Meier, H. (1998) *The Lesson of Carl Schmitt: Four Chapters on the Distinction between Political Theology and Political Philosophy* (Chicago, IL and London: Chicago University Press).
Montagu, A. (1997) *Man's Most Dangerous Myth: The Fallacy of Race* (Walnut Creek, CA and London: AltaMira Press).
Mouffe, C. (1993) *The Return of the Political* (London: Verso).
Mouffe, C. (Ed.) (1999) *The Challenge of Carl Schmitt* (London: Verso).
Muller, J. (2003) *A Dangerous Mind. Carl Schmitt in Post-War European Thought* (New Haven, CT & London: Yale University Press).
O'Sullivan, N. (1997) Difference and the concept of the political in contemporary political philosophy, *Political Studies*, 45, pp. 739–754.
Oakeshott, M. (1962) *Rationalism in Politics* (London: Methuen)
Sartori, G. (1989) The essence of the political in Carl Schmitt, *Journal of Theoretical Politics*, 1, pp. 64–75.
Scheuerman, W. (1993) The rule of law under siege: Carl Schmitt and the death of the Weimar Republic, *History of Political Thought*, 14, pp. 265–280.
Scheuerman, W. (1994) *Between the Norm and the Exception: The Frankfurt School and the Rule of Law* (Cambridge, MA: MIT Press).
Scheuerman, W. (1996) Legal indeterminacy and the origins of Nazi legal thought: the case of Carl Schmitt, *History of Political Thought*, 17, pp. 571–590.
Schmitt, C. (1950a) *Ex Capitivitate Salus*, (Cologne: Greven Verlag).
Schmitt, C. (1950b) *Der Nomos Der Erde* (Cologne: Greven Verlag).
Schmitt, C. (1996a) *The Concept of the Political* (Chicago, IL and London: University of Chicago Press).
Schmitt, C. (1996b) *The Leviathan in the State Theory of Thomas Hobbes* (Westport, CT: Greenwood Press).
Schmitt, C. (2002a) *Der Begriff des Politischen*, 7th ed. (Berlin: Duncker & Humblot).
Schmitt, C. (2002b) *Theorie des Partisanen* (Berlin: Duncker & Humblot).
Schwab, G. (1970) *The Challenge of the Exception: An Introduction to the Political Ideas of Carl Schmitt between 1921–1936* (Berlin: Duncker & Humblot).
Slomp, G. (2005) The theory of the partisan: Carl Schmitt's neglected legacy, *History of Political Thought*, 26(3), pp. 502–519.
Stirk, P. (1999) Carl Schmitt's Völkerrechtliche Grossraumordung, *History of Political Thought*, 22(2), pp. 357–374.

Friendship and Revolution in Poland: The Eros and Ethos of the Committee for Workers' Defense (KOR)

NINA WITOSZEK
Oslo University, Norway

You see, if we look at it in this way, that we've actually begun the most difficult battle – the first such battle in the history of mankind, one that nobody's tried – we, small, ridiculous people, then that's a big thing. That's the game that I'm passionate about more than anything else in the world. (Kuroń 1984: 208).

KOR vs Solidarity

This essay has been born thanks to the dedicated work of the secret agents of the Security Police in communist Poland. In the library of the Institute of National Memory, which stores countless files bursting with crimes and misdemeanours of the citizens of the former People's Republic, there is a folder with a Hollywood cryptonym: 'The Players'. The folder contains original reports of police investigations and stenograms of bugged meetings of a group of friends who are variously referred to as national traitors, political bankrupts, Judeo-masonry, political degenerates, provocateurs, the enemies of People's Poland, wastrels, usurpers and non-Poles. One of the meetings, recorded by a dutiful agent, took place on 26 May 1978 in the house of an eminent economist, Professor Edward Lipinski. The officer on duty reported with glee:

> The meeting was filmed by the TV crew from West Germany, but it was as querulous as usual. Michnik and Celinski especially threw themselves at one another's throats, and the others were even worse. Celinski said that everybody who looked at matters coolly had to see that Michnik and Kuroń had to stop lecturing at the Flying University because they put people's life in danger. Michnik answered that no, over his dead or mangled body. Kuroń said: 'Those who look at the world through a keyhole see nothing but a keyhole'. ['metaphor unclear,' added in parenthesis]. Celiński shouted: 'So you accept that the students will get a kick in the arse?' Kuroń said that everybody had the right to get a kick in the arse if it made sense. Then everybody yelled at one another, but they had to stop because Professor Lipiński said that it was 7 o'clock and he had to listen to a Brahms concert. The others protested, but Lipiński didn't pay attention and turned on the radio. (Meldunek operacyjny 1978: 164)

There was nothing unusual about this meeting, apart from the fact that the secret police had to listen to the whole Brahms concerto recorded on their tape to find out what happened next. The 'Players' used to argue, and they did it with gusto, in a feverish, inspired trance which would be suddenly detonated by an anecdote or a joke. They knew they were bugged so they followed a simple rule: say aloud the general, whisper the concrete, write down all the names and then throw the paper in to the toilet.

Some of the scurrilous nicknames coined by the police were justified. Four members of the 'Players', including the Brahms' lover and the host of this meeting, were masons,[1] about one-third were of Jewish origin, almost all had a dissident past and present. It may well be that it is precisely their in-betweenness as ethnic and social outsiders and as political outcasts that created a bond which was tighter than a hedgehog's bite. And it is certainly their hybridity which equipped them with sparkling rebelliousness and creative impudence so characteristic of the hyphenated species: the Anglo-Irish, the Anglo-Indians, the Latin-Americans.

There are two legends about the Committee for Workers' Defense (KOR). One, now almost nearly forgotten and shuffled under the carpet, is about a group of altruistic Don Quixotes who lay the foundations for the biggest anti-totalitarian revolution in Eastern Europe, led by Solidarity. The second legend – promoted by people of a deconstructive disposition who are now in majority – talks about the 'national traitors' who posed as saviours of the nation. Not only had the KOR dissidents little or no effect on Solidarity, the second story says; driven by lust for power and a sense of omnipotence, they distorted the intentions of Solidarity's rank and file and then bungled the project of decommunization. In a summing-up discussion published by the Institute of National Memory, it is dryly stated:

> So far nobody has spoken positively about the people of the pre-*Solidarity* opposition. They did not do so themselves because of modesty ... after all it would be out of place to say about themselves: 'We were wonderful and brave; we did great service to the cause of freedom, independence and democracy.' The communist propaganda wrote lies about them... When there was a system change in Poland, deep cleavages emerged in *Solidarity* before anybody said 'thank you.' ... And now we, historians, using extremely tendentious materials procured by the security police and the apparatus of repression, are supposed to write the truth and only the truth about them? What truth would it be? (Dyskusja 2003: 64)

Before we come closer to the 'spirit of truth', three questions are in order. What made the Players into an unsurpassed model of democratic opposition in East Central Europe? What turned them into a *bête noire* of Solidarity, and then into a cumbersome revenant that contemporary Poles would rather forget? And what role has their friendship played in this confounding rite of passage?

Listing the Virtuous

The predicament of the group is intriguing for three reasons. First, it touches upon the crooked relationship between ideas and politics – the relationship that can be captured only in hypotheses and suppositions. Secondly, it makes a fascinating case study of the role of intellectuals in social upheavals, displaying, in a brutal way, the un-photogenic side of the romance between the people and their leaders. Thirdly, and most importantly for our exploration, it offers a disquieting picture of the ethics and politics of dialogue which illuminated the work of the Committee for Workers' Defense. The dialogic mode – one of the holy imperatives of modern politics in the West – has been put to a test in pre- and post-Solidarity Poland in a way that forces us to rethink both its efficacy and limitations.

As Joseph Brodsky would have put it, in the beginning there was a can of meat. In June 1976 the communist government suppressed brutally a series of workers' strikes against the rise of food prices in Poland. The workers' protests such as those in Radom, Ursus, Lodz and Plock were followed by massive arrests, long trials and the sure prospect of unemployment for the strikers and their families. There was no chance of mercy or justice for some 2,500 arrested workers and no future for their families.

But not this time. On 23 September 1976, a group of 14 intellectuals publicly announced that they were taking the workers under their protection. They constituted themselves as the Committee for Workers' Defence (KOR) – a clever rhetorical ploy, invoking the romantic-proletarian tradition that the communists in Poland preached but did not practice. They issued an *Appeal to Society* calling for financial, medical and legal help for the oppressed workers. They went on tedious trips to Radom and Ursus, where they sat through the workers' trials as Samaritan witnesses of socialist ignominy and mock-justice. More importantly, they did it openly, publishing their own names and telephone numbers in a regular information bulletin which they circulated through their own network.

'A mouse challenging a lion', was the verdict. Jacek Kuroń, one of KOR's founders, admitted as much: 'In the beginning everybody, us included, thought that this was madness, a collective suicide ... We were told that if ten thousand were in jail and we found a 14 members' strong KOR, the effect would be that there would be ten thousand and fourteen in jail' (Kowalska 1981: 40).

Normally, intellectuals believe in giving the public what intellectuals want. Not this time. When distinguished professors, gifted poets and influential journalists in the West summoned their talents to convince the world that modern tyrants were liberators and that their crimes were noble when seen in the proper perspective, the Players were writing their 'satanic verses' to expose the beastly side of *Realsocialismus*. As early as 1976, they were trying to persuade the Poles to embrace Solidarity as the common man wronged by the all powerful state and with no recourse to justice. While European elites stayed at their desks developing interesting ideas to explain away the sufferings of peoples whose eyes they would never meet, the KOR men and women went to the defeated cities, sat at court trials, knocked on people's doors, gave out money, collected names and addresses of victims of state repression. They were eternal fugitives, watched, followed, arrested and released – to be arrested again. They mixed martyrdom with carnival. Their life was punctuated by rituals of hate: threats, beatings and terms in jail; and rituals of love: the magic of friendship, euphoric sprees after a success, long, inspired chats. Their story proves that intellectuals are like cream: they are at their best when whipped.

Why did they 'stretch' themselves in this way? For Plato, this is a deep psychological question, one to which the characters in his dialogues offer many different answers. Perhaps the loveliest is that given by the priestess Diotima and reported by Socrates in the *Symposium*, that some people have desiring souls and yearn to 'beget in the beautiful'. This yearning, this eros, may lead to a philosophy or poetry or towards 'the right ordering of cities and households'. This last is politics in the highest sense. Wherever we see human activity for the good, Diotima tells Socrates, there we will find traces of eros (Plato: 1993).

This can be translated into manifold terms. For Jacek Kuroń, the idealist architect of KOR, the opposition was a community-making act: 'I had a grand idea of love and friendship, both of them harnessed in a brotherhood, in a struggle for a cause' (Kuroń 1989: 23). For another oppositional genius, Adam Michnik, opposition was the act of self-making: 'I didn't search for an affiliation. First of all I wanted to see my own face, to find out who I was.' For the poet, Anna Kowalska, KOR offered a chance of a *meaningful* suicide: 'I thought that if I am to lose my life, then this would be the most illustrious way to go. I meant literally to "lose my life" because I didn't believe that an initiative like KOR would ever succeed' (Kuroń 1989: 23; Michnik 1995: 235; Kowalska 1983: 21). For many, membership in KOR was about the continuation of the noble family tradition: linking with a grandfather who took part in the insurrections against the tsar, or a mother who fought in the Warsaw Uprising. For the men especially, joining KOR was about charity, vanity and risk in the combined play at Zorro and Robin Hood. Some speak openly of their need for friendship: 'I joined in because ... I always aspired to a friendship with people like Jacek Kuroń, Adam Michnik, Sewek Blumsztajn, Janek Lityński. And it is their friendship I cared for, not just for being there' (Jankowska 2000: 305).

The Republic of Friends

Michnik summed it up as 'a community of hearts'. In fact, it was a community of minds. For the friendship of the Players was limited to the circle of the virtuous and the equal, with little or no place for intellectual mediocrity. It struggled to combine – with varying luck – the elitism and struggle for wisdom, as described by Cicero and Aristotle, with the Christian injunction to love your neighbour. In this, it challenged the Aristotelian claim that in a despotic city friendship could not thrive because all social relations are based not upon positive human sentiments such as justice or virtue, but upon the negative power of fear (Porter & Tomaselli 1994; King & Devere 2000). In the communist state this reclaimed friendship became a weapon against fear and a form of antipolitical politics. It was based upon a creative conception of common activities: totally open and transparent, focused on the collection of funds and legal help for the repressed workers, publication of a regular bulletin registering all cases of unjust repressions, and mobilization of international media (especially Radio Free Europe) to cover all abuses of justice *in extenso*.

Imagination let itself be surpassed by reality, as one Polish writer put it. Within a year the Players established a virtual 'Republic of Friendship' that included a wide national and international network of collaborators and patrons. *Robotnik* ('The Worker') – an independent newspaper published by KOR – was a hotline to the proletariat. The alliance with the 'Student Committee of Solidarity' ensured a constant influx of young activists. KOR's underground publishers and journals – such as NOWA, *Aneks* and *Krytyka* – promoted an uncensored version of Polish and European history and circulated translations and discussions of the cutting edge of contemporary Western thought. KOR's intellectual shockproofs – the 'Flying University' and *Towarzystwo Kursow Naukowych* ('The Society of Scholarly Courses') – circulated the best analytical achievements of independent thought. Support of international writers, such as Günther Grass, Heinrich Böll and Saul Bellow, gave KOR the status of a *cause celèbre*.

After the release of the last Radom and Ursus prisoners, KOR's project was revalued and the organization transformed itself into the Committee of the Social Self- Defense (KSS-KOR). Its aim was to create institutional conditions for the protection of civic rights and freedoms, which, in effect meant establishing an alternative *polis*. In designing its contours the architects of the new KOR took into consideration all previous sublime failures and disasters which had adorned the Polish struggle for independence. None of the Players' programmatic essays or postulates rested on a vision of a utopian society. There was a constant, cruel assault on illusions and consoling stories. As Michnik put it, 'since you already know that no spiritual groves or triumphant arches are to be expected, you won't believe in a pleasant lie about yourself or about the human condition' (Michnik 1995: 4). With all their skepticism and guardedness – and with constant police harassment which drove some KOR members to suicide attempts[2] – what was, then, the source of the Players' stunning success?

The simplest, and poorest, answer is that the communist authorities 'allowed' it in the same way Gorbachev 'allowed' the breakup of the iron curtain.[3] This, however, says very little about the genius of the people, or the magic of the deeds and words that prepared the emergence of the first free trade unions in the communist bloc. For in this case the historical drama had a Shakespearian dimension: action was the person.

From the beginning KOR was a friendship community which crossed generational, spiritual and ethnic boundaries, something which was both its strength and weakness. There were the 'older majesties' (*starsi państwo*) including eminent intellectuals and lawyers who were Second World War veterans (Aniela Steinsbergerowa, Edward Lipiński, Jerzy Rybicki, Stanislaw Pajdak, Jerzy Kielanowski, J.J. Lipski). There was Jacek Kuroń, the great pedagogue and the charismatic 'Godfather'. There was the 68 generation (*Komandosi*), people in their thirties with a dissident reputation (Michnik, Blumsztajn, Macierewicz, Lityński, Celinski, Belinski, Dorn, Romaszewski). There was Jerzy Andrzejewski, Poland's leading writer, who was *fanaberyjny* ('with homosexual leanings'), Halina Mikołajska, a famous actress who was a 'great lady', and a priest (F. Zieja) who was 'living proof of the existence of God'. In short, it was a very heterogeneous, subaltern team, bringing together socialists, agnostics and Catholics in a community acting out a bizarre family romance. They partied, smoked, drank and argued as passionately as they risked their lives and careers.

Friends with Multiple Personalities

The charismatic, and most hated, duo – Jacek Kuroń and Adam Michnik – were the Achilles and Patroclus of the group.

There were two Jacek Kuroń. One was a hobo who never took off his jeans, addressed every woman as *córeczko* ('little daughter'), a thug who shouted and coughed, smoked 100 cigarettes a day, and who 'learned English while doing push-ups, devouring breakfast and receiving phone calls'. The other Kuroń was a Christ-like figure who proclaimed himself a Jew, a Gypsy, Tibetan, Ukrainian and HIV positive to oppose the wave of hatred and persecution. One was a psychic terrorist who infuriated the whole KOR by chronically interrupting everybody and knowing better. The other was a reflexive democrat who said 'don't burn party committees, found your own' and proposed the idea of a 'self-organizing society'. 'Like all great pedagogues, he educated us with his very self', say his friends. 'We all wanted to be like him' (Blumsztajn 2004: 122). Kuroń had a twin soul, the extraordinary Gaja, who made him grow and flourish. There is an unwritten chapter about Gaya as a secret 'Holy Grail of KOR'. For there is no doubt that the unique love-friendship between the two coloured and sustained everything that Kuroń did and wrote during the 'times of contempt'.

There have been several Adam Michniks. One was an exalted dreamer and romantic patriot who, from his prison cells in Kurkowa or Mokotów or Białołęka, exerted a constant moral blackmail on the Poles. The camera of a Milos Forman or an Andrzej Wajda would capture a fifteen year-old boy who founds a 'Club of the Seekers of Contradictions' at Warsaw University to debate the right version of Polish history and politics. Or a young man standing on a box in the city of Otwock in 1981 and shouting: 'My name is Adam Michnik, I am an antisocialist element!' and thus stopping an infuriated crowd from setting fire to the headquarters of the security police. There was yet another Michnik, a carpet knight sparkling with wit and ready repartee, a seducer of women and men. Still other was Poland's most gifted snob, attracted to – and attracting - talent and fame home and abroad. 'At barely nineteen I became famous,' he ironized. 'I owe the communists everything – and I am not sure what I would have done if they hadn't been there' (Michnik 1995: 35). The fourth was an outstanding essayist with phenomenal memory, a man who paralyzed his interlocutors and opponents with quotes from international poets and sages. Still an other was a brilliant sophist, deciphering and unveiling deception and hypocrisy, navigating between contradictory views. His paradox – of a splendid orator who stammers – was a comical externalization of his hubris: an idealist errant knight who plots and schemes like Machiavelli.

The friendship between the two masterminds of KOR was built not so much on a harmony of souls as on endless arguments about strategies, books and choices. There is a story that captures in a nutshell the gist of their personalities. When in April of 1984 there was a chance of amnesty, Kuroń was escorted from prison by a group of jubilant friends, but Michnik refused to leave his cell. He could not accept the conditions of release set by the authorities: freedom in exchange for giving up oppositional activity for three years. 'If they put you up on a General Anders' white horse and the entire country is watching you,' he told Kuroń, 'you can't shit in your pants on the white horse. Especially if you are Jewish.'(Michnik 1998: 67). But this time Kuroń was not amused. 'In prison you sit with your friends,' he commented. 'You can't think solely about your honor and your dignity. You have to think about us all' (Kuron 1991: 351). In the last instance Kuroń's generous communitarianism tempered Michnik's principled megalomania - and vice versa. Socially, both men were a tonic; with their strong charisma and diabolic intelligence, they created a magnetic aura which mesmerized their followers and inspired venom in their opponents.

Apart from the aggregate power of 'Kuroniomichnik', the success of KOR was made possible thanks to the resourcefulness and dedication of the other members and collaborators. The scattered comments and reminiscences accrue to a picture. The action takes place in Kuroń's flat where people camp, work, argue, sleep and eat for twenty four hours. The phone doesn't stop ringing: students, journalists, possible collaborators, security police with threats, people offering money. When one walks through the yard in the evening, one hears the taktaktak of the typing machines. Many of the callers are madmen and loonies: a woman who claims her sex life has been ruined by the security police and Scotland Yard and demands that KOR provide her with a flat; a man who says that he has been poisoned by the Special Units; a gentleman who introduces himself as a representative of the common underground government of Lithuania, Latvia, Ukraine and Poland. As Kuroń put it, they were the 'distorted mirror of the disease we all suffered from' (Kuroń 1991: 45).

KOR as Moral Community

KOR conducted politics via unpolitical means: a bohemian community sharing things, money, food; a 'warm circle' which provided a sense of security and an awareness that 'you can risk everything because there will always be people who love you, who will help you and who will be with you to the end' (Kuroń, 2004:98). When all the 15 founding members of KOR were arrested, they were immediately replaced by the women: Gaya, Aniela Steinbergowa, Anka Kowalska. 'We could relax in prison' wrote Kuroń, 'because the movement not only didn't get stagnant but got a new lease of life.'[4] And Michnik observed: 'We could be simultaneously pathetic and ironic, patriotic and European because all these things were secondary. What was decisive was courage, mutual loyalty and solidarity' (Kuroń 2004: 122).

KOR's communal modus vivendi was regulated by a set of fragile, democratic principles. There were no more important and less important members, though, to the others' fury, Kuroń was often confused with a press spokesman of the group. The force of the combined, intractable personalities of Kuroń, Michnik and Macierewicz, was the reason why, when an important decision was to be made, the members preferred not to vote in order not to confront the unsavoury division into a minority and majority; they just kept arguing and hammering it out until everybody agreed. Though Kuroń describes it as a 'school of democracy', this was less a democratic and more a Socratic way of tackling problems, one which created havoc and splits, but also, paradoxically, forced the Players to develop and refine a 'dialogic imagination'.

The most impressive, and least studied, achievement of KOR is its spiritual-intellectual legacy. The Players acted consciously as a moral community drawing on and developing an original *paideia*. Four of the founding members had been connected with Czarna Jedynka – the patriotic scouts that had produced the heroes of the resistance during the Second World War. The other five had been former members of the Walterowcy, a legendary team of socialist scouts run by Kuroń in the 1950s and 1960s. The Walterowcy camps were Kuroń's attempt to build a children's utopia, where the 'law of the smallest' meant that the weakest had more rights than the stronger. 'That's how Kuroń understood justice: not as equality but as granting privileges to the weak' (Burnetko 2004: 105). Four older members of KOR had been the participants in the Warsaw Uprising who remained in opposition to the Soviet occupation.

Finally, almost all younger members were involved in the 1968 assault on the state socialism and had a prison 'apprenticeship' in their dossier.

Their patriotic-romanticism combined a general optimism of will with a pessimism of intellect. They perceived the cultural-political situation in Poland as analogous to the fall of the Roman Empire: the break-up of Western civilization and the onset of the reign of the barbarians. They drew on – and developed – the tradition of Polish democratic Romanticism, of early socialist thinkers, the humanist legacy of Camus, Chiaromonte, Bonhoeffer, Hannah Arendt, Leszek Kołakowski, and the vision of the two greatest bards of oppositional humanism, Czeslaw Miłosz and Zbigniew Herbert. KOR's often quoted motto came from Herbert's famous poem, 'The Envoy of Mr Cogito': 'You were saved not in order to live/you have little time you must give testimony.' Mr Cogito, the poignant persona in Herbert's poetic universe, is an emblem of the doomed rebellion inspired by the antiquarian virtues of honour, loyalty, civic duty, dignity, truth and beauty. He is an ironic, fragile spokesman of the central values of Western civilization which have been eroded by conformity, demolished by fashion, or eradicated by the barbarian hordes. With all reservations regarding the evolution of KOR's agenda, it would not be too much to say that both the lives and books of KOR members were an extension, if not a literal realization, of Mr. Cogito's moral codex. At the risk of simplifying a complex moral vision, I would roughly distinguish six pillars of this codex: (1) the Aristotelian conception of politics as a public struggle for values and interests carried through peaceful means; (2) The programme of Solidarity and self-organization designed by Kuroń in his 'Thoughts on the Programme of Action' (1976); (3) The reorientation of the oppositional struggle from one directed *against* authority to the one focused on creating the independent public sphere elaborated in Michnik's programme of the 'New Evolutionism' (1979); (4) The creative reworking of the values of original Christianity as the ethical platform of action codified by Kuroń in the influential essay 'Christians without God' (1975); (5) The ethics of dialogue elaborated by Michnik in *The Church and the Left* (1979); (6) The code of honour, exhumed by Michnik in his prison book *Z dziejów honoru w Polsce* ('From the History of Honour in Poland', 1976).

The Syncretic Wisdom of KOR

KOR's value premises were not some 'pap for the dispossessed', to use Seamus Heaney's phrase. They constellated into a concrete programme of action which was consistently realized over the four years of KOR's existence. One of the most striking dimensions of this axiology has been the endorsement of the Christian ethos despite the secular-socialist profile of the KOR leaders. It has been said about Kuroń: 'It is not important if Jacek believed in God; its important that God believed in Jacek.' Jan Józef Lipski wrote: 'We were convinced that if KOR's answer to arrests, provocations and slander was hatred, then KOR would have to lose because hatred is self-destructive. In no other matter has the influence of Christian ethics been as conspicuous as in this' (Lipski 1983: 67). While in prison, both Kuroń and

Michnik read voraciously Bishop Bonhoeffer's letters written in the death cell. Kuroń argued: 'Again and again, in Bonhoeffer's letters from prison there is a call to live like people who do without God ... One can live as a Christian *etsi Deus non daretur*' (Kuroń 1984: 32). One of the most dialogic – and underestimated – projects establishing a platform on which the Catholic Church and the secular Left tradition could meet and mutually de-dogmatize one another, has been Michnik's *The Church and the Left*. The book attacks both the Julianic, power-hungry and resentful Church, and the religious obscurantism of the Left. It emphasizes the common objective of the secular Left and the Catholic believers: the defence of individual dignity and freedom in a dehumanized world. At the same time it opposes expedient and mindless alliances, such as the religious fundamentalists uniting with the military dictators to fight atheism, or the liberationists romancing the communists in order to oppose the dictators (Michnik 1977b). This was an extended Thomas Jefferson: if you want to build democracy, first find citizens, if you want to recover the humanist project, first find Christians.

The complex, syncretic wisdom of KOR – first thrashed 'among friends' at riotous meetings, then ripened to an 'uncertain clarity' in prison conditions – has fallen prey to many simplifications. There has been a tendency to reduce it to a secular-left ideology or to the work of a sect of hotheaded 'radicals'. Matters are much more complex than that. First, a strong Christian ingredient and the redefinition of friendship as an instrument of politics, gives KOR's Weltanschauung a premodern touch. The ethics of *caritas* and the invocation of the tension between sacrum and profanum gesture towards the Renaissance rather than a modern worldview. So does the discourse of human dignity which laid the basis for the Solidarity revolution. The code of honour – explored in Michnik's programmatic book – gives a sublime, almost aristocratic ring to the oppositional philosophy. The interest in the concrete human being rather than, say, class or universal humanity, echoes sixteenth-century humanism rather than the values of the Enlightenment. The dislike of patriotic exhibitionism and reluctance to invoke the mantra of 'Motherland' is a departure from romantic obsessions and a reactivation of Erasmian cosmopolitanism. Ditto the appeal to the 'habits of the heart' as the corrective of abstract rationality. In short, there are many elements which bring KOR close to the Renaissance *republica litterarum*, that group of scientists, thinkers and aficionados of antique literature who knew and corresponded with one another, and were united by concrete tasks: promotion of European citizenship, religious reform and struggle against fanaticism through the invocation of the wisdom of antiquity. And just as the friendship of – and the argument among – Erasmus, Luther, Pico, Ficcino and Machiavelli contributed to a momentous change in European sensibility, so did the intellectual legacy of the Players created the basis for a historical breakthrough. After the meeting of KOR with the Czech dissidents which took place in the autumn of 1977, Kuroń wrote:

> Over there, the secret and open police and their agents. Here we, sitting at the table, on which there is rum, salami, cheese and bread, all of them pulled out

of Havel's bottomless bag. The fir trees are humming above us as we discuss how to overthrow the common enemy. It is as if at this moment the common dream of deliverance from servitude through friendship began to come true. (Kuroń 1991: 83)

The dream of deliverance came true – though in crooked ways. There is ample evidence to the effect that Solidarity was the KOR's child, 'albeit an illegitimate one' (Zuzowski 1996). It is not accidental that the founding event of Solidarity was the legendary strike in the Gdansk shipyard where KOR had a very strong programmatic basis and an active team of collaborators including Bogdan Borusewicz, Andrzej Gwiazda, Anna Walentynowicz and Lech Walesa. Without the Players' preparatory work promoting class solidarity, self-government, and peaceful resistance, the workers' strikes would have hardly led to a sustained and organized upheaval of 10 million people. Even taking into account the Pope's crucial role in reinforcing KOR's definition of solidarity as a struggle for human dignity, it is largely thanks to KOR's broad information and publication channels such as *Robotnik*, high quality journals like *Krytyka*, and a link with international media, that the image of resistance as a solidarity movement was established in the public consciousness. Zbigniew Bujak, one of the founders of *Solidarity* in Ursus, has observed:

When I went to check what's happening in the factory I saw that there was strike. But at the same time there was an atmosphere of uncertainty and fear ... Aha, I say, let's look at *Robotnik*. So I ran to get *Robotnik*, the issue which we had on the premises ... and I said this: Listen, there are names, telephone numbers in here, so if anybody's going to harrass you, these people are there to defend you! And the workers say: that's it, that's it!, and grab *Robotnik*. That's why our shift refused to budge. As I learned later, the workers were tremendously strengthened by this. By the consciosuness that if anything goes wrong, there's somebody to defend us. (Krytyka 1981:36)

Repudiation of the Players

Just when the KOR seems have reached a hard-won victory, it was either sidetracked or treated as a liability by Solidarity leaders. Why were the Players not feted and extolled, why wasn't their suffering acknowledged and rewarded and their writings studied and analyzed? The secret police that had bugged KOR's meetings and beat the guts out the members, must have been rubbing their hands with glee. In 1981 the attacks on KOR were coming from all fronts: the Communist Party, Solidarity's leaders and advisors, the best and brightest of the intelligentsia. This was a historical anticlimax. One of the brilliant communist ploys – the argument that KOR was a bunch of radical intellectuals who schemed to take over power on the workers' backs – was found so persuasive by some Solidarity local leaders that Lech Walesa strained to navigate between warring parties. Solidarity delegates did not hasten to erect a monument to their founding fathers: indeed there was quite a wrangle about mentioning Solidarity's debt to KOR in the report of the first Solidarity Congress. Many 'true Poles', who had a problem with the 'alien' element in KOR, were happy to add vitriol to a stream of slander. Leading Polish intellectuals took to unmasking the 'heroic amateurs' of resistance. Michnik writes:

> I remember a meeting in the KIK (The Club of the Catholic Intelligentsia), at which Bronek Geremek, Andrzej Wielowieyski, and Jadzia Staniszkis talked about the strikes in the shipyards. They spoke about KOR with such ironic superiority that I couldn't bear it and left slamming the door ... For those who had just been released from prison this irony was painful and inadmissible. (Michnik 1995: 299)

To add insult to injury, some Western scholars, mainly of Marxist persuasion, published sociological studies which demonstrated that KOR played little or no role in the creation of Solidarity (Touraine 1983; Ost 2005).

Surely, it was *not* the case of the revolution devouring its own children. It was the classical case of patricide. The begetters of the revolution were no longer perceived as a group of idealists who fought for 'deliverance from servitude through friendship'. They were reduced to what the security police always said they were: an omnipotent Jewish mafia conspiring to overturn the state, destroy Solidarity's Catholic soul, and take over power.

'There has never been a community built on enthusiasm which would not in the end turn into a community of folly', said Proudhon. It is possible in this case to point to some psychological and political mechanisms of this process. The first one – which in Poland has a rich tradition – is a fierce 'martyrdom race' combined with power struggle. There is no doubt that, in the conditions of uncertainty and impending Soviet invasion, the propagandist's image of KOR as manipulating the masses stood a chance to succeed, especially among the local Solidarity leaders who were anxious to become national heroes and did not like competition. As in every revolution, the atmosphere of mistrust and suspicion was further intensified by ubiquitous agents. 'The situation during Solidarity was such', Kuroń writes, 'that if the true news was spread that the government laid a golden egg, people would say: firstly, not golden; secondly not an egg; and thirdly, it didn't lay it but stole it' (Kuroń 1984: 201). The former defenders of Polish workers were very much discussed in similar terms: first, not the defenders; secondly, not of workers' interests; and thirdly, who are they working for anyway?

Tadeusz Mazowiecki, Solidarity's main advisor, believed the Players should not enter Solidarity's structures, not just because they were the Communist Party's Moby Dick, but because they 'had an overdeveloped instinct of group interest' (Jankowska 2000: 151). He touched the nerve of the problem. To many outside observers, KOR was first of all a tight and powerful group of friends 'who did the impossible' – a liability rather than an achievement in the crooked context of the revolution under siege. Last but not least, there was an air of haughtiness about them, 'an attitude of disdain towards the silent majority'.

Some of these perceptions were justified. Willy-nilly, the Players were the actors in the first Polish 'reality show' choreographed by the security police. The experience of being continuously watched and guarded by the security voyeurs, of having one's movements registered and studied, must have been a source of trauma and an ego boost, increasing the sense of threat – and of self-importance. The KOR members were well aware of the danger. Both Michnik and Kuroń speak of the threat of becoming 'the possessed from Dostoevsky's novel'' following 'the road which transforms a movement of the democratic opposition into a religious sect or a gang of bandits – the fate of the triumphant Jacobins, Bolsheviks or the bearded partisans of Fidel Castro' (Michnik 2004: 57). The tension between the temptation to think in terms of '*la nation c'est moi*' and the imperative of humility is especially evident in Michnik's writing. Once he stuns us with half-ironic statements such as 'for five minutes God put me in charge of the Poles' honour!' Then he redeems himself with brilliant polemical essays exposing dissidents' vanity (Michnik 1980: 178–185).

To sum up: there are manifold reasons behind the 'revolutionary patricide' executed on KOR. One of the most obvious is comprehensive envy of a group that stole the monopoly of martyrdom from the Church, the monopoly of compassionate socialism from the socialists, and the monopoly of patriotism and courage from 'true Poles'. There is, however, one more thread that is particularly suggestive. The Players challenged the 'natural order of things' with their cultivation of the dialogic. They were '*both–and*' dissidents, trying by all means to avoid the pitfalls of dogma and fundamentalism: They wanted to practice *both* politics *and* friendship. They were *both* patriots *and* cosmopolitans. They were *both* compassionate Christians *and* secular socialists. As 'liberal-conservative-socialists,' they fought *both* for socialism *and* capitalism with a human face. Even their attitude to the hateful communist rulers was characterized by tolerance, observes one of the former members (Jankowska 2000: 305). In short, the Players were perfect citizens in a utopia of 'dialogic democracy' as imagined by professors of multicultural studies. And here, precisely, lies the problem.

The Magic of a Warm Circle

The Round Table Agreement - signed by the Solidarity leadership with the members of the Communist Party in 1989 – was the crowning achievement of KOR's dialogic politics. The dialogic ethos, marshalled so fervently in countless appeals and essays, was part of Michnik's strategy to build a bulwark against the nation's – and his own – totalitarian temptation. The basis of this dialogue went beyond the readiness to find a pragmatic consensus; it invoked the Christian principle of 'charity before justice'. While settling accounts with the communist generals and apparatchiks, Michnik made a spectacle of forgiving his former oppressors and not bringing them to court. Persecuting them, he insisted, would mean that 'these people will never grow up ... that, being the victims of my fanaticism, they'll be locked in the ghetto of the damned in which there's no point to become better' (Michnik 1995: 96). This sounds persuasive, as always with Michnik. But whatever brilliant justification he conjures, there are understandable reasons why he has preferred to talk to the communist 'modernizers' – who, like him, were *both–and* people (though of a less noble sort) – than to the right-wing camp of nationalist Catholics ready to have him – and the whole of KOR – for breakfast.

It is surely ironic that on the twenty-fifth anniversary of Solidarity, the Round Table Agreement should be read, not as a masterpiece of a dialogic art but as a serious political and moral blunder on the part of the Solidarity leadership. Once an emblem of peaceful transition to democracy and the dawn of a humanitarian Poland without witch-hunts and reprisals, it has become the symbol of moral duplicity, a Mephistopheles' pact signed without consultation with the electorate. Released from Michnik's 'ghetto of the damned', the former communists swiftly returned to power and, with great alacrity, set out to implement the new politics by old means, i.e. through lies, robbery, misrule and cronyism.

There is something allegorical about the way in which a group of friends in a communist country put to test the best ideas of modern *dialogic democracy* – and revealed their problematic nature. We should perhaps add here that the dialogic mode lives on in Adam Michnik's *Gazeta Wyborcza*, the biggest quality newspaper in Poland and one of the greatest success stories in the media market world over. It is striking how many old oxymorons about KOR have been transferred on to *Gazeta*: the newspaper is seen as brilliant and manipulative, pluralist and flirting with the communists, tolerant and authoritarian – not to mention jibes about 'alien domination'.

One is, of course, tempted to inquire into the nature of the Players as 'power-players', to unmask the ways in which friendship became contaminated by politics, and dialogue compromised by ulterior motives. I wish, rather tendentiously, to propose another way of revaluating the phenomenon of KOR. There are two aspects of the Players' extraordinary friendship which deserve particular attention at the time when we are rethinking central values of Western civilization. One is the archetypal story of 'virtue unrewarded,' of Plato's 'desiring souls who yearn to beget in the beautiful' – and are hated for just that reason. We need only to think of Pascal who, risking being burnt on the stake, bravely defended the Jansenists. In return, the Jansenists censored his works and lost part of his scholarly output treating it as too this-worldly. This seems to be the terrible beauty of mankind's humanist project – desirable but resisted, often unacknowledged – and hardly ever rewarded. The cruel imperative inherent in this project has been captured in Herbert's summons:

Go where those others went to the dark boundary
for the golden fleece of nothingness your last prize
go upright among those who are on their knees
among those with their backs turned and those toppled in the dust
you were saved not in order to live

you have little time you must give testimony
be courageous when the mind deceives you be courageous
in the final account only this is important
and let your helpless Anger be like the sea
whenever your hear the voice of the insulted and beaten
let you sister Scorn not leave you
for the informers executioners cowards - they will win
they will go to your funeral with relief will throw a lump of earth
the woodborer will write your smoothed-over biography
...
repeat old incantations of humanity fables and legends
because this is how you will attain the good you will not attain
repeat great words repeat them stubbornly
like those crossing the desert who perished in the sand
and they will reward you with what they have at hand
with the whip of laughter with murder on a garbage heap
go because only in this way you will be admitted to the company of cold skulls
to the company of your ancestors: Gilgamesh Hector Roland
the defenders of the kingdom without limit and the city of ashes
Be faithful Go (Herbert 1993)

Whatever their 'hidden' agenda, one of the most unusual features of the Players' friendship was that it was inseparably connected with this humanist – and yet inhuman – programme, the programme which is not about being a winner but a witness. The twentieth century expired among declarations of humanism alongside wars and crises that unleashed suppressed repositories of violence and revealed weaknesses at the heart of the West's intellectual life. Today one returns again to the concepts of Renaissance thought – such as 'dignity', 'conscience', 'spirit' – but one is hardly aware of the difficult wisdom and frightening costs of humanism in action – one for which they 'will reward you with the whip of laughter with murder on a garbage heap'.

One of the most fascinating dimensions of the Players' legacy is their ancient, and yet novel conception of resistance. What makes KOR into a unique European movement of emancipation is its thought, which embraces not the spirit of the classical nationalist struggle but the spirit of modern cosmopolis. At the same time, however, it reaches back to the premodern values neglected by the Enlightenment: the importance of religion and of the 'habits of the heart', the centrality of human dignity and honour. The friendship of the Players was about politics, but it was first of all about the magic of a 'warm circle' which enabled people to overcome fear and passivity in a debased world. Kuroń recalls a poignant episode:

> In February 1978 a police broke into Boguś' flat and interrupted Adam's lecture. The participants closed their ranks, held Adam's hands, and he went on lecturing. Then the police threw gas bombs and began to beat the participants

with their clubs. But the crowd broke through the blockade, went down to the Floriańska street and, protecting Adam in the middle, walked in the streets of Krakow singing 'Poland is not dead yet' and 'Rota'. They marched like that, almost 200 people, and the others joined in until they brought Adam to the flat of Lilka Batka in the Grodzka Street. (Kuroń 1991: 65–66)

'Lawina bieg od tego zmienia/Po jakich toczy sie kamieniach' ('The avalanche changes its course/Depending on the stones it passes'), wrote Czesław Miłosz (Miłosz 1990). Ultimately, it was the Players' friendship, their unique eros and ethos – which was one of the stones that changed the course of the avalanche.

Notes

1. The masons in KOR included Prof. Edwad Lipiński, Jan Kielanowski, Ludwik Cohn and Prof. Jan Jozef Lipski.
2. Halina Mikołajska, the leading Polish actress and the member of KOR, attempted suicide after massive harassment by the security police.
3. There is evidence that there were plans to assassinate Adam Michnik and Halina Mikołajska, but there was seemingly a split between the security forces, which voted for the elimination of the KOR dissidents, and the party leadership. There are several reasons why Edward Gierek, the then First Secretary of the Communist Party, acted above the heads of the Political Bureau and the Kremlin and decided finally on a line of concessions with regard to KOR. One of the explanations is that, as a personal friend of Mitterrand and a leader who depended entirely on Western banks to solve an acute economic crisis, Gierek had to mind his international reputation. Furthermore, in 1978, after the choice of the Polish Pope, it was too late – and much too awkward – to harden the line. See Rolicki 1990.

References

Blumsztajn, S. (2004) Nasz ojciec chrzestny, *Zeszyty Literackie*, 88(4).
Burnetko, K. (2004) Obywatel K, *Zeszyty Literackie*, 88(4).
Dyskusja (2003): Opozycja demokratyczna w dzialaniach wladz PRL, *Pamiec i sprawiedliwosc*, 2(4).
Domosławski, A. (2001) Hieny, zdrajcy i terrorysci, *Gazeta Wyborcza*, 22 September.
Herbert, Z. (1993) The envoy of Mr Cogito, in: *Mr Cogito* (Oxford: Oxford University Press).
Jankowska, J. (2000) *Portrety niedokończone: Rozmowy z twórcmi Solidarności 1980–81* (Warsaw: Biblioteka Więzi).
King, P. & Devere, H. (2000) *The Challenge to Friendship in Modernity* (London: Frank Cass).
Kowalska A. (1981). Początki, *Kultura* 7/8, July–August.
Kowalska, A. (1983) Nie wierzyłam, ze sie uda. Rozmowa z Anką Kowalską, *Kontakt*, 5.
Kuroń, J. (1984) *Polityka i odpowiedzialność* (London: Aneks).
Kuroń, J. (1989) *Wiara i wina* (London: Aneks).
Kuroń J. (1991) *Gwiezdny czas* (London: Aneks).
Kuron J. (2004) Polityka według Kuronia, *Zeszyty Literackie*, 88(4).
Lipski, J.J. (1983) *KOR* (Warsawa: Wydawnictwo CDN).
Meldunek operacyjny (1978) Vol. 6, 26.V.1978 (Warszawa: Ośrodek Karta).
Michnik, A. (1977a) Nowy ewolucjonizm, *Aneks*, 13–14.
Michnik, A. (1977b) *Kosciół, lewica, dialog* (Paris: Instytut Literacki). English translation: *The Church and the Left* (1992), Trans. David Ost (Chicago, IL: University of Chicago Press).
Michnik, A. (1985) *Z dziejów honoru w Polsce* (Paris: Instytut literacki).

Michnik, A. (1998) *Letters from Freedom* (Berkeley, CA: University of California Press).
Michnik, A. (2003) *Wyznania nawrcónego dysydenta* (Warszawa: Zeszyty literackie).
Michnik, A. et al. (1995) *Między panem a plebanem* (Krakow: Znak).
Miłosz, Cz. (1990) Traktat moralny, in: *Poezje zebrane* (Warsaw: Czytelnik).
Porter R. & Tomaselli, S. (1994) The *Dialectics of Friendship* (London: Routledge).
Plato (1993) *Symposium and Phaedrus,* Trans. B. Jowett (New York: Dover Publications).
Ost, D. (2005) *The Defeat of Solidarity* (Ithaca, NY: Cornell University Press).
Rolicki, J. (1990) *Edward Gierek: replika. Wywiad rzeka* (Warsaw: BGW).
Touraine, A. *et al.* (1983) *Solidarity: the Analysis of a Social Movement 1980–81* (Cambridge: Cambridge University Press).
Zuzowski, R. (1996) *Komitet Samoobrony Spolecznej KOR* (Wroclaw: Ossolineum).

Civic Friendship: A Critique of Recent Care Theory

SIBYL A. SCHWARZENBACH
Department of Philosophy, City University of New York, USA

> Women's labor is considered a natural resource,
> freely available like air and water.
>
> Maria Mies

In recent years feminists have begun arguing for various political conceptions of 'care' (e.g. Tronto 1993; Bubeck 1995; Kittay 1999; White 2000). By contrast, I have argued for the intimate connection between the women's movement of the last century, and the growing realization of the necessity of civic friendship as a condition for genuine justice (Schwarzenbach 1987, 1996, 2005). I shall only repeat the outlines of my argument here, for my central goal in this piece is to look at various institutions which might help realize not merely 'public care' – contemporary theories of which I argue need a far more careful *normative* account – but a civic friendship between *all* citizens. Indeed, I argue that the ideal of civic friend provides precisely that normative account of political care lacking in contemporary theories.

The Argument for Civic Friendship

Central to my thesis on political or civic friendship is the concept of ethical reproductive labor or *praxis* (Schwarzenbach 1987, 1996, 2005). Although not confined to women, 'reproductive activity' includes the type of historical labor and activity predominantly performed by them. It refers in the limit case to childcare, but includes as well husband, extended family and general household care (food preparation, mending of clothes, etc.) and may be found to a large extent in neighborly activities, teaching, ministering, artistic performances, and the like. Reproductive labor is to be contrasted with the more familiar 'productive labor' of the market (craft or agricultural labor, commodity production, etc.), a concept that tends to be identified in the modern period with *labor per se* (Schwarzenbach 1996). In my account, distinguishing features of reproductive labor are, first, that is *not* biological, but a form of labor that centrally entails *logos* or reason (e.g. memory, planning, deduction, generalization, imagination etc.) and thus it is also 'ethical'. Secondly, such labor does not aim in the first instance at the production of physical objects, exchange value, or even 'social services' (where the aim is still characteristically some private good to the self) but at 'reproducing' particular human relations (Schwarzenbach 1996). Ethical reproductive labor includes all those actions that go towards maintaining flourishing relations (e.g. discussion and thought, cooking for another, tending to them when ill, etc.). In the best case, such aims to reproduce the best of human relations for their own sake: what I call relations of *philia* (the ancient Greek term for the 'friendship' between parents and children, siblings, lovers, as well as fellow citizens). Since ethical reproductive activity in the ideal case is done 'for its own sake', it emerges as a form of what Aristotle called *praxis*.

Although my account begins from the Aristotelian notion of *philia*, it does not end there. In Aristotle's view, recall, genuine friends exhibit three necessary and reciprocal traits: (i) awareness and liking of the friend *qua* equal, (ii) wishing the other well for *their* sake, as well as, (iii) practically 'doing' things for them (Aristotle 1984: 1380b). The paradigm of genuine friends in Aristotle's view, however, tends to be that of two autonomous, adult males, both of high virtue (*arête*) and who are roughly equal in those traits that affect *arête* (as do high birth, wealth, beauty, intelligence, moral virtue, etc.). One scholar has gone so far as to claim that Aristotle's ideal of *philia* is that of two male identical twins (Price 1989: ch.5). I believe this last interpretation goes a bit far, but let us nonetheless call Aristotle's paradigm – in which friends presuppose equality as well as objective similarity between them – the paradigm of *fraternity*.

If one takes seriously women's traditional reproductive *praxis* and the vast majority of her historical relations of *philia*, however, another picture emerges – nor is it necessarily (as Aristotle would have us believe) an 'inferior' one. Aristotle acknowledged that the relationships between virtuous mothers and children can be relations of genuine *philia* (as are all good family relations). For, when their relationship is conceived over a complete life, virtuous mothers and children can be said reciprocally to be aware of and like each other, wish each other well, and they certainly practically do a great many things for one another; good children at some point begin to reciprocate their parents' care and concern, and often even tend to the latter in old age, etc.

The central difference between such long-term filial relationships and Aristotle's paradigm, however, is that although aware of the other as possessing (in modern language) a moral equality, there is simultaneously an *awareness of great objective difference*: in age, status, power, perhaps in intelligence, natural capacities, looks, in realized abilities, etc. But why should this make the relationship 'imperfect'? On the contrary, *the goal* of the other's good and autonomy (and rough equality of those things that effect it) is necessarily still there and this despite myriad objective differences. A wealthier friend thus characteristically lends the poorer one money (or buys them a meal) while the latter might return the practical good will in other ways (say, by introducing the former to new friends). For all his profundity, Aristotle ultimately got the nature of friendship wrong. Genuine friendship need not presuppose objective equality between the friends, but it does necessarily *aim* at it (Schwarzenbach 2005).

This second ideal of friendship we might call *friendship through difference*, and it alone will account for those deep relations, say, between a 35- and an 80-year-old, or between two persons of different gender or race, or between those of antagonistic nationalities, etc. Here one friend will practically help the older (or weaker) or will fight against the injustices done to the other who reciprocates in other areas – a balance is always aimed at. And far from viewing this as the inferior form, it is the *friendship as sameness* that begins to emerge as narrow and narcissistic (not to mention chauvinistic) – particularly in a multicultural and rapidly changing world.

Having distinguished two different ideals of personal friendship – and keeping in mind that I will now stress the latter as the more comprehensive – what is Aristotle's argument that a political friendship between citizens is a necessary condition for the justice of the *polis*? For such is my analysis of Aristotle's claim

> for when men are friends they have no need of justice, while when they are just they need friendship as well, and the truest form of justice is thought to be a friendly quality. (Aristotle 1984, 1155a22ff; cf. Schwarzenbach 1996)

First, Aristotle clearly has no difficulty conceiving the three necessary criteria of all genuine friendship exhibited in a 'political' or civic form (unlike the modern methodological individualist). In the political version of friendship (*politike philia*) the traits of reciprocal awareness and recognition of equality, of wishing the other well and of practical doing for them, continue to operate only now no longer personally. Rather these traits are now evidenced *by way of* the constitution, the public laws and the social practices of the citizenry (Cooper 1990: 230). That is, these traits work *via* institutionally recognized norms concerning the proper treatment of persons in society, in what is concretely due them, in the content of their legal duties, etc., together with the knowledge and willingness of the citizenry to uphold these same norms in practice. Political friendship just *is* the *general and public concern* citizens reveal for one another by way of both the form and content of a society's laws, public institutions and social customs.

Objections and Replies

Since I have dealt with numerous objections to the above claims elsewhere, I shall here only note three common categories of criticism and give brief responses to each.

The Ideal of Political Friendship is Inapplicable

How can there be a political friendship in the modern nation state when citizens (unlike in the small ancient polis) can number in the hundreds of millions? This question typically confuses personal friendship with the civic form. Even Aristotle was not claiming that all citizens in the *polis* must personally know – much less like – all others (which is clearly impossible). Rather, in *politike philia* the 'awareness' and 'liking' and 'doing' work through legal and social standards of behavior regarding the treatment of persons, which public norms ultimately must rest on the individual citizens' goodwill. Nor must civic friendship necessarily entail (as some assume) what is known as 'face-to-face assembly' between all citizens (Mansbridge 1983: 10). Rather, the ideal of my liking each citizen in another part of the city (or country) would typically entail, first, that I am *informed* about the nature of that city's population, its citizens' general way of life, the standard of living, etc. So too, I would be concerned about their welfare (I wish them well) with a willingness to help to whatever degree. Such willingness might range anywhere from my not begrudging my fellow citizens the taxes I pay, to supporting public meals for all the poor (a favorite of Aristotle's), to actually helping in times of crisis, etc.

But if political friendship concerns such public norms of concern for all citizens (the characteristic way citizens experience each other's goodwill) they can equally well apply to a state of millions. Indeed, many public norms are higher today than in the ancient world; we no longer condone slavery, for instance. Surely the state here plays a critical role, for it is the universal state which ultimately regulates our awareness of the facts of other citizens' lives and our attitudes towards them (via a constitution, public education, through granting a common set of rights, etc.). Thus the modern state, like the ancient polis, stipulates what are to be considered citizens' minimal attitudes and responsibilities towards each other.

The Ideal is Undesirable

A second set of objections argues that one reason the moderns rejected Aristotle's account was because of the 'partiality' entailed in all friendship; political friendship can never lead to genuine (impartial) justice. It is true that in the ancient world an 'us and them' mentality (much like that of Polemarchus in Plato's *Republic*) prevailed de facto. Already Aristotle argued, however, that political friendship is governed by the 'rule of law' countering such untutored partiality; *politike philia* must be principled and apply to *all* citizens.

In the modern period, moreover, we have a further aid in hand: the doctrine (and culture) of universal individual rights. Far from the position of those (many Marxists and/or communitarians) who hold that individual rights and friendship are incompatible (c.f. MacIntyre 1981), I have argued that a doctrine of universal individual rights must be a necessary element of any *modern* form of political friendship under conditions of pluralism (Schwarzenbach 1996). That is, under conditions where individuals inevitably possess differing and conflicting conceptions of the good life, guaranteeing to each individual – simply on the basis of his or her humanity – a basic set of rights (including due process of law, etc.) and further, in the repeated efforts to uphold these rights and to see them realized in practice, citizens acknowledge and express their general concern and good will for the interests of each particular individual in the concrete. A doctrine of individual rights, far from revealing mere conflict or indifference, can embody an impartial, nonpartisan regard for the special interests of *every* human being – at least in principle.

In the language of Kant, individual rights (and even more so human rights) rest on the general recognition of the dignity of reasoning natures to set their own ends, and thus on the awareness that it is wrong to impose on any such creature a conception of happiness 'from without'. A lesser known theme of Kant's work, however, stresses that the recognition of universal human rights rests on a deep and abiding concern for human beings in general – on what Kant himself calls philanthropic love (*Menschenliebe*) (Kant 1991, Para. 399). Kant lists the sensitive capacity for such *Menschenliebe* among the necessary subjective conditions for the possibility of an agent's responding to moral notions in the first place. A culture of universal rights, may thus educate *against* partiality and favoritism (which is not to say that the *content* of such rights – e.g. whether they entail a right to 'opportunity' or to a job and health care, etc. is not of critical importance).

Stressing the role played by a doctrine of individual rights also helps mitigate against a variation of the above objection: the fear that stressing a political friendship will result in a 'thick brotherhood' á la Plato (with all things held in common) or worse (because closer to home) in one where all are forced to be 'comrades' as in the old Soviet Union. In the view presented here, however, friendship is to *supplement* fundamental freedoms, never replace them (which is not to say that our core set of individual liberties will not be affected). 'Civic friendship' necessarily refers to that form of political friendship that operates through a doctrine of universal individual rights. Moreover, in this account, it can never forcibly be imposed from 'above' (as in the Soviet Union) or 'from without'. On the contrary, as we shall see next, it involves an awareness and practice, which emerges primarily from 'within and below'.

The Ideal is Utopian and Unrealistic

Alright, my critic concedes, what you are arguing for is simply a virtuous citizenry who, although free, will yet concern themselves with their fellow citizens, as well as work to further the common good, etc. But, such is surely utopian given our advanced capitalist, individualistic society. Allow me two points in response. Granted, a genuine civic friendship is an ideal. If, however, one begins not from a productive model of labor (where the goal is some form of private property for the self) but from an ethical reproductive model, the charge of utopianism begins to loose much of its force. For, if I am correct, at least 50% of us have been trained for and operating on this model for centuries – in the midst of advanced capitalist society. Women have historically performed that kind of labor, which encourages and *develops the basic attributes of other persons*. How can such a motivation be called utopian? So too, the *general* awareness of the necessity of a civic friendship has its practical analogue with the mass movement (in the last century) of women into the various public spheres.

Finally, my claim is not merely that a civic friendship is indeed applicable to the modern state today, nor merely that it is desirable, nor that calling for it is not utopian. My claim is stronger: civic friendship is a *necessary condition* for genuine justice in *any* state. In the modern *democratic* state, such must be a civic friendship *between equals* (Schwarzenbach 2005). How does this argument run? As mentioned earlier, Aristotle writes, 'that the truest form of justice is thought to be a friendly quality'. On my reading, his point is that in a general atmosphere of distrust, ill will or even indifference, justice emerges as impossible because citizens lack the *subjective* conditions necessary to perceive and execute it. That is, in the midst of hostility, ill will or indifference, many will continue to perceive themselves as unjustly treated even if some narrower notion of justice (say, proportional equality) is strictly being adhered to. Again, justice by means of force – a fair distribution imposed on parties unwillingly – is clearly an inferior sort of justice to an arrangement *willingly acknowledged*. The former breeds resentment in turn, gives rise to instability, lawlessness, etc. Considering our natural and often unreasonable propensities to favor ourselves, genuine justice can *only* result if a flexible 'give and take' or friendly background exists to make us yield.

Thus, if any of the three necessary traits (reciprocal recognition of equality, good will, and a practical doing for) are absent from the background social institutions, laws and practices – e.g. certain groups go unacknowledged, or great inequalities in property or opportunities persist, or ill-will and suspicion are widespread – too many citizens will be unable to recognize and accept in practice *the burdens of justice* in any particular case. The rich will refuse to give up their undeserved privileges and the humiliated will be moved by resentment and fear. In such cases *what is called justice* emerges as nothing more than the imposition of the will of the powerful. A high degree of civic friendship is a necessary constituent of genuine justice.

The State of Feminist Theory

Theorizing the nature of the political state from a feminist point of view is still in its earliest stages. Nonetheless, at the dawn of the new millennium and together with the large-scale entry of women into the public spheres, we find not only the centuries-long demand that the traditional liberal values of freedom and equality apply to women also (the so-called 'catching-up' phenomenon), but we hear in addition the call for the politicization of certain formerly 'insular female' values. As noted above, numerous voices have begun calling for a political articulation of the value of 'care', for public acknowledgement of the importance of reproductive labor (Schwarzenbach 1987; Okin 1989), for a public theory of the emotions such as 'compassion' or 'sympathy' (Nussbaum 2001; Koziak 2000), and I am here arguing for the importance of a civic conception of friendship. It has even been suggested that the magnitude of the transformation ushered in by this recent turn of the women's movement may be comparable to such historic developments as the emergence of the idea of personal freedom among a bonded European peasantry, or the spread of the idea of democratic rights among the small farmers of the American colonies (Piven 1990). Whatever the ultimate significance of this transformation – and I believe it is very great – the question becomes how best to conceive it, as well as what further practical guidelines (if any) may be drawn. Next, I distinguish my position on the nature of the political state from various other contemporary feminist positions – at least in outline.[1]

I believe it is fair to claim that for much of the nineteenth and twentieth centuries, the women's movement focused on what ruling men historically possessed that women *lacked*: individual freedom from slavery and bondage, a right to property, public voice and recognition, the suffrage, protection from violence, decision-making rights in family affairs, a career, equal pay, etc. In general US women sought equal political rights as briefly summed up in the (failed) Equal Rights Amendment of 1972, as well as the social respect and individual dignity they perceived granted to the full-fledged (white) citizen. Not surprisingly, therefore, when mid twentieth-century feminist theorists first turned to an analysis of the distinctive nature of women's 'reproductive labor' in the home, the value and importance of the male *productive* model of labor remained a pervasive assumption.

Many Marxist feminists from the 1960s and 1970s, for instance, spent a good deal of time and effort showing that the work traditionally performed by women in child and family care (contrary to Karl Marx's own claims) is actually highly 'productive': of great economic worth, a creator of use value and wealth, and thus a central contributor to the exchange value and surplus profits of capitalists (e.g. Gardiner 1974; Hartmann 1981). Even such subtle thinkers as Ann Ferguson and Nancy Folbre – thinkers who explicitly criticized the narrow focus on the economic role of women's labor in the home in order to stress its broader sexual and affective side – continued to call such labor 'sex/affective production' (Ferguson & Folbre 1981); they failed to see that women's traditional activity is often of an entirely *different order* (i.e. closer to *praxis)*. As such, the issue became whether women should receive a wage for sex/affective production from a transitional socialist state or whether – consistent with radical Marxism – all work should in the end be non-waged and organized by councils of 'associated producers' as Marx himself had ultimately envisioned (the domestic labor dispute).

Even the 'radical feminist' rejection of orthodox Marxism by Catherine MacKinnon tends to leave the category of productive labor untouched, for MacKinnon claims that 'sexuality is to feminism what work is to Marxism' (MacKinnon 1983). In her analysis, sexuality becomes the central category of women's exploitation with the result that much of the original socialist account of productive labor and its value remains undisturbed. Moreover, it is not just socialist feminists (like Ferguson, Folbre or MacKinnon) who tended to assume this model as the standard of valuable laboring activity; liberal feminist theorists typically did so also. In her influential work *Justice, Gender and the Family,* for instance, Susan Okin argues for the value of what she now calls 'reproductive labor' (the labor of caring for children and the household), but she continues *to characterize such labor on the production model,* that is, labor worthy of a market wage (Okin 1989: Ch. 8). Okin accepts the present market system with one proviso; she proffers the novel solution that the wife as caregiver in the home should receive a 'co-pay check' from her husband's firm or employer for her efforts. Okin argues that the simplest way for the value of reproductive labor to be recognized and reimbursed (considering that in our society value and prestige is connected with monetary income) would be to require the husband's employer to 'split' the employee's pay check, sending half the monies in a separate payment directly to his wife.

The difficulties involved in Okin's suggestion are numerous. Not only does the scheme continue to make the wife's income depend *directly* on the individual husband's and hardly promotes her safety and independence from him (Frazer 1997: 66), not only does it afford no aid to those women who do not have husbands or male partners, nor to those women whose husbands or partners are unemployed, but the suggestion also does little if anything to alter the perception that care-giving in the home is 'woman's work'. Just as few men will likely stay home under Okin's scheme and choose care-giving work, despite the minimal new incentive, as do so today. Finally, and perhaps most importantly of all, the split-paycheck suggestion leaves the market place and our present class and race structure pretty much *as it is.* The women of minority or working-class background, even if she is lucky enough to have an employed husband, will characteristically receive a relatively small paycheck from her partner's employer for what could be a great deal of work, whereas the upper-class woman would characteristically receive a bonanza as her half of her executive husband's salary even though she is out playing tennis. In this latter case, the woman (typically white) might do almost *no* care work herself and simply hire other women (frequently women of color and from the Third World, who are in turn compelled to leave their own children behind thrust onto relatives, etc.) to do the nursing, housework and childcare. Although perhaps of help to certain middle-class, married, heterosexual women, Okin's proposal hardly proposes a fairer sharing of the joys and burdens of reproductive labor in general.

What these early Marxist, radical as well as liberal feminists have in common – despite very different analyses and conclusions – is a continuing awe of productive labor (and the wages it generates) and the need to justify the value of reproductive labor in terms of it. Nor do many theorists of the 'third wave' (women of color and the Third World), in their criticism of middle-class white feminist political theory, analyze the complexities of alternative conceptions of laboring activity, for they tend on the whole to focus on issues of 'recognition' and 'identity' (of race, class, culture or gender orientation) (e.g. hooks 1984; Lowe 1996; Lugones & Spellman 1986; Mohanty 2003; Moya 2002; Narayan 1997).[2] But thereby all these strands and movements failed to recognize how truly *radical* a transformation is underway in attempts to theorize the realm of women's historical labor and activity.

The more recent turn known as 'care theory' clearly makes headway towards the de-fetishizing of the production model and I believe it contains genuinely new and radical elements as well. Most importantly, it reveals the extent to which care labor is, not only of a different nature, but profoundly devalued in our society: thrust onto women, people of color and those of the Third World (e.g. nannies, housekeepers, gardeners, etc.) (Tronto 1993: 111–113). It is clearly in the interests of the ruling classes that care and reproductive labor *not* be theorized. Further, insofar as care is a critical element of all friendship, I am sympathetic with this movement. In the last decade, however, several tendencies have emerged that suggest to me that focusing on care alone – on care as *the* overarching notion or first principle – is inadequate for a democratic political theory. Allow me to mention three such tendencies, as well as illustrate them in various recent proposals for 'public care'. I shall argue that a political account of care cannot stand on its own, but must be embedded in a larger social and political theory of civic friendship.

Three Criticisms of Care

Continued Link with Biological Motherhood (or Parenthood)

Most theorists who focus on reproductive labor or women's work continue to conceive it far too narrowly. Women's work is characteristically still modeled on the activities surrounding biological motherhood, i.e. pregnancy, parturition, nursing and infant care (cf. Anderson 1990; Okin 1990; Satz 1992), and it is far too often conceived as highly particular and culturally and class specific (e.g. as taking place in the private home). The danger in such cases is that discussions of women's ethical reproductive *praxis* and labor become marginalized and relegated to the realm of childcare or nursing or special 'women's issues'; they soon loose their larger critical social and political potential.

Even more problematic is the link with the economic and political person. Thus Virginia Held writes that what we need now is to 'replace the paradigm of economic man with that of mother and child' (Held 1993: 195), and Eva Kittay aims for a political model based on the 'non-equalitarian, but caring relationship between mother and child' (Kittay 1999: 19). But surely for political purposes – and particularly for modeling the citizen relation – the model of mother and child is limited. The concept of friendship *(philia)* is more appropriate for a number of reasons.

First, the category of friendship is far more *general*. Everyone (but for perhaps the hermit) is profoundly motivated by the desire for friends (at least at most points in their lives) whereas not everyone wants to be a mother or parent (indeed, in recent years more and more women are foregoing it altogether). Friendship in its various cultural forms would appear a genuine candidate for a *universal value* (a universal desire and common need) whereas 'being a parent' or 'mothering person' is not. The non-universal character of motherhood takes on added significance when viewed from a global perspective: we do not *want* more and more parents – with more and more children – do we? The earth is dangerously overpopulated as it is (with near to one-third hovering on the edge of starvation). By contrast, *how to live together on the earth as political friends* may be seen as the new global challenge. Having noted this, let us recall that friendship relations also reveal an 'other-directedness', as well as a care and concern for particular persons and future generations – characteristics which are absent from the dominant economic and political models.

Friendship (as *philia*) is thus the more universal category and it encompasses the best parent–child relationships, whereas the reverse is not the case. Secondly, in contrast to our notion of *philia*, the category of 'mother' all too frequently entails 'physical likeness' as well as the 'extreme inequality' and dependency found in the biological reproductive unit of birth, growth and maturity. Whereas such extreme dependency relations, as well as racial similarity, pervades the natural realm of particular biological offspring, the diminishing importance of such physical and biological traits emerges as fully appropriate when we turn to the political domain of right – at least in the modern period. The ideal of the liberal, democratic state, after all, no longer views citizenship as grounded on blood ties or race, nor is *extreme* legal and political *inequality* acceptable between citizens. For, the political realm is now conceived as the most sustained and reasonable attempt ever undertaken of *rectifying* the inequalities and arbitrariness of the natural lottery. And we hardly want to reverse *this* aspect of liberal theory, do we?

For all these reasons the paradigm of mother and child emerges as the wrong paradigm for the citizen relation, whether in the political or economic sphere. By contrast there is nothing repugnant in the idea of thinking of one's fellow citizens as 'civic friends'. Indeed, the ideal of friendship between citizens – together with the values of freedom and equality – appears central to the ideal of genuine democracy itself (Schwarzenbach 2005). The category covers *all* members of a political community, including the young (potential citizens), the old (retired citizens), the poor, and even the severely handicapped (who often, despite not being productive, can contribute much, etc.). Here there is no biological (or racial or religious, etc.) requirement, but a moral-political connection. Moreover, the 'fact of dependency' that feminists are so fond of pointing to in the mother–child relation is included in the concept of friendship, at least to a certain degree. If I do not attempt practically to help my friend when they are young, old, ill or forsaken, I am simply not a friend. The *degree* to which a child might be dependent on its particular mother – especially considering how the (bourgeois) family is organized at present – is surely far greater than the degree of dependency found in other forms of *philia*. But the glorification of such *extreme dependency* by some feminists appears misguided.

Finally, as numerous thinkers have by now noted, this tendency to focus almost exclusively on mothers can function as an oppressive ideology for women. Rather than women critically reevaluating traditional roles and burdens thrust upon them – what is referred to as the 'cult of domesticity' – it simply glorifies such roles and burdens (Bubeck 1995; Koziak 2000).

Lack of a Clear Alternative and a Normative Account

Not all care theorists, of course, rest their notions of care on the mother–child paradigm; a growing number explicitly reject it (e.g. Tronto 1993; Bubeck 1995; White 2000; Koziak 2000). The problem that emerges now, however, is what might be termed the 'amorphous nature' of care: the problem of how to define it and contain its legitimate boundaries. Joan Tronto, for instance, clearly separates care from the motherhood model, as well as conceives it as a practice. However, Tronto, perhaps the leading proponent for a political ethic of care, continues to operate with a broad definition indeed.

> On the most general level caring is a species activity that includes everything we do to maintain, continue and repair our 'world' so that we can live in it as well as possible. That world includes our bodies, our selves, and our environment, all of which we seek to interweave into a complex, life-sustaining web. (Tronto 1993: 102; also 2003: 1).

This 'definition' of care is surely too broad, however, for it excludes nothing. 'Everything we do to maintain, continue and repair our "world"' includes the slaughter of beef cattle, Nazi death camps, the history of colonialism, as well as each of the United States' military escapades. A more promising venue is where Tronto describes four 'stages' of the practice of care (caring about, taking care of, care giving and care receiving, each with its respective virtue of attentiveness, responsibility, competence and responsiveness) (Tronto 1993: 105ff), but the difficulty of knowing when caring is appropriate and when not, and to what extent, remains. Particularly for political purposes, we must know how the value of care relates to competing values such as freedom and equality, efficiency and so forth. How to distinguish care from uncaring activities, and when to limit care to make way for other values – in short a *normative* theory of care – becomes the central political project. And here the norm of friendship may be of help.

The demand for an explicitly normative theory of care is another way of stating my second difficulty regarding its amorphous character. For there has been a tendency until now to incorporate *within* the concept of care itself numerous other values. Bubeck, for instance, has rightly argued that the concept of care entails some *harm minimization principle*; when one cares for someone or thing one wishes to prevent harm to it or to rectify harm done to it (Bubeck 1995: 202). But from this 'first principle of care' she claims to derive another*: the principle of equal care* (and discusses the case of a mother feeling pressed to spend equal time with her two children).

This further step is a non sequitur. There is nothing in the nature of care itself that mandates equality, whether between all persons or even for the same person at different times (although there may be something about the modern bourgeois family that mandates equal care between children). And the history of the concept of care reveals this. Care has frequently been (and continues to be) highly paternalistic: in feudal times the lord 'cared' for his serfs, the southern plantation owner for his slaves, and care has been distributed unequally (boy children were, and still are, given more care than girls worldwide, etc.) This is not to say that one should not try *to construct a model of reciprocal care among equals*, but here I want to claim we leave the realm of simple care and *begin to enter that of friendship*. For friendship – unlike care – has the goal of equality at its heart (Sec.2). The idea of a moral equilibrium, and a reciprocal practical good will, can here begin to function as a guiding norm for the democratic civic relationship itself.

Rejection of Principle

Finally, I must note one last tendency of much care theory from which I wish to distance myself: the eschewing of all principles and sometimes even of reason itself. Both Nel Noddings and Carol Gilligan, for instance, speak of a morality or ethic of care *in contrast to* that of justice or principle (Gilligan 1983; Noddings 1984). When considerations of care conflict (say, between sick child and a husband's needs), Noddings writes that a woman's 'decision is right or wrong according to how faithfully it is rooted in caring', which she defines as 'essentially non-rational in that it requires a constitutive engrossment and displacement of motivation' (Noddings 1984: 53, 25). Although critical of Noddings's view, Tronto too eschews abstract principles (Tronto 1993: 148ff). Even the virtue theorist Michael Slote writes:

> Anyone who needs to make use of some overarching principle or rule in order to act in a 'balanced' way toward his children can be suspected of an unloving, or at least a less than equally loving, attitude toward those children; and I am suggesting, by way of contrast, that equal concern for children by its very (unselfconscious) nature tends to lead a person to allot efforts and attention in a somewhat balanced way. (Slote 2001: 68).

Is Slote really suggesting that if I at times reflect on whether I actually treat my (very different) children 'equally', I can be suspected of an 'unloving attitude'? Do we not often find ourselves favoring one over the other (say, the youngest) despite our best intentions, a point at which we (or a friend) must remind us that we show favoritism?

This onslaught against 'principles' not only strikes me as seriously misguided, but more importantly, I believe it spells doom for the political project of extending care or practices of *philia* into the political realm. For, when it comes time to construct new social institutions and relations of civic friendship in the larger arena, we can hardly expect *personal feelings* to carry us very far (especially where no such prior social customs exist). Rather, we must reflect deeply, confer with others and *theorize* (replete with principles) what it means to incorporate greater practical care and civic friendship into public institutions without violating other precious values (such as freedom or equality). In current care theory, there is still far too strong a tendency of what many fear most: that our obligations to other citizens (as well as to those world wide) ends up resting – not on reason, reasoned discourse and principle as well – but on nothing more than contingent de facto personal 'feelings' alone.

Three Models of Public Care

I have suggested the ideal of flexible friendship as a political norm for the democratic citizen relation and I have suggested that it (and not care) can act as a determinate guide for (unlike care) genuine friendship has the goal of reciprocal equality at its heart. Let us now turn to various contemporary proposals for a 'public care' which (in my view) violate this central democratic goal. First, we should be clear why the political state today should directly concern itself with (support, oversee, fund) a fairer distribution of care, reproductive labor and *praxis*. While all reap the advantages of the good care of their fellow citizens (in terms of law abidingness, fairness, generosity, etc.), the burden of concrete physical and emotional caring tends to fall unfairly on individual women alone, and disproportionately on woman of color, the working class and Third World. But why must the state now take on – at least in part – such responsibilities?

Let us recall Hegel's words. In the modern period,

> civil society tears the individual from his family ties, estranges the members of the family from one another, and recognizes them as self-subsistent persons. Further, for the paternal soil and the external inorganic resources of nature from which the individual formerly derived his livelihood, it substitutes its own soil and subjects the permanent existence of even the entire family to dependence on itself and to contingency. Thus the individual becomes a son of civil society, which has as many claims upon him as he has rights against it. (Hegel 1967: Para.238 A)

Whereas many male workers were torn from the land already centuries ago – and in response society developed important supports of minimum wage, workman's insurance, unemployment compensation, social security, etc. – the claim here is that the social forces tearing masses of women from the bosom of the patriarchal family is far more recent. As the result of industrialized and expanding markets, legal divorce and abortion, inventions such as birth control, forces of global immigration, the women's movement, etc., not only are individual women ever more apt to find themselves on their own – without the help of relative or other family members, often as the sole provider of children, and with little or no customary support – but the state and civil society as a whole have not yet responded with the much needed new structures and institutions.

Conservatives, of course, long for women to return to the dependency of the patriarchal family unit, but feminists note not only the altered historical circumstances, but prepare for a far more just set of family arrangements. And although the latter are united in their claim that women can no longer shoulder the burden of family care-taking alone – the costs are simply too great – they divide when it comes to proposals for a more equitable distribution. In fact, at least three different models are currently operating in feminist literature: what I will call (i) the reimbursed private care model, (ii) community based care, and (iii) a civil service now devoted in part to reproductive *praxis*.

Private or State-Reimbursed Private Care

On this first model, personal care (for children, but also for the aged, the ill, the disabled, etc.) continues to be performed in the private home but now is directly supported or reimbursed by various agencies: by either a split pay check from the partner's employee (as we saw in Okin 1989), by reimbursement in the form of a government check (Kittay 1999) or, as in another popular version, by state subsidizes in the form of generous tax credits and privileges for dependency work (Fineman 2004). Fineman even advocates that the family unit be *legally redefined* around 'caretaking units': around those who do the actual care taking and their dependent charges (Fineman 2004: 246ff).

We have already indicated some of the problems with this first type of privatized scheme in Okin's proposal above (in terms of compounding pre-existing class and race injustices) and I believe similar criticisms adhere to both Kittay's and Fineman's versions. Difficulties with regard to forms of private reimbursed care may generally be summed up under three headings: issues of fairness, a return to the cult of domesticity, and finally, too, questions of feasibility and efficiency.

Eva Kittay argues, for instance, that 'dependency work' (the unpaid labor performed by women in the home for those individuals who cannot care for themselves) should be recognized *as work* and 'adequately compensated and given the same status and social standing as any legitimate employment' (Kittay 1999: 545). Kittay advocates a system whereby the taxpayer will support social programs that reimburse families and dependents, citing as justification the fact that we have all benefited from the vast amounts of the unpaid dependency labor of women in our lives. Kittay writes:

> Familial dependency workers must be permitted to devote themselves to caring for dependents, if that is their preference, without becoming impoverished and without irrevocably damaging their opportunities to engage in other labor if and when the period of intense dependency ends. Like other workers who are treated in an equitable manner, those doing familial dependency work should have available opportunities for retraining when the period of their charges' dependency is over; they also should have the equivalent of a paid vacation and time off for personal medical care, worker's compensation if they are injured,

and so forth. Such monetary compensation and benefits must be universal (i.e., they should not be limited to those who are impoverished); otherwise, they quickly deteriorate into stingy and stigmatized assistance such as welfare, both as we knew it and as we now know it. (Kittay 1999: 544)

Let us contemplate this suggestion for a moment. Kittay here describes a universal 'system of payment' for all dependency work (in theory including the work of not just mothers, but of fathers, aunts and even lovers). Beyond the practical difficulties of such a scheme (see below) there are critical issues of fairness that must be addressed. For, on the one hand, Kittay wants to grant dependency workers 'the same status' and treat them 'like other workers'. But which other workers are *entitled to* direct payment from the state? Street sweepers or secretaries also do labor from which we have all benefited, labor which is valuable and necessary, often underpaid, but they are hardly entitled (at least as things stand at the moment) to such a guaranteed reimbursement system. If we take this treat 'like-other-workers' strand of Kittay's argument seriously, either dependency labor in the home should be reimbursed by the market (for which it would receive very little), or other forms of useful work, should be state supported also. If care-work is truly 'like' other work why should not secretaries and street-sweepers and plumbers be supported by the state also, with paid vacations and medical insurance, subsidized re-tooling and higher education if desired? Following this line, we soon arrive at the idea of a *guaranteed basic income* for all workers. If we push further, why not guarantee a scheme of basic income *for all citizens* regardless of their ability to work? This last proposal is not so wild as it may seem; not only is a guaranteed basic income an old socialist ideal, but the movement for one is gaining ground today not just in Europe (BIEN), but in the United States (BIG) as well.[3] A guaranteed basic income for all citizens, however, is not the conclusion reached by Kittay.

For Kittay, on the other hand, wants to treat dependency labor and care-work *as special*. Secretaries and grocers and street-sweepers may continue to be reimbursed by the market, for presumably *unlike* such market relations 'the relationship between the dependency worker and the charge itself must be respected as nonfungible and of value, in and of itself' (Kittay 1999: 543). This claim reveals that Kittay does *not* really have 'all dependency work' in mind, but a far more particular form (hers is a politics, recall, 'grounded in the maternal relation'). For, *unlike* the work of the mother, the work of the professional nurse, childcare provider, geriatric aid, governess, etc. is typically *not* 'nonfungible'; these latter are replaceable and reimbursed by the market (even if poorly paid and less fungible than other types of work). The gist of Kittay's proposal can thus be stated: the state should reimburse parents – particularly the mother – for taking care of her own children and family members in the home. Fulltime *Kinder or Pflegegeld*, as it were, with paid vacations and the like.

At this point we are forced to ask: why should mothers (or parents) stay at home full-time and take care of their children with financial reimbursement and little risk to their careers (for they are guaranteed a seat on their return to the market) while the single women must work long hours at the office, or the male who makes shoes or solders pipes, etc., must deal with the vicissitudes and hardships of the market, ever fearful of being laid off, struggling with their boss (or the union) for a raise? This cannot help but cause resentment among other workers (Burkett 2000). Far from rectifying the injustices of private dependency labor, Kittay's 'politics grounded in the maternal relation' simply exalts such labor above all others, granting it unheard of security and privileges. And Fineman's proposal does much the same thing (Schwarzenbach forthcoming).

In both cases, the question remains why the state should support this form of labor and *not other types* as well. This is a difficulty proponents of a basic guaranteed income do not have, for the proposed guaranteed income is *universal and applies to all* (cf. van Parijs 2000). In the latter case, a women raising young children would be supplemented (in addition to her own income) by the income guaranteed to each child or ward as well; thus she would *indirectly* (via her dependents) be guaranteed X times more income than that of single persons. Short of this, however, unfairness reigns – particularly when one considers that having children is meant to be 'optional'.

So too, the above proposals perpetuate and further legitimize, through official state endorsement, 'the cult of domesticity' referred to above. Care for others is kept so private and individualized (and even focused on biology: Fineman 2004: 384) that it is doubtful many men (educated for the public realm) will be motivated to perform it. Not only do such proposals stigmatize those women who do *not* conform – those who wish to be physicists, say, or airline pilots – but, as one author notes, they even reverse the thrust of the 1964 US Title VII's anti-discrimination clause whose goal was precisely to *protect* women who want to perform *non-traditional work* (Williams 1999: 105). At best, such privatized schemes detract from the support and encouragement of women developing other abilities than parochial care taking; they allow women to escape any larger universal demands of the market, their fellow citizens or the global planet. At worst, such schemes legitimize women's traditional oppression.

Last but not least, the above proposals for privatized care-giving reimbursement emerge as prohibitively *expensive*, as well as simply unfeasible. Not only has the inefficiency of workers laboring in isolation (each under her own roof, etc.) been recognized since the time of Adam Smith – there is little or no pooling of hours, of resources or materials, much unnecessary reduplication takes place, the isolation leads to enervation and fatigue, etc.– but so too *who* is to determine whether a woman is doing real 'dependency labor' and not just hanging out, say, with friends? A *vast bureaucracy* would once again be needed to determine the 'deserving' from the 'not so deserving' laborer.

For all these reasons state reimbursement for private reproductive labor should be advocated as a minimum guarantee for all those women (and others) who suddenly find themselves alone with children or who must take care of elderly parents, relatives, etc., because there are no viable alternative arrangements. But it should not be advocated as a general rule – and certainly not *as an ideal* – to which we aspire in the new state, for there are alternative and far superior arrangements.

Community-Based Care

On this second model of public care, state or city funding would go primarily, not to individual private care provision (again, the latter would continue to hold for temporary or exceptional cases) but to local or community-based care centers. The advantages of some form of flexible community-based care over private provision are myriad. Such centers are generally in a far better position to share both the burdens as well as the advantages of various forms of child or elderly care. As community based they can utilize the skills and abilities of *many* individuals, as well as pool materials, resources and local knowledge; they thus emerge as far more 'efficient'. Importantly, such centers also begin elaborating in practice, not only wider ethical values (granted often those of a particular ethnic group), but ideally also an early education in the democratic values of equality, autonomy and civic friendship itself. There appears no reason, moreover, why successful experiments and models that already de facto exist in various educational settings, could not routinely be *extended* to the cases of early child and elderly care. Indeed, such reproductive *praxis* and organized caring activities seem natural extensions of a neighborhood's local public schools, community and religious centers, and even hospitals.

Let us take as one model of community-based care, the successful Beacons programs in New York City.[4] In 1991, in response to community concerns that children were growing up in dangerous neighborhoods with no place to go after school, the mayor of New York City allotted $10 million to establish ten school-based community centers. These centers – known as Beacons – were geographically located within the neighborhood and soon came to provide youth as well as adults with a mix of social services: educational, recreational and vocational. There are now 41 Beacon schools, operating in 32 school districts and located throughout the five boroughs of New York City. In fact, the program is so successful that the cities of Oakland, Savannah, Denver, Minneapolis and San Francisco are replicating it.[5]

What distinguishes these programs in particular is *community involvement*: a sharing of resources, as well as the breakdown of a permanent distinction between professional caregivers or social workers, on the one hand, and informal caregivers and social welfare 'recipients' on the other (White 2000). Public funds are largely 'handed over' to these community-based organizations, local school buildings are made available, and broad participation in decision making processes is encouraged; there is a strong sense that the work of care and concern should be done as much as possible *by* members of the community *for other* members. Although originally developed predominately for the care of older children (teenagers), a number of these programs are being extended to include early child day care, and even care for the elderly and the disabled. The advantages of such a system of community 'mutual care giving' – not only over private caregiver reimbursement schemes, but over the more traditional bureaucratic and paternalistic welfare services – are numerous and striking.

As already noted, in community-based care local resources and skills are shared and there is thus a marked *efficiency of care giving* over privatized models (i.e. one woman in a home taking care of X dependents). As a consequence, in the Beacon program, the *process of needs assessment* is far *less paternalistic*, since authority is widely shared and there is a focus on inclusion in the decision making process. Community members perform much of their own assessment of their needs, tapping a basic trust, loyalty and reserve of local knowledge that community members have for one another. Neither a professional elite arriving from the outside, nor a single 'mother knows best' model, has the last word in the interpretation of the community's or even a single child's needs, and hence too the general *quality* of care can be higher.

For instance, the fact that these caring and educative processes take place in and emerge out of a local community and in the neighborhood bodes well for those children or individuals who come, say, from abusive or in other ways deprived homes; basic protection as well as mentorship is just around the corner. Particularly important for many women and minority groups, collective pooling of community resources often avoids *two destructive poles* of full-time private care giving in the home: (a) the early inculcation of dominant racist, sexist or religious/ethnic societal values that can lead to a child's *lack of a sense of self* worth, or to (b) the opposite case, whereby parents glorify their own race, religion, etc. leading to a child's overly inflated or *false sense of self worth*. Both extremes tend to be mitigated, if the community takes greater responsibility in the care of all its children, for in this latter case the chances of exposure to opposed views are, although not guaranteed, at least enhanced, as are the chances that children are presented with various models of success, and not simply the dominant one.

Much recent literature by minority educators (whether Native American, Black or Hispanic, etc.) has stressed this twofold process in the successful education of minority children; the latter need *both* a sympathy with their particular cultural history, *at the same time* as they are taught how to negotiate the 'codes of power' leading to greater success and understanding in the majority culture and larger institutions (e.g. Moya 2002: Ch. 4). This twofold process community programs such as Beacons aim to provide. Finally, the likelihood of more *men participating* (not just in early education, but even in day and elderly care) is enhanced if care is community based for the labor and activity retains in this instance a public and organizational dimension, whereas few men are adapted to (nor trained for) the purely private labors of the traditional housewife.

In all these ways, federal or state funding *directly* to community centers (such as the Beacon programs) emerges as far superior to private reimbursement, whether in terms of social efficiency, of greater fairness to women in general, to *all* children, but also in terms of the cultivation of a greater democratic understanding and civic friendship between them. This is not to say that establishing such community-care centers would solve all problems; the possibility of *a whole community* or neighborhood being racist, sexist etc. is still all too likely. Nonetheless, it is to suggest that we rethink the present push of those well-intentioned feminists who argue for a privatized form of reimbursed care.

A Civil Service

Although far less prevalent than the first two, a third model of how to conceive of an adequate 'public care' has begun to surface in contemporary feminist thought: the model of a universal civil service now transformed to emphasize the activity of reproductive *praxis* and care (Schwarzenbach 1996: 127; Bubeck 1995: 295). A minimal amount of care and concern for fellow citizens could become a part of the civic obligation of each citizen across the board, much as defense of the nation has traditionally been the duty of the male citizen-soldier. Moreover, a number of the limitations that still adhere to the model of community care might here be rectified. The cult of domesticity, for instance, may well continue to flourish in many local communities (as well as a racism, xenophobia, etc.) whereas a universal care service would now *require* that care work not only be done by men also, but that it be in the service of all. A universal care service is not here meant to replace community-based care centers, but to supplement and complete them.

Traditionally, in addition to being instruments of war and defense, the armed services have always also been important means in the formation of a political or national civic identity. They are 'schools' of various patriotic and communal virtues, an education for a 'fraternity' between men from different parts of the country, walks of life, races and cultures. Historically, of course, women were excluded from such 'bands of brothers' and the virtues and activities taught there were decidedly 'male': a training in physical strength, hardship and deprivation, in discipline, hierarchical command and control, in the production and use of weapons, in strategic planning and so forth.

Let us now consider a possible alternative scenario. As women increasingly enter the public spheres, the professions and government *en masse* (and not individually one by one), the need for public support and funding of women's historical care and reproductive work will only *grow*. At some point, the demand will surely grow, that we begin to transform the goals of our traditional armed forces as well. Why, for instance, should we not divert *at least half* of our exorbitant military budget (in the US greater than the rest of the world's militaries combined) toward a universal citizen *ethical reproductive* service?

The idea of a universal civil service is one whereby each citizen across the board (all classes and genders) is required to contribute one year (or X months) to public service – say, between their 17th and 25th year of life. Unlike other proposals for a national service, however, the emphasis here would be on a different set of skills and abilities. The new civil service could be a training ground – not so much in physical and emotional hardship, in strategic planning or the use of weapons, nor even in the use of mechanics, agriculture and tools (Barber 1984: 300), but foremost in the creation and maintenance of what we have been calling the conditions of the possibility of civic friendship. That is, citizens would first be educated to an *awareness* of their fellow citizens and their communities. Beyond debating the constitutional essentials of the land and its common problems, they would get to know in greater depth its various diverse peoples, their histories and concerns, the background geography as well as ecosystems (including the nonhuman inhabitants), etc. Importantly, such growing awareness of fellow citizens would include a *practical doing* for them, one gauged to perceive and develop the capacities *of others*. This practical aspect might stress work in poorer neighborhoods or in the environment, in hospitals and drug clinics, but also in the routine care of young children, the elderly and disabled. Such an 'army' of young workers could thus help supplement the community care centers and even those individual women with dependents who, for whatever reason, must remain confined to their homes. Above all, such service would explicitly now stress the emotional and perceptual competence central to *politike philia*: the capacity not only to perceive and to understand, but to respond with goodwill (both abstractly and in concrete practice) to other persons who are very different from oneself. And such training in *philia* could not help but affect a nation's relations *outwards* as well.

Objections to this proposal for a universal care service will immediately arise. Just think of the bureaucratic nightmare, the expense, the extent of the state's intrusion into each individual's personal life and freedom, etc. Since I deal with many of such objections elsewhere (Schwarzenbach forthcoming) I will only here note that I find a number of them disingenuous. For one, we have such a vast bureaucratic organization *already*: it is called the US Armed Services. Although not mandatory at the moment in the United States (and hence membership largely determined by economics) such service could become so for 18 year olds at any moment. Why should not this largest and most extensive military in the history of the world be turned (at least *in part*) into a civil service – perhaps on Title VII's anti-sex discrimination and (unequal) funding grounds?

The typical response that we *need* such an exorbitant military begs the question, for it may just be that we *believe* we need one, only because we can imagine no other secure way of living with other peoples of the world – that is, as political friends. Finally, the claim that a mandatory care service would entail the illegitimate use of state power is, again, to argue in a circle for such a response assumes a predetermined answer to the question of the ultimate purpose of the state. At present, the modern state can require of its (male) citizens that they risk their lives in order *to kill* distant others (as well as destroy their things, families, animals, etc.) if the need should so arise. This is no simple feat. Whatever reluctance the individual might feel in leaving the warmth of his home, whatever natural sympathy or commonality he might experience when confronted with fellow human beings on the battle field, his physical, mental and emotional being must be carefully trained and socially prepared, his behavior channeled and formed into something ideally approaching a war hero's action. The tremendous social resources, time and cooperative effort involved in this production of 'fighters' is mind-boggling.

I am thus not referring only to the vast material resources or technological knowhow required to teach a young person, say, to maneuver an F-16 *Falcon* or a stealth bomber. I am pointing to the extensive *emotional training* required as well. If such training is acknowledged and considered legitimate, however – if the political state has the authority to require, in times of crisis, that its citizens actually risk their own lives for the defense of their fellow citizens (and kill other humans in the name of this goal) – there is no doubt it has the rightful authority to require, for limited periods of time and in specified places, that its members also care for fellow citizens in need.

The New State

I have argued that in response to various historical (and surely irreversible) trends, the modern liberal political state must be reconceived so that its central organizing principle shifts away from being an instrument of productive competition and war, and takes on an *explicit* concern with the conditions of civic friendship and a public function of care. This is so, I have argued, not only on grounds of fairness (because women can no longer shoulder their historical burden of reproductive *praxis* alone), but as a necessary condition for genuine justice as well.

Clearly, however, not just any conception of public care will do. In particular, we need a *normative theory* of care, one that carefully analyzes and distinguishes legitimate from illegitimate (or better and worse) forms. *All* existing societies, after all, reproduce themselves and perform caring labor: whether the Nazi mother in the service of the Third Reich or the black mammy slave of the old South. We hardly want to reproduce *such* forms, do we? It is thus necessary for feminists to go *beyond* the category of care itself and to integrate it with other values – particularly with those reigning democratic values of freedom and equality (and now also sustainability). I have attempted to do so in this piece by delineating a civic conception of friendship relations: these are the political ties we should encourage, reproduce and embody in our institutions for they emerge (as noted above) as central to genuine democracy itself.

Finally, the particular proposal for 'public care' proffered here – publicly funded community care centers supplemented by a universal civil service – I consider part of a distinctively *feminist* conception of the state for a number of reasons. With such an arrangement, not only would the cult of male patriotism and production be disrupted on the one hand, but so too, on the other, would that of female domesticity (which still adheres to all European versions of the state). With a mandatory civil care service young men would be schooled – for the first time in history and *en masse* – in the intricate labor and *praxis* of caring for the most vulnerable members of society. Even if such civic schooling and practice were only for a relatively short period of time, it could nonetheless be life transforming.

Taken together with various other necessary economic and representative measures,[6] the new state could begin to move beyond its historical foundations in the gendered division of labor. Simultaneously, we move beyond conceiving the state's justification in terms of the values of freedom and equality only, and begin to embody and realize in its public norms and institutions the forgotten value of friendship as well. Finally, such a major restructuring of the central priorities of the modern political state could never occur without a simultaneous transformation in our conception of the political person or citizen. Perhaps most importantly, this new citizen would be one who, from the start, is carefully nurtured, respectfully educated, and thoroughly grounded in the ways of civic good will, reproductive *praxis* and democratic cooperation – long before it learns anything of the arts of war.

Notes

1. For a far more detailed account, see Schwarzenbach forthcoming, esp. Ch. 7.
2. There are some clear exceptions to this rule, e.g. Mies 1986.
3. See http://www.usbig.net/. Also, Cf. my (2004) The limits of production: justifying basic income in: Standing, G. (Ed.), *Guaranteed Basic Income in Europe and North America*, pp. 97–114 (London: Anthem Press).
4. This account of the Beacon program is indebted to the careful study by White 2000, esp. Ch. 4.
5. See http://www.nccic.org/ccpartnerships/profiles/beacons.htm.
6. Cf. Schwarzenbach forthcoming.

References

Anderson, E. (1990) Is women's labor a commodity?, *Philosophy and Public Affairs*, 19(1), pp. 71–92.
Aristotle. (1984) *The Complete Works of Aristotle*, Ed. J. Barnes, Vol. II (Princeton, NJ: Princeton University Press).
Barber, B. (1984) *Strong Democracy: Participatory Politics for a New Age* (Berkeley, CA: University of California Press).
Bubeck, D. (1995) *Care, Gender, and Justice* (Oxford: Clarendon Press).
Burkett, E. (2000) *The Baby Boon: How Family Friendly America Cheats the Childless* (New York: The Free Press).
Cooper, J. (1990) Political animals and civic friendship, in: Patzig, G. (Ed.), *Aristotle's 'Politik'*, pp. 220–241 (Friedrichshafen: Vandenhoeck & Ruprecht).
Ferguson A. & Folbre, N. (1981). The unhappy marriage of patriarchy and capitalism, in Sargent, L. (Ed.), *Women and Revolution*, pp. 1–41 (Boston, MA: South End Press).
Fineman, M. (2004) What place for family? in: Schwarzenbach, S. (Ed.), *Women and the United States Constitution*, pp. 236–254 (New York: Columbia University Press).
Frazer, N. (1997) *Justice Interruptus* (New York: Routledge).
Hartmann, H. (1981) The unhappy marriage of Marxism and feminism: towards a more progressive union, in: Sargent, L. (Ed.), *Women and Revolution*, pp. 1–41 (Boston, MA: South End Press).
Gardiner, J. (1974) Women's domestic labor, *New Left Review*, 89(1), pp. 47–58.
Gilligan, C. (1983) *In a Different Voice* (Cambridge, MA: Harvard University Press).
Hegel, G. (1967) *The Philosophy of Right*, Ed. T.M. Knox (Oxford: Clarendon Press).
Held, V. (1993) *Feminist Morality* (Chicago, IL: University of Chicago Press).
hooks, b. (1984) *Feminist Theory: From Margin to Center* (Boston, MA: South End Press).
Kant, I. (1991) *The Metaphysics of Morals*, Ed. Mary Gregor (Cambridge: Cambridge University Press).
Kittay, E. (1999) *Love's Labor* (New York: Routledge).
Koziak, B. (2000) *Retrieving Political Emotion: Thumos, Aristotle and Gender* (University Park, PA: Pennsylvania State University Press).
Lowe, L. (1996) *Immigrant Acts: on Asian American Cultural Politics* (Durham, NC: Duke University Press).

Lugones M. & Spellman, E. (1986) Have we got a theory for you! Feminist theory, cultural imperialism, and the demand for 'the woman's voice', *Women's International Forum,* 6, pp. 573–581.
Mansbridge, J. (1983) *Beyond Adversary Democracy* (Chicago, IL: University of Chicago Press).
MacIntyre, A. (1981) *After Virtue* (London: Duckworth).
MacKinnon, C. (1983) Feminism, Marxism, method, and the state, *Signs* 8(4), pp. 635–658.
Maria, M. (1986) *Patriarchy and Accumulation on a World Scale: Women in the International Division of Labor* (London: Zed Press).
Minow, M. (1997) All in the family and in all families: Membership, loving and owing, in: Estlund, D. & Nussbaum, M. (Eds.) *Sex, Preference, and the Family,* pp. 249–276 (Oxford: Oxford University Press).
Mohanty, C. (2003) *Feminism Without Borders: Decolonizing Theory, Practicing* Solidarity (Durham, NC: Duke University Press).
Moya, P. (2002) *Learning from Experience: Minority Identities, Multicultural Struggles* (Berkeley, CA: University of California Press).
Narayan, U. (1997) *Dislocating Cultures; Identities, Traditions, and Third-World Feminism* (New York: Routledge).
Noddings, N. (1984) *Caring: A Feminist Approach to Ethics and Moral Education* (Berkeley, CA: University of California Press).
Nussbaum, M. (2001) *Upheavals of Thought: The Intelligence of the Emotions* (Cambridge: Cambrdige University Press.
Okin, S. (1989) *Justice, Gender and the Family* (New York: Basic Books).
Okin, S. (1990) A Critique of Pregnancy Contracts, *Politics and the Life Sciences,* 8, pp. 205–210.
Philippe van Parijs. (2000) *What's Wrong with a Free Lunch*? (Boston, MA: Beacon Press).
Piven, F. (1990) Ideology and the state: women, power, and the welfare state, in Gordon, L. (Ed.), *Women, the State and Welfare,* pp. 251–252 (Madison, WI: University of Wisconsin Press).
Price, A. (1989) *Love and Friendship in Plato and Aristotle* (Oxford: Oxford University Press).
Ruddick, S. (1989) *Maternal Thinking* (New York: Beacon Press).
Satz, D. (1992) Markets in women's reproductive labor, *Philosophy and Public Affairs,* 21(2), pp. 107–131
Schwarzenbach, S. (1987) Rawls and ownership: The forgotten category of reproductive labor, *Canadian Journal of Philosophy,* 13, pp. 139–167.
Schwarzenbach, S. (1996) On civic friendship, *Ethics* 107, pp. 97–128.
Schwarzenbach, S. (2005) Democracy and friendship, *Journal of Social Philosophy,* 36(2), pp. 233–254.
Schwarzenbach, S. (forthcoming) *On Civic Friendship: Including Women in the State.*
Slote, M. (2001) *Morals from Motives* (Oxford: Oxford University Press).
Tronto, J. (1993) *Moral Boundaries: A Political Argument for an Ethic of Care* (New York: Routledge).
Tronto, J. (2003) Care as the work of citizens: a modest proposal, paper presented to the Yale Political Theory Workshop, 15 April.
Van Parijs, P. (2000) *What's Wrong with a Free Lunch*? (Boston, MA: Beacon Press).
White, J. (2000) *Democracy, Justice, and the Welfare State: Reconstructing Public Care* (University Park, PA: Penn State University Press).
Williams, J. (1999) *Unbending Gender: Why Family and Work Conflict and What To Do About It* (Oxford: Oxford University Press).

Friendship, Mutual Trust and the Evolution of Regional Peace in the International System

ANDREA OELSNER
Department of Politics and International Relations, University of Aberdeen, UK

Friendship and International Relations: Incompatible?

There seems to be an insurmountable obstacle to even thinking in terms of friendship about relations taking place at the international (interstate) level: the alleged anarchic structure of the international system. International Relations (IR) realism, both in its classical and structural versions – arguably *the* dominant theory in the field over the last 60 years – has made anarchy an unquestioned assumption.[1] Indeed, anarchy has been the driving force behind IR (neo)realist theorizing.[2] This has had at least three important consequences. First, it has led to a particular understanding of the functioning of the international system. Secondly, and closely related, it has resulted in a biased research agenda. As Alexander Wendt (1999: 298) asserts, 'relative to "enemy", the concept of "friend" is undertheorized in social theory, and especially in IR, where substantial literature exists on enemy images but little on friend images, on enduring rivalries but little on enduring friendships, on the causes of war but little on the causes of peace, and so on'. Finally, despite realism's claims of being an objective, non-normative approach, it has led to a particular set of prescriptions regarding how states should behave if they want to survive in the international arena.

According to neorealism, anarchy is a structural feature of the modern international system. Under anarchy, units (states) are sovereign – they recognize no higher authority such as a world government – and functionally similar, in that they differ in their (military) capabilities rather than in their responsibilities. By contrast, in a hierarchic system units serving different functions are organized under a clear line of authority. Additionally, states are assumed to be unitary and rational actors seeking survival and security. Given the condition of anarchy, every state is solely responsible for its own security, and thus, for the sake of caution, should consider other states as potential threats. The anarchic international system, as described by (neo)realism, is a *self-help* system where states should accumulate power for defensive and deterrence purposes. An unsolvable problem of this perspective – and of the realist world – is that this defensive move easily results in a *security dilemma*. By trying to ensure their own security, states make the system as a whole more insecure, since other states may (mis)take defensive for offensive build-up efforts and be inclined to strengthen their own military capabilities as well. The likely outcome is arms races and the emergence of balances of power.

If the world is as (neo)realists describe it, these rational, self-interested states do well not to trust one another. In this context, it is clear that the emergence of any interstate relationship resembling a friendship is simply impossible, or else suicidal.

However, sometimes states do maintain friendly relationships with each other, and even commit themselves to fighting in the name of other states. Arnold Wolfers suggests that alliances and cooperation between states amount to international amity. Yet he warns, 'terms like "amity" and "enmity" – even more, terms like "friendship" and "hostility" – must be used with caution in discussing interstate relationships ... Diplomatic postures of amity and enmity do not depend on emotional conditions and may in fact contradict them' (Wolfers 1962: 25). According to Wolfers (1962: 33–34), 'most states most of the time ... maintain amical [sic] or inimical relations with others on the basis of calculations of interest rather than in response to popular sentiments whether of gratitude or resentment'. Thus, active cooperation – relationships of 'going it with others', in Wolfers' words – mostly result from 'the desire to meet an external threat by co-operative effort; here co-operation is predicated on the continuance of the threat'. However – and this will prove more helpful when trying to trace friendship in international life – cooperation can also arise from a different incentive, namely 'a desire to improve relations within the co-operating group' (Wolfers 1962: 27). While both are possible, Wolfers admits – 'to the disappointment of idealists' (1962: 27) – that the former, outward-directed cooperation proves much more potent than the latter, inward-directed, and when the latter takes place, it is usually pursuing outward-directed defensive purposes as well.

Outward-directed arrangements clearly conform to the traditional definition of alliances as 'formal associations of states for the use (or nonuse) of military force, in specified circumstances, against states outside their own membership' (Snyder 1997: 4). IR thought on alliances rests on (neo)realist premises, according to which alliances result from the systemic balance-of-power mechanism that works to prevent one state or group of states from becoming too strong and dominant. Were this to happen, there could be a structural change in the international system from anarchy to hierarchy, and along with it, a change of system itself. However, weaker states may ally, thus pooling their capabilities and precluding world domination by one strong state or coalition, thereby restoring the balance needed for their survival as sovereign units and the survival of the system as a whole. Explicitly enough, John Mearsheimer (1991–1992: 220) contends, 'peace is mainly a function of the geometry of power in the international system, and certain configurations may be very peaceful while others are more prone to war'. However, balance-of-power theorists are not in agreement on whether bipolar configurations are more stable than multipolar ones, or vice versa.

There is additional disagreement on whether states join alliances to balance against power or against threats, and indeed on whether states join alliances for balancing purposes or, under certain conditions, in order to bandwagon with the stronger side. Nor does it seem to be all that unequivocal that states are more likely to enter into alliances with culturally, politically and/or ideologically similar states, or whether similarity makes for more cohesive alliances. There are cases that show and scholars who argue that the opposite is true (for these debates, see Walt 1985). What is clear is that what drives the formation and maintenance of alliances is some sort of rational calculation seeking the unit's and system's survival. For this same reason alliances are only temporary: as soon as the balance of power (or of threat) shifts, so states shift alliances.

The unstable nature of interstate alliances had already been noticed by Thomas More in 1515:

> no confidence is put in alliances, even though they are contracted with the most sacred ceremonies. The greater the formalities, the sooner the treaty may be dissolved by twisting the words, which are often purposely ambiguous. A treaty can never be bound with chains so strong, but that a government can somehow evade it and thereby break both the treaty and its faith. (T. More reproduced in Wolfers & Martin 1956: 6)

Not just alliances, but also international agreements more generally have been seen as equally precarious. Edmund Burke, reflecting on the possibility of peace in Europe, drew attention to the fact that,

> in the intercourse between nations ... we lay too much weight upon the formality of treaties and compacts. We do not act much more wisely, when we trust to the interests of men as guarantees of their engagements. The interests

frequently tear to pieces the engagements, and the passions trample upon both. Entirely to trust to either is to disregard our own safety, or not to know mankind. (E. Burke, reproduced in Wolfers & Martin 1956: 111).

Indeed, more contemporary writings often do not differ from Burke's observations.

In sum, there seems to be agreement that alliances and international treaties, at least by themselves, provide at best only thin grounds for true and long-lasting mutual understanding. In contrast, we would expect friendship, or its international equivalent, to be built on more stable bases. As will be seen below, I will argue that the key is to be found in what More identifies as missing from alliances – mutual confidence and trust.

Arnold Wolfers' caution, if not scepticism, about the chances of successful inward-oriented cooperation in the absence of external threats nicely reflects the general prudence that dominates IR scholarship when it comes to international friendship. Nonetheless, even Wolfers (1962: 28–29) eventually acknowledges that 'some form of regular and institutionalized political co-operation among nations ... may be able under certain circumstances to assure a high degree of amity among the participants'. Similarly, an increasing number of IR scholars have come to recognize that relations comparable to those of friendship have grown in certain regions of the world where the condition of anarchy has taken a different form from what realism predicts (see, for instance, Deutsch et al. 1957; Adler & Barnett 1998b; Wendt 1999; Kacowicz et al. 2000).[3]

In the remainder of the article I focus on the development of what Wolfers called regions of inward-oriented cooperation. I see this reflected not necessarily in actual agreements, but in states' ability and willingness to maintain regional peace. Drawing upon the securitization approach developed by Barry Buzan, Ole Wæver and their colleagues of the so-called Copenhagen School, I argue that the maintenance of stable regional peace is connected with domestic processes of desecuritization taking place in a given region. The second section briefly reviews the concepts of securitization and desecuritization. The following section turns to the concept of peace, and proposes a peace typology to identify different qualities of regional peace. Finally, I explore the connection between desecuritization and the evolution of regional peace, emphasizing the role of mutual trust. I suggest that the improvement of regional peace can be understood as a two-phase process, and I illustrate this with the case of the rapprochement in the Southern Cone of South America. Indeed, following a protracted history of rivalry and hostility, in the late 1970s Argentina and Brazil began a process of bilateral détente that resulted, about ten years later, in the creation of Mercosur, the common market of the South.

Securitization, Desecuritization and the Domestic Construction of Asecurity

The securitization approach has initially been developed in various articles by Ole Wæver (among them, see Wæver 1995, 1998), eventually fully materializing in a volume published in 1998 written in collaboration with Barry Buzan and Jaap de

Wilde, *Security: A New Framework for Analysis*. The theory is to be understood in the context of a debate flourishing during the 1990s regarding the definition of security and the need to expand it or keep it narrow. Rather than proposing a new, longer list of threats, the securitization project entailed a search for the logic that drives the securitization process; that is, the process by which issues come to be seen as security matters.[4] Building upon language theory, Wæver argues that security can be regarded as a speech act: the mere invocation of something using the word 'security' declares its threatening nature, 'invokes the image of what would happen if [security] did not work' (Wæver 1995: 61), thereby justifying the use of extraordinary measures to counter it.

Hence, security is the realm where emergency measures beyond ordinary political procedures become permissible. When an issue makes it into the sphere of security because it has been successfully presented as a threat, it has been *securitized*. Using the jargon of this approach, securitization is the process by which a *securitizing actor* succeeds in presenting a threat or vulnerability as an *existential threat* to a *referent object* that has a legitimate claim to survival, thereby attaining endorsement for *emergency measures*. These measures would otherwise not have been granted the necessary legitimization (approval) by the *securitizing audience*.

Although the authors deliberately leave the definition of emergency measures open and implicitly play down the link between these measures and violence, I think that there is a case to be made for reconnecting the two.[5] The idea that securitization internalizes the logic of war is more forcefully presented in an earlier work by Wæver (1995). There, the author contends that 'the logic of war – challenge-resistance(defense)-escalation-recognition/defeat – could be replayed metaphorically and extended to other sectors. When this happens, however, the structure of the game is still derived from the most classical of classical cases: war' (Wæver 1995: 54). Yet following this argument, the logic of a game called 'competition' would not substantially differ from Wæver's war game. I would claim that what indeed makes them two different games is the inherent component of violence of the logic of war. Successful securitization legitimizes emergency measures that make reference to violence, either because the audience agrees to the recourse to violence, or because it agrees to extraordinary action that should avoid later violence.

However, more interesting for the present discussion on friendship is the concept of desecuritization, on which the authors, unfortunately, do not expand very much. In principle, desecuritization involves 'the shifting of issues out of the emergency mode and into the normal bargaining processes of the political sphere' (Buzan et al. 1998: 4). Yet using our revised understanding of emergency measures, it can be said that the process of desecuritization implies that issues, for which the potential use of force had been legitimized before, now start to retrace their steps taking the opposite direction, whereby violence ceases to be a legitimate option. This time, the aim will be to remove certain issues from the security agenda. When these issues involve (aspects of the) relationships with neighbours, the domestic process of desecuritization may advance positive changes at the regional level, in a similar fashion as securitization moves may provoke regional escalation and crises.

Three conditions (or states) of security can be identified. First, when one feels to lack adequate defences to counter perceived threats, the situation is one of *insecurity*. If, by contrast, sufficient counter-measures are felt to be available, the situation has evolved to one of *security*. A common feature of insecurity and security is the presence of perceived threats, rendering necessary an alert attitude; precluding serenity. Conversely, by the slow erosion of the perception of threat a situation of *asecurity* emerges; one in which neither the security language nor logic apply (Wæver 1998: 81).

Perhaps because both securitization and desecuritization are processes that take place inside states, the reference to (regional) peace has been remarkably absent from the literature on this approach. While desecuritization is a domestic process, peace is an inherently relational concept, as will be seen below; it compels us to look beyond state behaviour, towards regional patterns of interaction.

Types of Peace

The decision to focus on regional peace rather than on regional agreements partly follows from the earlier discussion. As many scholars have stressed, the fact that states can walk away from, or violate the terms of, agreements without their co-signatory partners feeling *emotionally betrayed* can be explained by the absence of a global enforcer (anarchy). However, it can be also explained because states need not conduct friendly relations, let alone be friends, in order to sign agreements. In contrast, the link between regional peace and friendship is more intertwined. Regional peace, I suggest, is a necessary condition for regional (interstate) friendship, although not a sufficient one. It is necessary because without regional peace we cannot talk about regional friendship. However, we may find regions where the absence of interstate violence, even if for extended periods of time, is the product of relationships very different from friendship: a regional balance of power (Job 1997: 171), the presence of an overriding regional hegemon that sorts out disputes short of war (Aron 1966), strong influence of an extra-regional power with the same effect (Buzan 1991: 219–221),[6] or alternatively impotence, geographical isolation, or sheer strategic irrelevance (Kacowicz 1998: 34–39). The fact that we still talk of peace in these circumstances points to the need of distinguishing between different kinds of peace. If not just *any* type peace is a sign of mutual trust, mutual responsiveness, etc., but only *some* types, then we need to qualify peace.

The recognition of different types of peace is by no means a novel idea. Several scholars have constructed typologies or scales that typically cover all the range from a very fragile and unstable peace to situations of consolidated and stable peace. A possible further step that some authors consider in these gradations is the establishment of pluralistic security communities, alluding to the situation in which war has become unthinkable due to the emergence of a sense of transnational community among both elites and societies of the states involved. The typologies are not fundamentally divergent in essence. They all point, with slight differences in emphasis, to similar stages of one same peace continuum. Variations relate more to each scholar's research interests than to fundamental conceptual disagreements (see, for instance, Holsti 1996; Kacowicz 1998; Boulding 1978; George 2000; Miller 2000a,b; Morgan 1997: 31–38).

Drawing upon existing peace scales, I have found that a more detailed analytical typology would help to better capture the different stages of a peace relationship (see Table 1). Before turning to that, the following assumptions should be made explicit. First, no particular type of domestic political regime is indispensable for the maintenance of a zone of peace, broadly defined. Liberal democracies seem to favour it, but other types of regimes have been equally capable of avoiding war, conducting peaceful relationships, and even initiating a process of peace stabilization, as the example of the South America's Southern Cone will show below.

Secondly, peace at the international level refers to the type of relationship that two or more states maintain. When the talk is about peace, rather than about pacific foreign policy, clearly more than one state has to be involved. Thus, international peace is a *relational* concept. It is necessary that two or more states conduct some sort of relationship or interaction to be able to assert that it is peaceful. The mere absence of war, as observed earlier, may be pointing to lack of relationship rather than to meaningful peace. In a regional context, nonetheless, it is rare to find neighbouring states with no relationships at all.

Finally, peace is a *process*, and as such, *dynamic*. To be maintained, peace demands constant attention and commitment. There is nothing in even the most stable type of interstate peace that makes it irreversible. On the contrary, it is an inherently fragile process, much easier to reverse than to build. Nonetheless, if successfully built, peace tends to be self-reinforcing, resulting in an increasingly stable and consolidated type of peace.

An initial broad distinction can be made between negative and positive peace.[7] Negative peace refers to the situation where the absence of threat or use of force is not necessarily expected. Domestically, bilateral or regional relationships are securitized, and the security lens and language permeate all perception of them. Under negative peace there is no war, but there are preparations and contingency plans for war. Depending on how frequently and how distant in time violent clashes last occurred, I subdivide this category into *fragile*, *unstable* and *cold or conditional peace*.

Highly securitized visions of the neighbour(s) will translate externally into *fragile peace*, where pending disputes survive, armed forces work on regional conflict hypotheses, and states prepare for war. Peace is occasionally interrupted by military

Table 1. Peace categories.

Negative peace	Fragile peace
	Unstable peace
	Cold or conditional peace
Positive peace	Stable peace
	Pluralistic security community

clashes, but they are kept below the level of international war – hence it can still be called a zone of peace. Yet the resort to violence to resolve or protect securitized issues is seen domestically as a legitimate option. The chances of escalation are high, and the situation is perceived as one of insecurity; war may indeed break out. For instance, until a few years ago Israeli–Palestine relations could have been said to be in fragile peace, later becoming a zone of war, and more recently moving again into a fragile peace situation.

Under *unstable peace*, preparation and contingency plans for war are also present, but with no armed confrontations having occurred, or only in the distant past. Nevertheless, confrontations and even war have not only *not* been ruled out, but also deterrence and threats play a critical role in this type of relationship. This is what makes this peace unstable. Domestically, it still is the security language that defines the relationship, and thus the situation is perceived in terms of insecurity or security – depending on how one's own capabilities are assessed vis-à-vis the adversary – but never in terms of asecurity. Clearly, US–USSR relations during the tensest periods of the Cold War would fit into this category.

When the situation is no longer perceived in terms of insecurity, either because one's own defensive capacity is seen as superior, or because a gradual process of détente has begun, the situation is one of *cold or conditional peace*, i.e. a less extreme type of non-war. Relationships are still characterized by the absence of war rather than by the presence of mutual confidence, but violent confrontation does not appear as such a realistic eventuality. In other words, although the use of 'extreme measures' has not been discarded and issues in the relationship continue to be securitized, violence does not appear to be as likely an outcome as in fragile and unstable peace. Display of force can be used as a means to apply pressure during negotiations, and parties have no reason not to expect this. Argentina and Britain conducted such a relationship in the years that followed the Malvinas/Falkland Islands war of 1982.

If negative peace and its three subcategories (fragile, unstable and cold peace) are defined by the absence of war, then positive peace is defined by the presence of confidence and trust. It is in situations of positive peace that states can achieve relationships resembling those of friendship. In positive peace, states do not prepare for war, nor do they expect other states in the zone to do so. They do not read bilateral or regional issues in security language. This does not necessarily mean that all disputes have been resolved. Issues and disagreements may persist, but no party conceives of force to sort them out. Zones of positive peace can be subdivided into zones of *stable peace* and *pluralistic security communities*. In both, their members have ruled out the possibility of war among themselves, and are confident that their fellow members have done so too. They are all certain that any potential changes to the status quo will be peaceful and agreed.

A *pluralistic security community* stands out as a more 'participatory' kind of stable peace in that not only has war become unthinkable, but also the societies involved have developed links, mutual sympathies, and some sort of common identification[8] that makes them perceive each other as members of the same community. In addition, states may be bound by common political institutions, similar political systems, and considerable economic interdependence. To be sure, all pluralistic security communities are zones of stable peace. However, not all zones of stable peace are pluralistic security communities (Kacowicz & Bar-Siman-Tov 2000: 22). An example of stable peace are relations among members of the Association of the Southeast Asian Nations (ASEAN) since the late 1970s. On the other hand, members of the European Union, as well as Canada and the United States are cases of pluralistic security communities, whereas Argentina and Brazil can be said to be part of an incipient security community, as I will argue below.

Trust, Desecuritization and the Evolution of Regional Peace

The categorization presented above implies the consideration of mainly two variables: the stability of peace, temporally determined by the duration of the absence of military confrontation, and the solidity of peace, signalled by the presence or absence, and degree, of trust in the relationship. Of the two, I consider the solidity of peace to be the crucial element in distinguishing among the different types of peace and the one moving the desecuritization process forward.

The factor of time plays a weightier role in situations of negative peace, where aggressive behaviour may have occurred in a recent past. Collective memory of past aggression influences the degree of trust between states and peoples. Therefore, issues are more likely to remain securitized. While it holds true that recent armed conflict makes the development of trust more difficult, the opposite is not necessarily the case. Even relationships with a long record of absence of actual military conflict may be dominated by mistrust. Thus, time, while important (especially if there have been recent confrontations), tends to influence only indirectly the type of peace, mostly by affecting the level of mutual trust.

Consequently, the development of mutual confidence is critical to understanding the process of desecuritization implied in the transformation of negative into positive peace, and in the stabilization and later consolidation of peace. The level of mutual confidence indicates the solidity of the peace upon which the relationship rests. In other words, the higher the degree of mutual confidence, the more solid the peaceful relationship, and the harder (although not impossible) it will be for the process to be reversed. Conversely, the higher the degree of distrust – and therefore the less solid the basis for peace – the easier that even minor misunderstandings or misinterpretations develop into military violence and possibly war.

Although stability can be measured in years of absence of conflict, I am reluctant to set a fixed number of years to indicate whether peace has become unstable, cold or stable. Rather, I understand it to be a delicate blend of stability (time) and solidity (trust) pointing to one type of peace or another. Nevertheless, one might say, following Kacowicz, that a zone of peace, whether negative or positive, is one in which

> a group of states have maintained peaceful relations among themselves for a period of at least thirty years – a generation span – though civil wars, domestic

unrest, and violence might still occur within their borders, as well as international conflicts and crises between them. (Kacowicz 1998: 9)

A quantitative measurement of trust is even more difficult. Instead, one has to rely on the examination of certain indicators.[9] For instance, the deployment of troops along a common border is most probably a sign of securitized relationships and of fragile or unstable peace. The presence of a system of mutual accountability through confidence and security building measures (CSBMs) is likely to be indicative of cold or stable peace, in which some issues remain securitized and are to be closely monitored. Common institutions, high level of interdependence, compatible domestic regimes, withdrawal or absence of troops on common borders, among others, point to the existence of trust, and thus to a situation of stable peace. Furthermore, they may point to a pluralistic security community, or rather, as Wæver called it, an *asecurity* community (Wæver 1998: 104).

The existence of pending disputes need not in itself indicate distrust. Certain issues may be disputed without being securitized if, for instance, there is a firm commitment to find agreed solutions. Conversely, distrust can define a relationship even in the absence of apparent conflict. Short of producing an exhaustive list, I suggest that the presence or absence of the following indicators should be taken into account when the solidity of regional peace is to be assessed:

- recent war, repeated exchanges of cross-border fire, deployment of troops in border areas, arms races, existence of contingency plans for war, few and distant (in time) diplomatic visits, mistrust and antipathy between societies, obstacles for the mobility of persons;
- diplomatic visits and public speeches pointing at the easing of tension, CSBMs, problem-solving mechanisms;
- fluid communication channels, common projects involving expectation of joint benefits (e.g. a common market), common institutions, high degree of interdependence and exchange, compatible self-images, easy or free mobility of people.

The first set of indicators reveals a situation of either fragile or unstable peace, depending mainly on whether force was used in the recent past or not. In either case, it reveals a high degree of distrust and suspicion, high levels of securitization, and the relative ease with which peace can be reverted. The second set of indicators show the parties' clear intention to avoid potential misperceptions, implicitly acknowledging that they can indeed occur. Mutual confidence is not high, but actors have developed common mechanisms for making their behaviour more predictable and transparent, if not accountable. These mechanisms represent the basis for whatever degree of mutual confidence might exist. States in such a situation have a relationship of cold or conditional peace. If one of these mechanisms fails, peace can revert into an unstable or fragile type, and even war can break out. Conversely, states may make explicit efforts to increase the degree of mutual confidence and trust, and in this way succeed in transforming their negative peace into positive peace. However, states might choose to stay in conditional peace and not pursue closer links. They may leave some issues securitized and remain alert and vigilant, yet behave carefully not to make peace unstable. Even in this case, I argue, peace is a dynamic process, in that its maintenance will require an active effort on the part of governments.

The last set of indicators signals a high level of mutual trust, which suggests a relationship of stable peace, or even the existence of a pluralistic security community if a sense of 'we-feeling' and community among states and societies has also developed. The most important feature of such a high level of mutual confidence is that the use or threat of force has become unthinkable to resolve disputes and disagreements, and indeed all parties perceive it in this manner. States in a situation of stable peace or in a security community neither expect this situation to change, nor are they prepared to resort to the threat of force in their mutual relations. Such perceived certainty makes positive peace resemble friendship, despite the constraints of the international system. Figure 1 shows the links between different levels of securitization and different types of peace, and the role of time and trust.

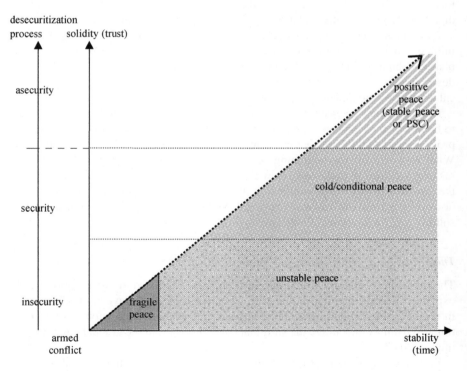

Figure 1. Desecuritization and the peace process.

So far, I have set out a descriptive framework indicating connections between stages in the processes of desecuritization and of peace stabilization/consolidation. Explicitly and simultaneously studying both processes allows for a more comprehensive perspective; one that focuses more consciously on the reciprocal effects of domestic and regional developments. The causal relationship between these two levels is more complex. While in some cases domestic changes promote transformations at the regional level, in others the origin of the process takes place in the region (or beyond, on the global level) and encourages domestic desecuritization from the 'outside' (see, for instance, Miller 2000b). In other words, the process can start at either end, thus being a bottom-up or a top-down process. Nonetheless, once in motion, domestic and regional dynamics start feeding back into each other, rendering the distinction between *domestic* desecuritization and *regional* peace stabilization merely an analytical one. Indeed, for all practical purposes, they become so mutually influential and intertwined that they come to constitute two dimensions of a complex and delicate *single* process.

Moreover, I would argue that we need to distinguish two phases in the desecuritization/peace process. This will help us to understand the different mechanisms at work at each stage enabling the advancement of peace. The first phase accounts for the initiation of the process. This moment is critical, since it entails overcoming inertia. In fact it is more difficult than that. This phase involves a 'change of direction' from a negative relational pattern to a gradually improving one.

By contrast, the second phase refers to the period after which the process has been initiated; that is, the moment of its development and consolidation. While the former phase is about regional peace stabilization and the first few steps towards domestic desecuritization, the latter phase is about peace consolidation, expansion of reciprocal desecuritization, and growth of mutual trust.

Distinguishing between these two phases allows for different types of questions to be raised at each stage. A key issue in understanding the initial part of the peace process refers to how it is that governments decide to change their regional attitudes. What accounts for the beginning of détente? At the second stage of the process, instead, we need to understand how the solidity of this peace expands. What keeps the process going? Explanations of the mechanisms triggering the process of desecuritization/stabilization of regional peace, and those of the expansion of its solidity are, I will argue, of a different nature.

The First Phase: Desecuritization/Peace Stabilization

The question of how the beginning of a process of positive transformation can be explained implicitly assumes that even when regional states have not been involved in regional wars, such eventuality has been part of their calculations and preparations. What may encourage the shift that can later result in the gradual emergence of mutual trust?

Rationalist approaches to International Relations, both in their (neo)liberal and (neo)realist versions, offer strong explanations for the absence of war and the beginning of détente. In what follows, I propose to borrow some rationalist arguments in order to shed light on the mechanisms at work in this first phase of rapprochement. This resort to rationalist arguments does not imply an endorsement of realist or liberal ontologies, let alone their epistemologies.

Theories of interdependence and institutionalism take on a liberal stance. They argue that states – or at least economically developed and prosperous states – are inclined to avoid war because they hold absolute gains higher than relative gains, and regard negatively the costs of going to war and positively the benefits of international trade. Furthermore, it is argued that these states recognize the importance of a peaceful environment for the achievement of the latter. Such states value more the benefits of exchange and commerce than those of territorial conquest (Rosecrance 1986; Keohane & Nye 1971). In addition, neoliberal institutionalists emphasize the role that international institutions play in achieving common goals and overcoming the difficulties created by interdependence (Keohane 1984). In short, war avoidance and even cooperation can take place in the context of anarchy mainly because actors see more instrumental advantages in peace and cooperation than in a different international conjuncture (Hurrell 1998: 228–229). Through this lens, peace and cooperation are more *convenient* than war, and therefore are preferred by actors.

Realism too offers solid arguments to explain the absence of war, as seen earlier. Moreover, with its emphasis on rational models and strategic alliances, it can also explain the first stage of détente and desecuritization. Indeed, bilateral or multilateral rapprochement can be seen as the outcome of power, interests and capability calculations, according to which strategic cooperation is evaluated as more efficient for the accomplishment of certain goals than alternative means, such as war.

These rationalist claims bear important explanatory weight when it comes to the motivations of regional adversaries to start easing tensions. Against a backdrop of hostility, if a state is to revise its attitude towards its neighbour-slash-rival without experiencing it to be a political defeat or at best a political concession, it needs to perceive strong incentives. In regions of negative peace states will be more willing to start working towards détente if they identify concrete and material rewards for doing so, rather than for moral or normative reasons. Interdependence theorists will define these rewards in economic terms, whereas neorealists will cast them in terms of military power and capabilities. In any case, the importance of rivals conceding that détente might bring about potential benefits must be stressed again, since it renders possible – maybe for the first time – a different type of relationship to enter into their scope of foreign-policy options. Envisaging the option of advancing rapprochement with a hitherto rival already is valuable in itself.

The case of Argentina and Brazil in the late 1970s is illuminating in this regard. It allows for a fairly conventional power/interest-based interpretation of détente, but one that took shape in an atypical context. After a long history of rivalry and competition, shortly following a significant deterioration of bilateral relations and with both countries under military rule, détente between the neighbours evolved quickly, and indeed opened the door to more committed, long-term cooperation between these former rivals.

Since before becoming independent states, Brazil and Argentina constructed their relationship upon negative mutual perceptions, which reinforced the dominant relational pattern defined in terms of rivalry. The emergence of a dispute over water resources on the River Paraná in the 1960s made both countries' militaries update their 'war hypotheses' against one another; a fact that was aggravated by the context of their race to develop nuclear technology.

By then, the cold peace that had prevailed between the two countries began to deteriorate. If so far competition, display of military capacity, and zero-sum calculations had dominated the military's and politicians' frame of mind, during the 1970s, when the Paraná dispute escalated, the relationship reverted to a situation of unstable peace. Bilateral tension increased to the extent of making dialogue very difficult and the threat of resorting to violence more credible.

However, it was also during this period that international, regional and domestic circumstances concurred to generate a favourable environment for cooperative postures to gain influence on domestic decision-making circles. These postures can be read in terms of power-balancing strategies and rational calculations on the part of both states.

Internationally, US pressure on nuclear development matters clearly made possible the identification of a common ground for policy coordination. Brazil's 'special relationship' with the United States, which had historically played a role in the Argentine–Brazilian confrontation, had come to an end in 1967, when Brasilia refused to join the Treaty for the Prohibition of Nuclear Weapons in Latin America and the Caribbean (Treaty of Tlatelolco). In the second half of the 1970s the 'special relationship' had only worsened as a consequence of Jimmy Carter's human-rights and nuclear-proliferation policies, which were also punishing Argentina. Additionally, by the late 1970s there were clear signs of exhaustion of Brazil's economic boom and its model of inward-looking industrialization. These developments, combined with the government's decision to deepen the gradual *abertura* (or liberalization) of its political system and strengthen relations with Latin America, as well as its recognizing the superiority of Argentina's nuclear programme, encouraged Brasilia to reorient its foreign policy, seeking to ease tensions with Buenos Aires.

In turn, Argentina was facing a critical period. Internal politics were in a state of havoc, and relations with Chile were deteriorating rapidly. The Videla government had recognized Brazil's industrial, economic and conventional superiority, and some sectors – such as the pragmatic liberals in charge of the economy and the nationalist-developmentalists in charge of the military industry – were exerting pressure upon the junta for an entente with the larger neighbour. Confrontation with Brazil implied a race that they were no longer certain to win, while rapprochement could bring about some material advantages, in addition to helping balance Santiago de Chile.

In the face of these adverse circumstances, decisive actors in both states favoured a process of gradual abandonment of contending perceptions, and adoption of more positive mutual images with the prospective goal of easing tensions and pursuing cooperation. As securitization theorists predict, this development involved a bargaining process. Being both states under authoritarian rule, it was not public opinion the desecuritization audience. Instead, the bargaining took place between different factions within the military governments, and between each government and the local economic and scientific (nuclear) elites. In any case, through this mechanism a slow process of bilateral desecuritization evolved.

In October 1979 Argentina, Brazil and Paraguay signed the Tripartite Agreement on Itaipú-Corpus, bringing the Paraná dispute to an end. In May 1980, President João Figueiredo visited Buenos Aires, in what constituted the first visit of a Brazilian president to Argentina in 40 years. In August, President Jorge Rafael Videla reciprocated the visit. These summits were of paramount importance. They lasted several days, and the presidents travelled with large delegations of ministers and state secretaries. On the occasion of the visits, 22 documents establishing cooperation in 11 areas were signed; among them, an agreement on nuclear fuel-cycle cooperation, which – despite being rather symbolic – represented the end of competition and the beginning of collaboration on nuclear matters. In addition, joint infrastructure enterprises were agreed, such as the construction of a bridge over the River Iguazú linking Puerto Iguazú (Argentina) and Porto Meira (Brazil), the first of its kind since 1947; hydroelectric cooperation, the export of Argentine gas to Brazil, and the interconnection of their electricity systems. Other important gestures that eased rapprochement were Brazil's agreement to represent Argentine interests in London during and after the Falklands/Malvinas war and its support for Argentina's sovereignty claim at the UN and OAS, as well as its decision not to authorize British airplanes flying to the South Atlantic to schedule a regular refuelling stop in Brazilian territory.

Even though these rationalist approaches may help to understand the unfolding of détente, its first few steps, their accounts tend to imply the presence of a somewhat contingent type of peace based on circumstantial calculations rather than on some deeper commitment. As a consequence, détente might not be durable, nor necessarily encouraging of further advancements of the peace/desecuritization process.

Yet, as mentioned earlier, although these incentives do not take us much further than to a negative type of peace where mutual trust is still absent, they do play a very important role. By bringing to the forefront and highlighting the potential advantages of easing existing tensions, they make rapprochement a conceivable option. They make it be seen as a possibility; an alternative that might not have been imaginable to the parties at an earlier stage. Once desecuritization is perceived as a convenient, and thereby feasible, policy option, the process of domestic desecuritization and regional stabilization of peace may unfold. This first stage already opens the door to a different type of relation between regional states. Mutual trust is still absent, but interaction, exchange, more fluid relations, and, of course, strong political will may work positively towards its gradual emergence.

The Second Phase: Towards Asecurity and Peace Consolidation

If the initial changes continue to develop in a positive manner and become sustained, they will facilitate the advance to the second stage of the process, the one involving a redefinition of the relationship. It is this latter phase that leads to more durable changes, which in turn will result in a consolidated type of peace and a domestic situation dominated by a sense of asecurity, that is, a situation that has transcended security codes.

To redefine the relationship means not just to reassess how one perceives the other(s). Rather, it implies to simultaneously re-evaluate the vision one has both of the other and of the self. An important move in this direction will already have taken place during the first stage, when a different type of relationship will have been envisaged as possible. Once this has happened, interaction and exchange will feed back into the process, encouraging parties to further revise self and mutual images, which can lead to the gradual emergence of mutual trust – the key to understanding peace consolidation and the establishment of a situation of asecurity.

The resort to social constructivist theory helps to understand the process at work here. Constructivism incorporates into the analysis of IR the role of identities, ideas and perceptions, and understands that they are transformed through interaction. Furthermore, it claims that neither identities nor interests are static or invariable, but that they are altered through practices and habits.

As Emanuel Adler and Michael Barnett point out, transactions as well as international organizations and institutions facilitate processes of social learning. These imply a re-assessment of actors' meanings, beliefs and understandings (Adler & Barnett 1998a) – i.e. of their cognitive structure – influencing the way they perceive others and themselves. This in turn constitutes and constrains (or broadens) their perceived range of policy options. When this is a positive process, it redounds to the expansion of trust, which will be reflected in policy decisions, such as withdrawal of troops from common borders, expansion of cooperation, and so on.

According to Kacowicz and Bar-Siman-Tov, this complex learning process 'requires a redefinition or re-evaluation of the parties' national interests, so that each party will perceive a mutual interest in establishing and maintaining the peace between them as the most important factor in assuring each other's security and even existence' (Kacowicz & Bar-Siman-Tov 2000: 24–25). Thus, the development towards a more consolidated peace involves 'an active process of redefinition or reinterpretation of reality – what people consider real, possible and desirable – on the basis of new causal and normative knowledge'. During this process social actors 'manage and even transform reality by changing their beliefs of the material and social world and their identities' (Adler & Barnett 1998a: 43–44).

Crucial actors in this process are policy-makers and other political, economic, and intellectual elites who will try to convey to the public (audience, in securitization theory language) their re-interpreted perception of reality – that is, their modified cognitive structure – with the aim of producing concrete policy, broadly legitimized. Although differently put, this was also observed by Wolfers:

close and effective interstate amity as among allies should tend to promote emotional friendship. The mere experience of successful common effort can make for mutual confidence and sympathy although it does not necessarily do so; old grudges, suspicions, resentments, and jealousies may prevail at least in some parts of the population. But then, even democratic governments need not wait passively for the spontaneous development of public sentiments of friendship to complement their policies. There are many ways in which a favourable image of another nation can be sold to the public, even though anything as radical as the way totalitarian governments manipulate public opinion is incompatible with democracy. (Wolfers 1962: 33)

In this phase the domestic and the regional interact very clearly. As regional relationships become (domestically) desecuritized and regional states show themselves ready to trust one another, coordinated positions, shared discourses, common projects, and even common institutions can be expected to evolve. Regional peace thus becomes *positive* peace; not only have neighbours ruled out the possibility of war among themselves, but also they are confident that the other states in this zone of stable peace have done so too.

In this way, regions that were previously characterized by mistrust, hostility and competition can gradually evolve into zones of stable peace. Moreover, once mutual trust, links, and interdependence have grown among regional states, they may trickle down to these states' civil societies. As indicated earlier, deeper and stronger ties among civil societies are the basis of pluralistic security communities, in which mutual sympathies, solidarity, and some sort of common identification exist, so as to make participating publics perceive each other as members of a shared *community*.

Indeed, the second phase of the Argentine–Brazilian rapprochement can be interpreted along the lines of the emergence of mutual trust, complete (military) desecuritization of bilateral relations, establishment of stable peace, and incipient emergence of security community facilitated by the construction of shared projects and discourses. Partly because democracies seem to be better at developing reciprocal trustful relationships, and partly because of the evolution of events in the Southern Cone in the early 1980s, the unfolding of positive peace had to wait until 1985, once both countries had initiated their democratic transitions.[10] Also, it was after the fall of the military governments and with the restoration of democratic rule that both states were in a propitious moment to reassess identities and perceptions of both themselves and the other.

Under the leadership of Raúl Alfonsín (Argentina) and José Sarney (Brazil) mutual gestures of goodwill multiplied. While initially these declarations and gestures did not translate into an immediate programme of action, they constituted crucial signs that these governments were sending to one another and to their domestic publics. Indeed, in addition to overcoming a history of mutual mistrust, the governments needed to persuade newly empowered public opinion in both countries that the neighbour no longer represented a rival. To this end, two factors – rhetoric as the manifestation of political will on the one hand, and the construction of cooperative institutions and organizations on the other – proved useful in helping to build up trust and confidence, and develop these into viable policies backed by the public.

Regarding the first factor – manifestations of political will – the second half of the 1980s offers plenty of examples. In 1985 the presidents signed a Joint Declaration on Common Nuclear Policy stating their commitment to developing nuclear energy with peaceful purposes and reiterating the goal of close cooperation and mutual complementation. The following year, among numerous cooperation protocols, they signed one on immediate information and reciprocal assistance in case of nuclear accidents. In 1987 and 1988, for the first time in Argentine–Brazilian relations, Presidents Sarney and Alfonsín carried out mutual visits to their nuclear facilities; a most significant event given both the bilateral history and the sensitive nature of the issues involved.

In addition, the two presidents resolved to revive the old project of Latin American cooperation and integration by starting with a bilateral Programme for Economic Integration and Cooperation (PICE) in 1986. This signalled the culmination of the process of détente that had gained momentum since 1979, when the negotiation of the Paraná dispute came to a satisfactory end. After 1986 the relationship became firmly grounded on the 'positive half' of the peace continuum.

Despite its name, PICE was not promoted by the ministries of the economy, but by the ministries of foreign affairs. This highlights the profound political commitments lying at its core, as well as a broader convergence of foreign-policy orientations and of perceptions of shared domestic and external challenges. Goals such as strengthening peace and discouraging regional arms races, keeping Latin American outside of the strategic conflict of the superpowers, consolidating continental representation instances, and advancing Latin American integration came to constitute a shared vision. Argentina and Brazil took common stances on the crisis in Central America, the Uruguay Round of negotiations on the General Agreement on Tariffs and Trade (GATT), nuclear-proliferation regimes, and the South Atlantic peace zone. Regarding common domestic and external challenges, both governments shared concerns about issues such as high inflation, democratic transition, improving their international images, the external debt crisis, and the developed countries' trade protectionism. Regional integration was conceived of as a strategy with multiple purposes, as much political as economic (if not *more* political than economic), and domestic and regional as well as international.

The early 1990s, in turn, was the time of the construction of a common institutional framework, including both formal organizations with material entities and common social practices. The new presidents, Carlos Menem (Argentina) and Fernando Collor (Brazil), agreed on a Joint System of Accountability and Control that included reciprocal inspections to be applied to all nuclear activities, which was administered by the Argentine–Brazilian Agency of Control and Accountability (ABACC) created in 1991. Furthermore, later that year Argentina, Brazil, the ABACC and the International Atomic Energy Agency (IAEA) signed an agreement on full-scope safeguards; something the two states had hitherto refused to do.

Additionally, by 1994 Argentina, Brazil and Chile had ratified the Tlatelolco Treaty. With these developments, the nuclear issue definitely moved to the category of asecurity in regional relations.

While in the 1980s PICE had not gone far beyond good intentions – partly as a result of domestic programmes of economic stabilization and reform – in the 1990s it felt a new impetus when Menem and Collor implemented unilateral trade liberalization. In 1990 they agreed to accelerate PICE's scheduled timetable for the establishment of the bilateral common market by the end of 1994. In 1991, Paraguay and Uruguay joined the project, and the four countries signed the Treaty of Asunción creating Mercosur. During the first half of the 1990s genuine dynamics of interdependence became evident in Mercosur. In turn, increased exchange, interaction and interdependence brought the business communities closer together, increasing communication and making dialogue more fluid. During this period, as Mercosur consolidated an external agenda a shared sense of regional bloc matured. The incorporation of Chile and Bolivia into Mercosur as associated member (1996), and the decision to play as one single actor in international negotiations – such as those on the formation of the Free Trade Area of the Americas (FTAA), and on economic cooperation with the EU – reinforced this feeling.

Finally, Mercosur's evolution came to include slowly (and limitedly) social and cultural areas, which are key to the development of compatible identities and potential emergence of a common identification between societies. It is more directly through social and cultural activities – such as arts, music, languages, literature, cinema, television, academia, student exchanges, holidays, etc. – that societies get to know more about one another than through international trade treaties and commercial exchange. Thus, at the level of societies, cognitive structures may be more easily transformed by social learning in these areas, bolstering positive changes in the mutual visions of societies, and in turn, rendering possible a security community.

In Mercosur the construction – however limited – of compatible identities has been mostly promoted by its two larger members, Argentina and Brazil. It was pursued through initiatives that ranged from exchanges of trainee-diplomats, to the promotion of Spanish and Portuguese language courses in schools, the training of Spanish teachers from Brazil in Argentina and of Portuguese teachers from Argentina in Brazil, the recognition and homologation of degrees across the region in order to facilitate mobility, and the organization of festivals and arts exhibitions with artists from the region. Likewise, in other events and competitions only Mercosur residents were eligible to participate, such as literary awards, photography competitions, and a science and technology prize for young researchers. All this contributed to unfolding a new, distinctive geographic scope, gradually awakening a perception of common or shared destiny not only among political and economic elites, but also in wider circles of society.

This rather optimistic scenario requires a note of moderation. Processes of cognitive change and construction of mutual confidence, whereby former adversaries become true friends, take a long time to reach societies and even longer to

160 *Friendship in Politics*

consolidate within them. Just when such developments were beginning to take hold in the Southern Cone, Mercosur's profile became increasingly commercial. Argentine and Brazilian foreign policies proved to be too divergent in the years of Carlos Menem and Fernando Henrique Cardoso for Mercosur to keep up the pace of its political progress. In the late 1990s, Mercosur's political content and base of support seemed to be thinning down, diluting the timid feeling of community that was only just starting to arise. Nonetheless, it must be stressed that relations between the states of the Southern Cone have improved to levels which were unthinkable only 25 years earlier. Although no peace process is ever irreversible, the development that began in the late 1970s with the Argentine–Brazilian détente has consolidated into a stable and strong regional peace in the 1980s and 1990s.

Final Remarks

This discussion has highlighted the difficulties of defining friendship at the international level. However, as Thomas More observed almost 500 years ago, while 'alliances do not cement friendship' because they make it seem 'as if men who are separated by only a hill or a river were bound by no tie of nature, ... the fellowship of nature among men serves instead of a treaty, and ... men are bound more adequately by good will than by pacts, more strongly by their hearts than by their words' (T. More reproduced in Wolfers & Martin 1956: 6). That 'good will' appears to be more decisive when states and peoples are bound by shared interpretations of their social realities. Ultimately, this was already present in Burke:

> [Men] are led to associate by resemblances, by conformities, by sympathies. It is with nations as with individuals. Nothing is so strong a tie of amity between nation and nation as correspondence in laws, customs, manners, and habits of life. They have more than the force of treaties in themselves. They are obligations written in the heart. They approximate men to men without their knowledge, and sometimes against their intentions ... The conformity and analogy of which I speak, incapable, like everything else, of preserving perfect trust and tranquillity among men, has a strong tendency to facilitate accommodation, and to produce a generous oblivion of the rancor of their quarrels. With this similitude, peace is more of peace, and war is less of war. (E. Burke reproduced in Wolfers & Martin 1956: 111–112)

Allowing for the constraints set by international anarchy, I have advocated for focusing on constructed mutual trust and confidence – the central elements in stable and peaceful regions – to find relationships resembling friendship at the international level. The emergence of trust and confidence amongst states marks the transformation of zones of *negative peace* into zones of *positive peace*. Moreover, if civil societies are so closely interconnected that in addition to their national identities some kind of regional community identification emerges, then that zone of *stable peace* has also become a *pluralistic security community*. Where this is the case, a sense of shared destiny explains the long-term stability of a consolidated peace.

Is this too optimistic an approach? Does it all sound like once the process begins there is something inevitable about the improving quality of regional peace and the expanding nature of regional trust? In this article, I chose to trace the move in its direction away from 'securitization-negative peace' and towards 'desecuritization-peace stabilization' in order to highlight that it is possible to construct regional relationships that resemble friendship. However, the opposite route is not only also possible, but it is easier. The process towards peace stabilization and consolidation is demanding, fragile, easily reversible, and needs a great deal of political will. In contrast, securitization and destabilization of peace are a likely outcome in the anarchic context – although not a necessary outcome, as this essay has shown.

There are a number of significant historical instances in which former rivals, and even former enemies, have succeeded in achieving stable peace, if not security communities, in their regions. A more thorough understanding of how such a transformation works, what encourages it, and what makes it sustain itself in time may offer valuable insights to the search for solutions to protracted conflicts. This article has sought to contribute to this debate by sketching out the development of peace processes and by stressing factors that only too often are underplayed or overseen.

Finally, supporters of the democratic peace theory (in its many variants) will complain that this argument emphasizes the role of trust at the expense of type of regime. This is partially true. More often than not, even non-democratic regimes have succeeded in keeping external relations short of war, as South America in general and the Argentine–Brazilian case in particular have demonstrated. Democracy is not a sine qua non for the maintenance of a zone of negative peace. Nor is it a necessary condition for improvement in the first stage of the peace process – stabilization of peace – when a zone of fragile or unstable peace becomes one of cold peace. Moreover, although democracy seems to favour the emergence of mutual trust, it is not necessary for the existence of a zone of (positive) stable peace. For long periods during the Cold War some governments in Eastern Europe established trustful relationships among themselves and with the USSR.

Nonetheless, democracy is indeed crucial for the emergence of security communities as defined above. The role and participation of civil societies, and their linkages in regional relations is what turns a zone of stable peace into a pluralistic security community. Hence, it seems reasonable to claim that members of such a community have regimes that allow a great deal of participation and involvement of their civil society and public opinion in all aspects of political and social life.

Notes

1. IR realism builds upon the Hobbesian state of nature to draw an analogy between it and the world's lack of a Leviathan.
2. Structural realism is also called neorealism, and both terms are often used interchangeably. For this approach, see Waltz 1979.

3. Alexander Wendt, in particular, makes the argument that international anarchy can have three different predominant cultures; Hobbesian, based on a role structure of enmity, Lockean, based on the logic of rivalry, and Kantian, based on one of friendship.
4. Also Jef Huysmans (1998: 226) argues that 'although the debate on expanding the security agenda to non-military sectors and non-state referent objects launched an interesting discussion about the security (studies) agenda, it has not really dealt with the meaning of security.'
5. It is not surprising that the authors leave this definition open. They are trying to avoid the easy association between security and the military sector. If security is about a specific logic, it can also apply to the other sectors of security – political, economic, environmental and societal. See Buzan et al. 1998.
6. Buzan calls this 'overlay'.
7. This distinction was first made by Kenneth Boulding (1978: 3), for whom positive peace involves 'good management, orderly resolution of conflict, harmony associated with mature relationships, gentleness, and love', whereas the negative peace implies 'the absence of something – the absence of turmoil, tension, conflict, and war'.
8. I prefer to use the term 'identification' rather than 'identity', as the former suggests a looser conceptual understanding, implying a common perception of shared potential benefits and costs, mutual sympathies, recognition of areas of common interests that promote cooperation and co-ordination in different fields, both at the public and private levels, growing familiarization with the other's politics, culture, society, etc. reflecting a growing interest in the other as such, and in general, a positive image of the other that tends to advance cooperation rather than competition, and that facilitates absolute- rather than relative-gain logics.
9. For a conceptualization of trust in interstate relations see Hoffman 2002.
10. Among the events 'diverting attention' from rapprochement were the Falklands/Malvinas war, the untidy fall of the Argentine military regime, and the death of Trancredo Neves – the first President elect of Brazil after 20 years of military rule – shortly before taking office.

References

Adler, E. & Barnett, M.N. (1998a) A framework for the study of security communities, in: Adler, E. & Barnett, M.N. (Eds), *Security Communities*, pp. 29–65 (Cambridge: Cambridge University Press).

Adler, E. & Barnett, M.N. (Eds) (1998b) *Security Communities* (Cambridge: Cambridge University Press).

Aron, R. (1966) *Peace and War: A Theory of International Relations* (New York: Doubleday).

Boulding, K.E. (1978) *Stable Peace* (Austin, TX & London: University of Texas Press).

Buzan, B. (1991) *People, State and Fear: An Agenda for International Security Studies in the Post-Cold War Era*, 2nd. ed. (Boulder, CO: Lynne Rienner).

Buzan, B., Wæver, O. & de Wilde, J. (1998) *Security: A New Framework for Analysis* (Boulder, CO: Lynne Rienner).

Deutsch, K., Burrell, S.A., Kann, R.A., Jr, Lichterman, M., Lindgren, R.E., Loewenheim, F.L. & Wagenen, R.W.v. (1957) *Political Community and the North Atlantic Area: International Organization in the Light of Historical Experience* (Princeton, NJ: Princeton University Press).

George, A. (2000) Foreword, in: Kacowicz, A.M., Bar-Siman-Tov, Y., Elgström, O. & Jerneck, M. (Eds), *Stable Peace Among Nations*, pp. xi–xvii (Lanham, MD: Rowman & Littlefield).

Hoffman, A.M. (2002) A conceptualization of trust in international relations. *European Journal of International Relations*, 8(3), pp. 375–401.

Holsti, K. (1996) *The State, War, and the State of War* (Cambridge: Cambridge University Press).

Hurrell, A. (1998) An emerging security community in South America?, in: Adler, E. & Barnett, M.N. (Eds), *Security Communities*, pp. 228–264 (Cambridge: Cambridge University Press).

Huysmans, J. (1998) Security! What do you mean? From Concept to thick signifier, *European Journal of International Relations*, 4(2), pp. 226–255.

Job, B.L. (1997) Matters of multilateralism: implications for regional conflict management, in: Lake, D.A. & Morgan, P.M. (Eds), *Regional Orders: Building Security in a New World,* pp. 165–191 (University Park, PA: Pennsylvania State University Press).
Kacowicz, A.M. (1998) *Zones of Peace in the Third World: South America and West Africa in Comparative Perspective* (Albany, NY: State University of New York Press).
Kacowicz, A.M. & Bar-Siman-Tov, Y. (2000) Stable peace: a conceptual framework, in: Kacowicz, A.M., Bar-Siman-Tov, Y., Elgström, O. & Jerneck, M. (Eds), *Stable Peace Among Nations,* pp. 11–35 (Lanham, MD: Rowman & Littlefield).
Kacowicz, A.M., Bar-Siman-Tov, Y., Elgström, O. & Jerneck, M. (Eds) (2000) *Stable Peace Among Nations* (Lanham, MD: Rowman & Littlefield).
Keohane, R.O. (1984) *After Hegemony: Cooperation and Discord in the World Political Economy* (Princeton, NJ: Princeton University Press).
Keohane, R.O. & Nye, J.S. (1971) *Transnational Relations and World Politics* (Cambridge, MA: Harvard University Press).
Mearsheimer, J. (1991–1992) Back to the future, part III: Realism and the realities of European security (correspondence), *International Security,* 15(3), pp. 216–222.
Miller, B. (2000a) Explaining variations in regional peace: Three strategies for peace-making, *Cooperation and Conflict,* 35(2), pp. 155–192.
Miller, B. (2000b) The international, regional, and domestic sources of regional peace, in: Kacowicz, A.M., Bar-Siman-Tov, Y., Elgström, O. & Jerneck, M. (Eds), *Stable Peace Among Nations,* pp. 55–73 (Lanham: Rowman & Littlefield).
Morgan, P.M. (1997) Regional security complexes and regional orders, in: Lake, D.A. & Morgan, P.M. (Eds), *Regional Orders: Building Security in a New World,* pp. 20–42 (University Park, PA: Penn State University Press).
Rosecrance, R.N. (1986) *The Rise of the Trading State: Commerce and Conquest in the Modern World* (New York: Basic Books).
Snyder, G.H. (1997) *Alliance Politics* (Ithaca, NY: Cornell University Press).
Walt, S. (1985) Alliance formation and the balance of world power. *International Security,* 9(4), pp. 3–43.
Waltz, K. (1979) *Theory of International Politics* (Reading, MA: Addison-Wesley).
Wendt, A. (1999) *Social Theory of International Politics* (Cambridge: Cambridge University Press).
Wolfers, A. (1962) *Discord and Collaboration: Essays on International Politics* (Baltimore, MD and London: The Johns Hopkins University Press).
Wolfers, A. & Martin, L.W. (1956) *The Anglo-American Tradition in Foreign Affairs: Readings from Thomas More to Woodrow Wilson* (New Haven, CT: Yale University Press).
Wæver, O. (1995) Securitization and sesecuritization, in: Lipschutz, R.D. (Ed.), *On Security,* pp. 46–86 (New York: Columbia University Press).
Wæver, O. (1998) Insecurity, security, and asecurity in the West European non-war community, in: Adler, E. & Barnett, M. (Eds), *Security Communities,* pp. 69–118 (Cambridge: Cambridge University Press).

The Institutionalization of International Friendship

ANTOINE VION
Institute of Labour Economics and Industrial Sociology, University of Aix, France

Introduction

Friendship is often neglected in international relations. If it is assumed that violence cannot be eliminated, international friendship may only be analyzed as a temporary agreement to bypass enmity (see essays by Slomp and Van der Zwerde in this volume) or to solve a security dilemma (see essay by Oelsner in this volume). From the ontological perspective of elective affinity, international friendship would exemplify the human condition of Love (St Augustine) or *Agape* (Boltanski 1990). Modern approaches seek peace through the management of equivalence: equivalence of status for Mill, equivalence of goods to be exchanged for Ricardo or Smith, or equivalence of rights for Kant. More hermeneutic perspectives deal with international friendship as a question of the possibility of sharing common interpretations of universal brotherhood (Derrida 2006; Dallmayr 2000) or bypassing collective 'being for the Death' (Koselleck 1979). The purpose of this essay (pragmatic and analytical) is to analyze international friendship empirically through institutional facts.

Institutional Facts and Political Institutions

Searle (1995) insists that collective intention creates institutional facts. Agentive functions are status based and go on through time. This makes institutional facts stable. Three dimensions of his analysis are relevant to processes of institutionalization. The first is the distinction between facts which depend on language and facts which do not. Only the first category can found institutional facts, according to Searle, because institutional facts cannot be thought without symbols and words. The second is the temporal dimension through which Searle establishes distinctions within institutional facts. Here, he explains that institutional facts may go on, or break off by decline, destruction, or the ending of a mandate. He also explains that institutional facts are so because they are systematic. Thus, thirdly, he qualifies the structure of institutional facts as in terms of power relations.

The emergence of institutional facts allows us to understand the way principles and practices structure institutions and are affected by them. Institutions refer to formal rules between and among individuals in the polity. From this theoretical perspective, the evolution of bonds of friendship may be analyzed across time and space as a result of interactions consolidated through institutions. This kind of historical institutionalism (Thelen & Steinmo 1992; Immergut 1998) is an attempt to overcome the limits of group-based pluralist explanations of political phenomena. Criticism of historical institutionalism is well known: this theoretical framework would not furnish any theory of action. Fisher argued against these criticisms by claiming 'it is not that institutions cause political action, it is their discursive practices that shape the behaviours of actors who do.' (Fischer 2003). Macrosociological approaches like theories of path dependancy are very uncomfortable with the questions of policy change. This is why it is preferable to focus on local interactions and institutional facts. So, of course, this kind of context explains emerging or changing configurations, though it explains few stable institutions made of routinized formal rules (Lahire 1996).

Mainstream political science takes a neo-classical approach to this nebulous set of bonds and agreements. Such an analysis emphasizes the potential for these agreements to fail as a result of information asymmetry, incomplete contracts, moral hazard and agency problems. From a sociological point of view, bonds of friendship cannot be seen as contracts, even when they lead to trade and classical contractual relationships. Thus I contend that, whatever the levels of cooperation and types of bonds involved, there are significant internal factors at work in the implementation of these relationships. Our theoretical framework is thus closer to neo-institutionalism than to neo-classical theory. These two approaches are outlined in the following comparative table (Table 1).

Table 1. Comparative analytical framework.

	Neo-classical Framework	Neo-institutional Framework
Method	Individualism	Institutionalism
Status of Action	Constrained or favoured by contracts (subordination/incitement)	Oriented by rules and social patterns
Evaluation	External: allocative efficiency/ prevention of *hold up* effects/ reduction of social cost	Reflexive (coming out from the situation)
Information	Endowment analytically given to agents involved in the relation	Construction processed by the relation
Rationality	Maximization of utility	Bounded
Relationship	Produced by an inter-individual agreement	Produced by institutional facts

Two Main Fields of Investigation: Town Twinning and Cultural Institutes

The study presented in this essay focuses on the role of local institutions in the structuring of international bonds of friendship. The role of cities as actors in the international relations' system has been questioned in the literature since the 1960s (Boulding 1968). In a more institutional perspective, studies have also taken into account the importance of subnational entities in the definition of foreign policies, but mainly in federal states (Duchacek 1986; Duchacek et al. 1988; Hocking 1993). Even when initiatives of municipalities have been studied (Hobbs 1994), friendship initiatives have rarely been the main centre of interest.

Historical investigation through the four decades of the Cold War period[1] furnish data in two main fields: involvement in town twinnings and local support to cultural institutes. The role of local authorities in initiating the development of town twinnings since the 1940s has been fully explored in recent works (Vion 2002; Bautz 2002). Previous papers (Vion 2002; Vion 2003) have shown that this movement in France has been the main source of local foreign policies or paradiplomacy. Local support to cultural institutes is a difficult question, because it is much more tied to the implementation of cultural diplomacy initiatives and national foreign policies. The essay will only suggest how such organizations impact social life culturally as well as politically and economically. The role of such institutes in the promotion of Arts, intellectual exchanges and democratic values is well known, notably in the Franco-German case (Defrance 1994). But links with firms and economic exchanges may also be observed in some cases.

International Friendship Through Twinning Feasts

A previous paper (Vion 2002) explains how the invention of town twinning established a municipal 'tradition' through which the opening of international friendly relationships among municipalities could be read. That paper stressed that twinning fits Eric Hobsbawm's definition of an invented tradition: a set of ritual and/or symbolic practices, normally governed by openly or tacitly accepted rules and designed to inculcate certain values and codes of behaviour by dint of repetition, automatically suggesting the idea of continuity with the past (Hobsbawm 1983). If 'inventing tradition' means anything it must mean a rational intention to use reference to past situations as a basis for the creation of new practices which may then become routine – *become* a tradition. Genuine 'tradition', according to its etymology – 'passing on' a message – is in origin simply a chain of links, from the spoken word to the written word and back again, or vice versa (Ricoeur 1983). It can leave room for innovation as long as the chain, going back into the mists of time, remains unbroken. 'Invented' tradition, on the other hand, has a discernible origin: it is a 'link' of innovation which, by virtue of its own creation, establishes the fiction of a 'chain'. It gathers up the fragments of a more or less imaginary past and puts them at the service of a social, cultural or political innovation (Bayart 1995). The invention of tradition is a dynamic process which gives rise to political debate and doctrinal controversy. In the invention of town twinning it is important to note that the ideological disputes over the choice of partners and the parameters for the exercise of the tradition were much more lively and decisive than disputes over the form of the rite. Nonetheless they did oppose two very different concepts of what made a municipality. In Christian Europe municipal liberties were forged by the experience of centuries: indeed, the municipality or commune was the natural seat of liberty. For *Monde Bilingue* the municipality was a location for popular initiatives, where equal citizens could take the destiny of the world into their own hands.

Municipal institutions, beyond national debates and controversies, practically structured bonds of friendship. Town twinning is generally conceived as a kind of folklore celebrated by rituals and feasts. Isambert (1982) suggests that any celebration consists of symbolic valorization, which means a form of collective insistence on events combining solemnity and enjoyment. For Searle feasts are a kind of institutional fact, a form of collective intention ascribing a function.

Fêtes as Rituals

Official ceremonies have been a very important concern in the first decades of town twinning. As already explained (Vion 2002), the solemnity of rituals has been promoted by organizations, which emphasize the needs of protocol, oath and acting. The main symbolic resources mobilized in these rituals are the vestiges of medieval communes:

> In Reims, one could see exterior decorations of the City hall made of 'lis' from Reims and Florence, banners of the corporations from Champagne, the prestigious gonfalon of the City of Florence, the reception of the mayors on the square of the Cathedral, the flight of jets coming back from Florence and

dropping the two towns flags trimmed with the arms of the communes. (*Le Figaro*, 3 July 1954)[2]

In the central lounge of the City Hall, the Municipal Council, the two prefects, the roman delegation and the Ambassador of Italy strode towards the top of the room, as the trumpets of the Capitole heralded their arrival. A hand drew back a violet and golden canopy, revealing a bronze She-wolf giving Romulus and Remus the first milk of our civilization. In the conference room, councillors of Rome sat amongst councillors of Paris. The Mayor of Rome, whose loins were girt by the green-white-red sash, sat down in face-to-face with the Mayor of Paris, while the Ambassador of Italy took a seat between the Prefect of Paris and Prefect of Police. Mr Rebecchini and Mr Feron read the twinning oath in French to a round of applause ... At the end, Mgr Feltin read a telegraph addressed by His Holiness Pious XII: 'We are feeling great satisfaction to have been told of this new bond of friendship between the councillors of Rome and Paris, and we are pleased, on this occasion, to recall the history of our two cities, which worked at promoting Christian civilization in the world'. (*Le Figaro, l'Aurore*, 31 January 1956)[3].

In every ceremony, solemnity is expressed in unusual decorations (sprays of flowers, garlands, and so on) in city halls and their surrounds. In flower-filled rooms, flags and badges are flanked by the arms of the communes. A foreign mayor then may be given the keys of the commune, or medal struck with its arms, or any other object expressing a privilege. In other cases, it may be a symbolic exchange of clothes: the vestments of French and English ushers, suits and 'boubous' in Franco-African twinnings. All these things concretize the promise. In any case, the communal imaginary is made concrete by clothes: 'Let's remind the councillors of the fact that they must have their sash and their rosette. The ushers must wear their formal dress and every thing must be prefect.'[4]

Music plays a big role. When everybody is seated, the municipal orchestra plays a fanfare. All of this means that achieving international friendship is not only discursive. Aesthetic experiences are an important part of the process. And what is exemplified by such rituals is not simply state diplomacy but communal autonomy.

In such a framework, friendship cannot be achieved without collective participation, what Eisenhower used to call 'people-to-people'. In order to guarantee the success of such a ceremony, the city hall must be full of more or less representative people (see Table 2), exemplify what Searle (1995) means by logical operations within institutional facts imposing a structure of power.

Such a crowd is not peculiar to Franco-German celebrations. What is unusual in this case is the presence of the Ambassador and all the protocol precautions taken by the municipal elites, in context of reconciliation:

There should be an official presentation of the delegation of Erlangen with a welcome speech of the Mayor of Rennes and an answer from the Mayor of

170   *Friendship in Politics*

Table 2.   First reception of a German delegation (from Erlangen) in the city of Rennes, 8 September 1964 (AMR 7/81-3. Préparatifs du jumelage Rennes–Erlangen)

The German delegation
  The mayor (CSU)
  Two CSU councillors (one man and one woman)
  One CSV-GDP councillor
  One FDP-GUW councillor
  Three SPD councillors (two men and one woman)
  One municipal architect
  One assistant professor in roman languages

Locals and VIPs participating in the ceremony
  Meeting of the whole municipality (except Communists)
  The German Ambassador
  The Belgian Consul
  The Prefect and his wife
  The Recteur d'Académie and his wife
  The General and two Colonels of the Regional Headquarters
  The President of the Judicial Court
  The President of the Commercial Court
  Eight journalists from regional and national newspapers
  The President of the Chamber of Trade and Industry
  The Deans of the Faculties of Health, Literature and Chemistry, and the Institutes of Agriculture and Trade
  The regional head of Tourism
  A clergyman
  The Director and one civil servant from the Prefect's office
  The Inspector of Academy
  Two civil servants of the Ministry of Youth and Sports
  Eight municipal servants (including the General Secretary, his Adjunct and the Director of the Financial Service)
  The Head of the Chamber of Crafts
  The Head of the Union of Trade
  The Head of the Chamber of Agriculture
  The Head of the Union of Young Patrons
  The Director of the Tourism Office
  The Head of the Regional Academy of Music and of the Youth Orchestra
  The Proviseur du Lycée Préparatoire aux Grandes Ecoles
  Three Directors of high schools
  One German teacher, also interpreter
  Twenty-four teachers
  Nineteen members of associations

Erlangen. I remind you of the fact that during the official twinning ceremony in Germany, Mr Lades introduced me as Chairman of the ceremony, so he and his first assistant Sponsel stood up at my right and at my left. A German Chair of our ceremony is of course irrelevant. I even doubt that Lades should be the Chairman of the unofficial part of the ceremony, but it seems to me that fairness should lead you, as Chairman, to welcome the German delegation, and then, to invite him to take your place in order to give his speech.[5]

As one can see in Table 2, the protocol issue concerns the obliteration of political divergence. In every ceremony, bonds of friendship mean that a whole council is united by the expressing of common values. As Van Gennep pointed out, rituals renew feelings of community membership. By celebrating international friendship, communal institutions celebrate themselves as political bodies. to bring politics into this is considered inappropriate. Parties are represented in delegations. The expression of political opposition is unusual, and when expressed it is done so by boycott – as with the Communist councillors protesting Franco-German ceremonies.

Rhetorics of Friendship: Bridging Some Philosophical Gaps

Through a corpus of about 50 official speeches, remarkable regularities may be observed. Though the contexts of the ceremonies may change a lot, these speeches have very similar frameworks. The part of such a speech usually describes the genesis of the twinning oath in the history of the friendship between the two peoples. Alternatively, it recounts the need to overcome hostility, to consolidate the peace. The historical narrative often refers to religious history, such as previous links between missionaries or pilgrims. These narratives about progressive reconciliation between religions allows both believers and agnostics to stress the conciliatory effects of twinning ceremonies. These speeches emphasize friendship as a way to transcend political oppositions. We need not privilege Schmittian objections to such processes.[6]

The second part of these speeches is generally based on exemplifications of bonds of friendship favoured by the relationships between the two cities. Figures of success are the increase of the number of individuals involved and the regularity and density of such exchanges. Arguments are here much more basic, made of anecdotes, difficulties in learning languages, sports' results, and so on. This may allow us to bridge the theoretical gap between private friendship and political friendship (Goodman & Elgin 1988). A particular relationship may, without loss of particularity, carry some broader significance. So that private links between A and B, which (like marriage) are genuinely private, may also have significance for the international relations of the different countries which the parties to this union represent.

The conclusions of the speeches often project friendship bonds in the future, referring to expected 10th, 20th and 30th birthday celebrations, on the model of what usually happens in conjugal life. Rhetorics thus appear as embedding bonds of friendship simultaneously in what Koselleck (1997) calls 'topics of experience' and 'horizon of expectation'. This links us to the second way (the temporal one) by which Searle establishes distinctions within institutional facts. Empirically, friendship bonds structured by twinnings are very rarely destroyed, never end through the end of a mandate, but, may naturally decline. So that international friendship is always supposed to be steadfast, until it appears that it has disappeared.

Beyond Ceremonies: Fun

Transitions between ceremonies and collective fun are often managed by a banquet, in which people taste typical dishes. In France, French wine has always been a matter of pride at such events. In Germany, such dinners coincide with 'beer festivals'. Drinking together is a usual way to share emotions far beyond protocol frames and barriers of foreign languages. Drunkenness is an ancient way to fraternize – although it may not feature in theories of friendship.

Festivals also take place in streets and squares, with folkloric ballets, orchestras, beauty queens, and so on. Cities of the north of France may have shown their cortèges of Giants. Cities from Brittany may have asked their *bagadou* (traditional music bands) to play. In any case, even when there is no current tradition, municipalities actively restore such local habits. In Rennes, for example, although the city has never been a centre of the Briton culture, traditional bands have been encouraged. In Lille, the immense carnival mannequins called Giants are involved in every reception or trip to sister cities. As with Lyderic and Phynaert, the most famous ones, who are supposed to have founded the commune, all these Giants have legendary heroic lives. A French ethnologist, Marie-France Gueusquin, showed that Lille had never been a dominant place of gigantic figures, unlike cities such as Douai, Cassel, Dunkerque or Bailleul. She pointed out that Lille 'is noticeable by the predominance of the municipal institution, by the fact only the City Hall promotes these festive mannequins, whereas in other cities, support and promotion belong to official groups'. Marie-France Gueusquin stresses that administrative reform led by Mauroy in 1975 marked the beginning of the creation of Giants. This enjoyable activity has been linked to the organization of festivals, those to do with twinning festivals being the most important.

Sports competitions feature as a major activity at twinning festivals. Just as Durkheim said that 'not everything in the contract is contractual', we could say that 'not everything in friendship is friendly'. Many cities organize special tournaments, such as soccer and rugby matches and water tourneys (more likely in southern cities), which are very closely fought. Little clubs have always been active participants in such events, because that allows them to prepare for international matches. Such competitions are everything but anecdotic. Elias and Dunning have shown how rugby inculcated aggressiveness, sublimated rivalry, and the warlike urges. Anyone, not just professional athletes, may take part in peaceful or, at least, fair-play fights. That is one dimension of what Elias called civilizing habits. This historical practice of organizing popular competitions and games between cities has inspired some popular TV shows invented in the 1960s, like *Intervilles* and *Jeux sans frontières*, created by the famous French compères Léon Zitrone and Guy Lux. Zitrone himself, who was born in Russia, got the idea of such games from presenting radio reports on East–West twinnings of the *Monde Bilingue* in 1955.

Local Support for Cultural Institutes

Local support for cultural institutes is tied to cultural-diplomacy initiatives and national foreign policies. The following case studies show that the durability of such organizations depends on their social anchorage in localities and notably on municipal efforts to promote them.

Franco-German Institutes

French mayors were ready, even as early as 1947, to translate their desire for peace between France and Germany into action (Vion 2002). Though their initiative was not universally supported, it led to a new international association, the Union Internationale des Maires (UIM), dedicated to Franco-German reconciliation and understanding among nations. From 1947 to 1950 its efforts were isolated. In 1947, for example, two eminent Swiss supporters, the writer Eugène Wyler and Dr Hans Zbindon, organized a discussion session for French and German mayors with the aim of launching an exchange programme in a spirit of reconciliation. After the First World War there had similarly been a few scattered attempts by municipalities to re-establish dialogue between French and German youth movements (Tiemann 1989) in the wake of political discussions between the two countries (Delbreil 1994). But such direct exchanges between the two peoples at municipal level had remained very much the exception. The Mont Pèlerin meeting witnessed the mayors' willingness to reinitiate them. It led to a solemn mutual undertaking to simplify visa formalities and encourage exchanges among young workers, and annual study trips by mayors and local government officers. The French contingent was led by the mayors of Montbéliard (M. Tharradin), La Flèche (M. Montgascon), and, most important of all, the Gaullist MP René Radius, deputy mayor of Strasbourg. The participants were not delegated by their town councils and attended in their personal capacity; those who had AMF responsibilities took care not to mention the fact.[7]

The association was drawn into the orbit of French cultural diplomacy in Germany.[8] From 1948 onwards, the UIM worked with the French Institute at Ludwigsburg, founded by the Franco-German jurist Carlo Schmid, head of the first government of Würtemberg-Hohenzollern. After the inauguration of the German Federal Republic in 1949, there was a heavy demand for exchanges among German mayors, but the implementation of these plans was hedged around with precautions by the French Foreign Office, which supported the idea in principle but feared French local reactions might disturb the peace.[9] Up to the Stuttgart Congress in June 1950 the UIM's activities remained modest; but this congress was supported and attended by French and German representatives at the highest level,[10] and it led to the organization of a first official exchange between the municipalities of

Montbéliard and Ludwigsburg at the end of 1950. As early as 1948, the strong local links between the mayors of Ludwigsburg and Montbéliard provided strong support of the activities of the Institute. This was the first expression of the municipal ethic of peaceful co-existence, but there were other initiatives in the pipeline. The French Germanophile milieu, made up of Christian Democrats and youth movements, Socialists, some Gaullists, planners, civil servants, trade-unions, associations of German teachers, and journalists, promoted public support for Goethe institutes and youth exchanges.

The French Official History considers that bonds of friendship between France and Germany were by the signing of the Elysée Peace Treaty in 1963. People who studied this field (Defrance, Ménudier, etc.) have shown that this treaty was more the outcome of postwar exchanges than itself the cause of closer ties with Germany. Local archives show that institutes and exchanges benefited from the political support of municipal teams (except the communist ones, who began to promote links with GDR at the end of the 1950s) and from the financial support of the Franco-German Office.

Franco-American Institutes

Franco-American institutes were part of US cultural diplomacy after the Second World War in Europe. In France, they were created mostly in the 1950s, in cities where Marshall Plan offices were opened.

The US Embassy supported the creation of libraries, English lessons, arts and photographic exhibitions, American movie shows and so on. These institutes functioned in the context of the quick spread of American culture and American way of life through magazines, radio and cinema. They also encouraged youth exchanges, such as Eisenhower's 'People-to-People Program' created in 1956, a few weeks before his reelection. All of these activities made these institutes popular. French public high school teachers did not participate in their functioning as much as they did in Franco-English town twinnings. Marxist and anti-imperialist theories which had been popularized by the Communist Party and Left movements and trade-unions led a majority of them to proclaim their anti-americanism, or, at least, to keep their distance from the American people. This might be a reason why these institutes did not find many active supporters when the Congress, involved in the Vietnam War efforts, voted budget cuts in 1966. American support for these institutes was no longer considered a priority by anyone. President Charles de Gaulle decided that France would quit the integrated force structure of NATO. Most of these institutes were closed at the end of the 1960s, causing few demonstrations, revealing again the decisive importance of local volunteer associations.

What is interesting is that the only remaining institute is one that the US services had not wanted to create in the 1950s. This institute, in Rennes, was supported by local institutions from the beginning, contrary to the others, which were entirely financed by the United States. The mayor of Rennes, Henri Fréville, who was a Christian-Democrat, negotiated this outcome after his city and its universities had twinned with Rochester, in New York State, in 1958. The Rennes Institute was not a priority of the US Embassy, but the mayor was supported by his predecessor, who was the chairman of the local *France–Amérique* Committee, and the boss of the French branch of Kodak, whose global head office was in Rochester. They secured from the Americans use of the ground floor of the local office of the Marshall Plan to have an American bookshop, *Brentano's*. The French local institutions (commune and department) paid for the functioning of the Institute, which meant recruiting a director and assistants, supporting exhibitions and youth exchanges. Local contacts with Rochester helped open the institute. The City of Rochester gave materials for exhibitions and books. The global head office of Kodak supported youth photo competitions by offering films and cameras as prizes to the winners. All these local arrangements made the arrangements quite original. This explains why the Rennes Institute remained the only Franco-American Institute at the end of the 1960s. This centre has developed many activities for 40 years (teaching, training periods, exchanges, exhibitions, conferences, translation, political debates about American elections, etc.).

Since the 1980s, the director has been associated with all the local efforts to attract American direct investment. When the location of production units of Kodak, Rank Xerox, or Motorola were negotiated, he was the leader of the welcome team. The Institute also tries to attract American firms in international trade fairs and shows.

So, if one looks at the link between transnational organizations and intergovernmental cooperation (Risse-Kappen 1995; Keohane & Milner 1996), they should pay attention to local institutions too as part of a larger understanding of multi-layered diplomacy (Hocking 1993).

The Institution of Friendship Reinforces Communities

There has been an increase in international official exchanges between cities, growing from only a few in the 1950s, to very many more since the 1970s, and still more since the 1980s (Figure 1).

When Bonds of Friendship Keep Alive Local Communities

What can be noticed, when studying the development of these practices from the 1950s to the 1980s, is that the more innovative municipal councils have been those that celebrated international friendship.

Such bonds of friendship have often been considered as elements of professional exchanges, or even trade. In some cases, exchanges through corporations or professions have been the spearhead of the twinning process, such as exchanges between hosiery firms of Troyes and Tournai or glass artists of Chartres and Varenne. Universities have intended to multiply their links in this way, too. Such exchanges strengthened local professional organizations, and stimulated the international circulation of 'know-how'. French bakers learned to make pretzels, Spanish wine

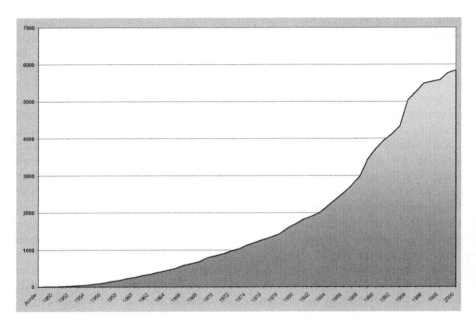

Figure 1. International agreements signed by French local authorities (1947–2001) (Baraize et al. 2002).

growers learned French methods of wine-making, judges compared their law systems. These relations were often occasions for reasserting the value of corporative traditions. Professors, judges and attorneys have enjoyed wearing their regalia in professional twinning ceremonies. Brotherhood rituals have been restored, for example in wine-growing. This kind of corporative folklore is all the more surprising given that the corporatist experience of the fascist Vichy regime made unsuitable corporatism distinctly unpopular after the Second World War in France (Kaplan 2001).

Promoters of Friendship: Tocqueville's Paradox

French local councillors who favour local interventionism in social, cultural and sports policies also tend to favour the twinning of their cities. Studies of the associative movement in France (Héran 1988) have demonstrated higher representation of teachers and liberal professionals in associations. My own local interviews and observations in Rennes, Lille and Toucoing show that these individuals have been the main promoters of international friendship since the 1950s. Studying local interactions allows us to go further than macro explanations. If one explains political change by the changing social structure of cities, one will not pay attention to the social structure of local activism, which may be different from basic demography.

In his famous book *La Démocratie en Amérique*, Tocqueville stressed the paradoxical situation of voluntaristic associations. He noticed that people promoting universal values could be organized in very closed *milieux* or communities. The experience of French cities of twinning and international friendship associations are evidence for this conclusion. One of the militants interviewed in Rennes said:

> If we sum-it-up it, I did the whole tour of twinning committees. I gave a new start to Rennes-Sendaï exchanges in the seventies and I even became the Chairman of the Committee. I became a member of Rennes-Mopti after taking part in the Catholic Committee for Development and the Third World commission of the Associative Office. I went to Erlangen for the twentieth birthday, in Alma Ata, too. So, I travelled all over the world '. On the contrary, simple members with simple projects are pushed to the margins of the system, as students explain: 'People make it too serious. It's too bureaucratic. All these chairmen of twinning committees in the International House, creates a hierarchy that is unnecessary.'

Conclusion

The politics of friendship is not to do with what Walzer (1983) calls 'the sphere of money' and is something different from contractual links. Emotions allow interindividual relations to extend beyond social roles. That flexibility is not supposed to happen in the case of monetary exchanges according to Simmel (1987). Of course, institutional bonds of friendship may favour such flexible exchanges, but it is only a secondary effect.

Rituals constitute a dominant kind of institutional fact from which emerges political friendship. Scheffler (1981) has pointed out that rituals penetrate hearts as a form of is what Goodman (1978) calls expressive reference.

A wide range of moral ideals may be at stake, but should theorists forget fun? Searle (1995) has shown events are perceived through expectations. What is interesting in the most popular expression of international friendship we studied is that attempts are often disturbed, so that friendship is made of unusual events (such as dancing the gigue with a Scottish man wearing a kilt, travelling by coach with Carnival Giants, and so on).

Studying international friendship as a pattern of institutional facts invites attention to the specific contexts in which they emerge. In Europe, after the Second World War, the embeddedness of friendship politics in local communities went through a process of invention of communal traditions. European communal history has been a major symbolic resource in this process.

The embeddedness of international friendship in local communities promotes stronger ties. Governmental initiatives may have big impacts, but are unsuitable without local support. Yet, achieving friendship may not favour a broad and open community.

Notes

1. Historical investigations were undertaken in the French Diplomatic Archives (Ministry of Foreign Affairs), Municipal Archives of Rennes, Lille and Puteaux, and newspaper archives. Interviews were conducted with 60 persons, and direct observations conducted mainly in Rennes and Lille. Published sources include *Communes d'Europe*, 1953–1963; *Cités unies*, 1957–1986; *La Revue administrative*, 1950–1968; Débats A.N., 17 November 1959, pp. 2439 and 2456, Débats Sénat, 9 December 1959, p. 1550; J.O., Débats Sénat, 18 November 1961, pp. 1556–1558; J.O. Débats Sénat, 13 March 1962, p. 44. Notes concerning the examples given in this essay are: Lille Municipal Archives: AML, 1 D2 156, CM, 31 October 55, no. 411, pp. 863, 827 (débats); A.M.L., 4 D3 1, Jumelages, Contacts divers: Lettre de J.M. Bressand à Augustin Laurent, 7 September 1955; Lettre d'Augustin Laurent à Melle Poulain, chez Miss J. Krone, York, 13 September 1955; Lettre du secrétaire d'ambassade des Etats-Unis en France, 9 May 1956 (confirmation de l'accord de Pittsburgh); Lettre de Jean-Bernard Piobetta à Augustin Laurent, 16 May 1956; Lettre du maire de Pittsburgh annonçant la décision de son conseil + résolution no. 207 (translation), 28 May 1956; Lettre de Douglas Dillon, ambassadeur des Etats-Unis à Augustin Laurent, 22 June 1956; Lettre d'Augustin Laurent à Jean-Bernard Piobetta, 9 August 1956; Lettre d'Augustin Laurent au maire de Pittsburgh, 9 August 1956; Lettre de Jean-Marie Bressand à Augustin Laurent suite à une entrevue, 15 October 1956; Extrait de compte-rendu du conseil municipal du 19 octobre concernant le report de la discussion vue l'heure tardive. Lettre d'Augustin Laurent à Denise Poulain, 17 September 1957; AML, 1 D2 150, CM 11 March 1949, p. 273; AML, 1 D2 150, CM 11 March 1949, pp. 279–280; AML, 1 D2 151, CM 24 January 1950, p. 273; AML, 1 D2 151, CM 30 November 1950, p. 1234; AML, 1 D2 154, CM 19 June 1953; AML, 1 D2 155, CM, 26 February 1954, no. 648, pp. 244–246; AML, 4 D 3. 1 to 4 D 4. 54. IN Rennes Municipal Archives: AMR, Bor. 23.87 all boxes; AMR, 43 W 19; AMR 15 W 1/27, Échanges de courriers et discours d'inauguration de l'Institut Franco-Américain prononcé par le premier adjoint Georges Graff; AMR 19/86. Note Jean Raux sur le projet de fonctionnement de la MIR; AMR 19/86, Préparatifs du Xxe anniversaire du jumelage Rennes-Erlangen. Voyage à Erlangen, 4–9 June 1984. See also the comptes-rendus dans Ouest-France, 4–10 June 1984; AMR 17 W 1. Discours d'inauguration de la rue d'Erlangen, 10 September 1964; AMR 7/81-3. Préparatifs des cérémonies du jumelage Rennes-Erlangen, octobre 1964. Note de Victor Janton à Henri Fréville; AMR 7/81-3. Préparatifs des cérémonies du jumelage Rennes-Erlangen, octobre 1964, dernières instructions du maire; AMR 6/81-48; in the Archives Diplomatiques Quai d'Orsay: Europe, RFA, Carton 1581; Europe, RFA, Carton 1571, 24.1. Relations politiques franco-allemandes 1961–1963, chemise 1; Carton 1577. 24.1.4/1.5, Commission interministérielle pour la coopération franco-allemande.
2. 'A Reims la décoration extérieure de la mairie avec les lys de Reims et Florence, les bannières des corporations champenoises, le prestigieux 'gonfalon' de la ville de Florence, la réception des maires sur le parvis de la cathédrale, le passage à l'heure du serment d'avions à réaction revenant de Florence et jetant sur les deux villes un pavillon orné de leurs armes'.
3. 'Dans le salon du centre de l'Hôtel de ville, le Conseil Municipal, les deux préfets, la délégation romaine et l'ambassadeur d'Italie se dirigèrent vers le fond de la salle, tandis que les trompettes des hérauts du Capitole ouvraient le ban. Une main écarta un velum mi-partie violet et or et alors apparut la Louve de bronze donnant à Romulus et Remus le premier lait de notre civilisation. Puis cette "session extraordinaire" de quelques instants. Dans la salle des séances les élus de Rome s'assirent parmi les élus de Paris. Le Maire de Rome, ceint de l'écharpe vert-blanc-rouge, se plaça en face du maire de Paris pendant que, entre le Préfet de la Seine et le préfet de police prenait place l'ambassadeur d'Italie. M. Rebecchini, en italien, et M. Jacques Feron, en français, lurent le serment de jumelage parmi les applaudissements ... A l'issue du Service Mgr Feltin a lu le texte d'un télégramme adressé à l'archevêché par SS Pie XII: "Nous apprenons avec une grande satisfaction ce nouveau lien d'amitié qui se noue aujourd'hui entre les élus de Rome et ceux de Paris et nous nous plaisons, en cette circonstance, à évoquer l'histoire de nos deux cités, qui ont travaillé à promouvoir la civilisation chrétienne dans le monde."'
4. Municipal archives of Rennes 7/81-3. Préparatifs des cérémonies du jumelage Rennes-Erlangen, octobre 1964, dernières instructions du maire. The original text is: 'Il y a lieu de rappeler aux

conseillers qu'ils devront être, mardi, munis de leurs écharpes et de leurs cocardes. Les huissiers devront être en habit et tout devra être impeccable.'
5. Municipal archives of Rennes 7/81–3. Préparatifs des cérémonies du jumelage Rennes-Erlangen, octobre 1964. Note de Victor Janton à Henri Fréville). The original text is: 'Il faudra bien une présentation officielle de la délégation d'Erlangen avec un discours d'accueil du maire de Rennes et une réponse du maire d'Erlangen. Je te rappelle que lors de la cérémonie officielle du jumelage, M Lades m'en a d'autorité donné la présidence, lui même n'occupant que la place à ma droite et le premier adjoint, M. Sponsel celle à ma gauche. Il n'est pas question évidemment d'une présidence allemande pour notre séance publique. Je ne crois même pas qu'il serait judicieux de donner d'emblée à M. Lades la présidence de la partie officieuse de la cérémonie mais il me semble qu'il faudrait lui rendre sa politesse et que tu pourrais, après avoir pris la présidence et salué la délégation allemande, l'inviter à prendre ta place pour prononcer son discours de réponse.'
6. We may follow Ricoeur (1983) against Heidegger, in claiming that accounts and narratives are the epistemological conditions of ontology and not the reverse. So when Schmitt builds an ontology of enmity, he can only do so through experiences, accounts and narratives of war periods. Can anyone talk about the threat of total war without knowing anything of war experiences? If not, there is no good reason why we should assume *a priori* an ontology of enmity.
7. Subsection Central Europe (Seydoux) to Minister's office, summary note on 'Visit to Germany by French mayors and to France by German mayors', 28 July 1950, Archives du Ministère des affaires étrangères (France), Series Europe (1944–1960), Subsection Central Europe, Subseries Germany, April–July 1950.
8. On the overall programme of French cultural diplomacy in Germany, aimed at the political re-education of young Germans (and of which the Gaullist Raymond Schmittlein was one of the principal architects), see the comprehensive study by Corinne Defrance, *La politique culturelle de la France sur la rive gauche du Rhin 1945–1955* (Strasbourg: Presses Universitaires de Strasbourg, 1994).
9. Subsection Central Europe (Seydoux) to Minister's office, summary note on 'Visit to Germany by French mayors and to France by German mayors', 28 July 1950, Archives du Ministère des affaires étrangères (France), Series Europe (1944–1960), Subsection Central Europe, Subseries Germany, April-July 1950.
10. Report by the French High Commissioner in Germany, 2 June 1950, Archives du Ministère des affaires étrangères (France), Series Europe (1944–1960), Subsection Central Europe, Subseries Germany, April-July 1950. André François-Poncet, 'Address to the Congress of French and German Mayors at Stuttgart, 2 June 1950', *Réalités Allemandes* 18 (1950),pp. 25–27.

References

Abbott, A. (1992) What do cases do? Some notes on activity in sociological analysis, in: Ragin, C. & Becker H. (Eds) *What is a Case? Exploring the Foundations of Social Inquiry*, pp. 53–82 (Cambridge: Cambridge University Press).
Arendt, H. (1969) *Philosophy and Politics: What is Political Philosophy?*, Lectures and Seminar, 1969, Library of Congress, Hannah Arendt Papers, Series: Subject File, 1949–1975.
Bautz, I. (2002) Die Auslandsbeziehungen der deutschen Kommunen im Rahmen der europäischen Kommunalbewegung in den 1950er und 60er Jahren. Städtepartnerschaften Integration Ost-West-Konflikt, Siegen: internet publications of Siegen University's Library.
Bayart, J.F. (1995) *L'illusion identitaire* (Paris: Fayard).
Boltanski, L. (1990) *L'amour et la justice comme compétences* (Paris: Metailié)
Boulding, K. (1968) The city as an element in the international system, *Daedalus*, 97(4), pp. 1111–1123.
Bourdieu, P. (1982) Les rites comme actes d'institution. *Actes de la Recherche en Sciences sociales*, pp. 58–63.
Coninck, F. (1998) La métaphore de l'ouvert et du fermé chez Max Weber. Questions préliminaires pour une sociologie de l'action, *Cahiers internationaux de sociologie*, 104, pp. 139–165.

180   Friendship in Politics

Dallmayr, F. (2000) Derrida and friendship, in: King, P. & Devere, H. (Eds), *Thinking Past a Problem*, pp. 105–130 (London: Frank Cass).
Defrance, C. (1994) *La politique culturelle de la France sur la rive gauche du Rhin 1945–1955* (Strasbourg: Presses Universitaires de Strasbourg).
Delbreil, J.C. (1994) Les premiers rapprochements franco-allemands 1919–1932, in Vaïsse, M. (Ed.), *Le pacifisme en Europe* (Bruxelles: Bruylant).
Derrida, J. (2006) *The Politics of Friendship*, (London and New York: Verso).
Derrida, J. (1994) *Politiques de l'amitié* (Paris: Galilée).
Duchacek, I.D. (1986) *The Territorial Dimension of Politics: Within, Among and Across Nations* (Boulder, CO: Westview).
Duchacek, I.D., Latouche, D. & Stevenson G. (1988) *Perforated Sovereignties and International Relations: Transsovereign Contacts of Subnational Governments* (New York: Greenwood Press).
Elgin, C.Z. (1983) *With Reference to Reference* (Indianapolis, IN: Hackett).
Elgin, C.Z. (1992) Comprendre: art et science, in: Pouivet, R. (Ed.), *Lire Goodman. Les voies de la référence*, pp. 49–67 (Paris: Editions de l'Eclat).
Elias N. & Dunning, E. (1999) *Sport et civilisation. La violence maîtrisée* (Paris: Agora Pocket).
Fischer, F. (2003) *Reframing Public Policy: Discursive Politics and Deliberative Practices* (Oxford: Oxford University Press).
Goodman N. (1978) *Ways of Worldmaking* (Indianapolis, IN: Hackett).
Goodman, N. & Elgin, C.Z. (1988) *Reconceptions in Philosophy and Other Arts and Science* (Cambridge, MA: Harvard University Press).
Gueusquin, M.F. (1994) Tradition et artifice dans les fêtes urbaines du Nord de la France: les mannequins de cortège ou les raisons d'un échec à Lille aujourd'hui, in Corbin, A., Gérôme, N. & Tartakowsky, D. (Eds), *Les usages politiques des fêtes aux XIX–XXe siècles*, pp. 263–268 (Paris: Publications de la Sorbonne).
Héran, F. (1988) Le monde associatif, *Economie et Statistique*, 208, pp. 15–44.
Hobbs, H.H. (1994) *City Hall Goes Abroad* (Thousand Oaks, CA: Sage).
Hobsbawm, E. (1990) Inventing traditions, in Hobsbawm, E. & Ranger. T. (Eds), *The Invention of Tradition*, pp. 1–14 (Cambridge: Cambridge University Press).
Hocking, B. (1993) Localizing *Foreign Policy: Non-Central Government and Multi-layered Diplomacy* (New York: St Martin's Press).
Immergut E.M. (1998) The theoretical core of the new institutionalism, *Politics and Society*, 26(1), pp. 5–34.
Inglehart, R. (1977) *The Silent Revolution. Changing values and Political styles among Western Publics* (Princeton, NJ: Princeton University Press).
Isambert, F.A. (1982) *Le sens du sacré. Fête et religion populaire* (Paris, Minuit).
Kaplan, S.L. (2001) Un laboratoire de la doctrine corporatiste sous Vichy: l'Institut d'Etudes Corporatives et Sociales, *Le Mouvement Social*, 195(2), pp. 35–77.
Keohane, R. & Milner, H. (1996) *Internationalization and Domestic Politics* (Cambridge: Cambridge University Press).
Koselleck, R. (1979) Kriegerdenkmale als Identitätstiftungen der Überlebenden, in: Marquard, O. & Stierle, K. (Eds), *Identität*, pp. 255–276 (Munich: Wilhelm Fink).
Koselleck, R. (1997) *L'expérience de l'histoire* (Paris: Seuil).
Lahire, B. (1996) La variation des contextes dans les sciences sociales. Remarques épistémologiques, *Annales HSS*, 2, pp. 381–407.
Négrier, E., Vion, A. (2002) 7[E] Congres de l'AFSP, Lille La coop´ration décentralisée, un nouvel étage du jeu diplomatique, Alelier *Les ncuvelles forme de la diplomatie*, (Marc Dixneuf & Isabelle Lebreton).
Powell W.W. & Di Maggio P.J. (1991) The new institutionalism in organizational analysis (Chicago: University of Chicago Press).
Ricoeur, P. (1983) *Temps et récit* (Paris: Seuil).
Risse-Kappen, T. (1995) *Bringing Transnational Relations Back In* (Cambridge: Cambridge University Press).

Scheffler, I. (1981) Ritual and Reference, *Synthese International,* 46(3).
Schmitt, C. (1932) *Der Begriff des Politischen* (Berlin: Duncker & Humblot)
Searle, J. (1995) *The Construction of Social Reality* (New York: Free Press).
Segalen M. (1998) Rites et rituels contemporains (Paris: Nathan Université, coll. 128).
Simmel, G. (1987) *Philosophie de l'argent* (Paris: Presses Universitaires de France).
Steinmo, S., Thelen, K. & Longstreth, F. (Eds) (1992) *Structuring Politics. Historical Institutionalism in Comparative Analysis* (New York: Cambridge University Press).
Thelen, K. & Steinmo, S. (1992) Historical institutionalism in comparative politics, in: Thelen, K., Steinmo, S. & Longstreth, F. (Eds) *Structuring Politics: Historical Institutionalism in Comparative Analysis,* pp. 1–32, (Cambridge: Cambridge University Press).
Tiemann, D. (1989) Deutsch-*französiche Jugendbeziehungen der Zwischenkriegszeit* (Bonn: Bouvier, Röhrscheid).
Tocqueville, A. de (1986) De *la démocratie en Amérique* (Paris: Folio Histoire).
Van Gennep, A. (1909) *Les rites de passage* (Paris: Emile Noury).
Vion, A. (2002) Europe from the bottom up : town twinning in France during the Cold War, *Contemporary European History,* 2(4), pp. 623–640.
Vion A. (2003) L'invention de la tradition des jumelages: mobilisations pour un droit (1951–1956), *Revue Française de Science Politique,* 53(5), pp. 559–582
Walzer, M. (1983) *Spheres of Justice. A Defense of Pluralism and Equality* (New York: Basic Books).
Weber, M. (1986) *La ville* (Paris: Aubier).
Weber, M. (1995) *Economie et société* (Paris: Plon, Agora Pocket).
Zelinsky, W. (1988) The twinning of the world: sister cities in geographic and historical perspective, *Annals of the Association of American Geographers,* 81(1), pp. 1–31.

INDEX

abortion 129
Adler, E. 156
Africa 169
agendas 31, 95, 113, 141, 145
agonism 46–8
agriculture 10, 118, 135
Alfonsín, R. 157–8
Algeria 86
aliens 11
Allies 2
America 10, 123
amigocracy 43
anarchy 47, 141–4, 146, 160–1
ancient settings 9–14, 34, 120
Anders 105
Andrzejewski, J. 104
anomie 13
Ansell-Pearson, K. 34–5
anthropology 42
anti-essentialism 47
Aquinas, T. 54
Arendt, H. 37, 43–4, 46, 107
Argentina 144, 148–9, 153–5, 157–61
Argentine-Brazilian Agency of Control and Accountability (ABACC) 158
aristocracy 43, 53, 61–2, 108
Aristotle 11, 27, 32, 34
   care theory 118–20, 122
   equality 51, 54–6, 61–2
   politics 36–7, 44–7
   responsibility 70–3
   revolution 103, 107
arms races 142, 150, 158
asecurity 144–6, 150, 156–60
Association of the Southeast Asian nations (ASEAN) 149
Asunción Treaty 159

asymmetrical sharing 22
atheists 108
Axis 2

Bacon, F. 55, 57–8
Balakrishnan, G. 83
balance of power 142–3, 146, 154
bandwagons 143
Bar-Simon-Tov, Y. 156
Barnett, M. 156
Batka, L. 114
Bauman, Z. 37, 44
Beacons programmes 133–4
Belinski 104
Bellamy, R. 93
Bellow, S. 103
Bendersky, J. 91
Bible 25
biology 11–12, 26, 125–9, 132
Blumsztajn, S. 103–4
Boétie, É de la 44
Bogús 113
Bolivia 159
Böll, H. 103
Bolsheviks 111
bondage 123
bonding 2, 12, 14, 37, 46
   institutions 166–7, 171–2, 174–7
   polemics 85, 87, 90–1, 94–5
   responsibility 71
   revolution 100
Bonhoeffer, D. 107–8
Borusewicz, B. 109
Bounds, E. 42
bourgeoisie 126, 128
Brazil 20, 144, 148–9, 153–5, 157–61
Britain 10, 155

Index

Brodsky, J. 101
Bubeck, D. 127
Buber, M. 12
Bujak, Z. 109
bureaucracy 12, 132, 134, 136, 177
Burke, E. 143–4, 160
Bush, G.W. 10, 24
Buzan, B. 144

Camus, A. 107
Canada 149
capitalism 111, 122–3
Cardoso, F.H. 160
care theory 118–38
carers 5, 16
Caribbean 154
Carter, J. 154
Castro, F. 111
catching-up phenomenon 123
Catholics 26, 104, 108, 110, 112
Celinski 100, 104
Central America 158
chauvinism 119
Chiaromonte, N. 107
childcare 118, 123–5, 128, 130–3, 136
Chile 154, 159
Christianity 25, 37–8, 53
    institutions 168–9
    responsibility 66–7, 73
    revolution 103, 107–8, 111
Cicero 31–2, 36, 44–5, 48, 103
citizenship 46, 126
city-republics 43
civil service 130, 135–7, 174
civil society 27–8, 35, 42, 45, 92, 129, 157, 161
Clausewitz, C. von 88
Clinton, B. 16, 24
codes of power 134
Cogito, Mr 107
cold peace 147–8, 150, 154, 161
Cold War 88, 92, 148, 161, 167
Collor, F. 158–9
colonialism 10, 86–7, 93, 123, 127

Committee for Workers' Defense (KOR) 99–114
communes 168–9, 172, 175
communication 11, 87, 90, 150, 159
communism 5, 47, 99, 101
    institutions 171, 174
    revolution 103–5, 108–9, 111–12
Communist Party 109–11, 174
communitarianism 32, 37, 42, 105, 121
community 148–9, 151, 157
    care 130, 133–7
    institutions 171, 175–7
    trust 159–61
competition 137, 145, 153, 155, 157
comrades 121
conditional peace 147–8, 150–1
confidence and security building measures (CSBMs) 150
conservatives 38, 111, 130
constitution 61, 119–20, 136
constructivism 156
cooperation 142, 144, 153–5, 158–9, 166, 175
Copenhagen School 144
corporations 27–8, 37
Critchley, S. 34–5
cronyism 5, 20, 112
cultural institutes 173–5
Cupit, G. 53
Czechs 108

Danish language 65
Däuber 91
de Gaulle, C. 86, 174
debt 158
decommunisation 101
Defrance, C. 174
democracy 2, 5, 10, 13, 27
    care theory 122–3, 125–6, 129, 133–4, 137–8
    equality 61
    institutions 167
    polemics 84–5, 90, 92
    politics 32, 37–8, 42–8

revolution 101, 106–8, 111–12
  trust 147, 157–8, 161
Democrats 19
demography 54, 176
dependency 20, 126, 130–2, 136
Derrida, J. 32, 34, 44, 48, 84, 93–4
desecuritization 144–6, 149–61
despotism 27
deterrence 148
diagnostics 83–96
Diogenes Laertius 44
Diotima 102
diplomacy 142, 150, 159, 167, 173–5
Disney, W. 16
dissociation 41
divorce 129
Dorn 104
Dostoevsky, F. 111
drives 68–73, 76
drunkenness 172
dualism 87
Dunning, E. 172
Durkheim, É. 172

Easter Islands 10
Eastern Europe 100–1, 161
economics 11, 33–4, 36, 42–3
  care theory 123, 125–6, 136–7
  equality 52
  polemics 87–8
  trust 153–6, 158–9
economists 100
ecosystems 136
education 21, 53, 55–6, 131–4, 136, 138
egalitarians 60–2
Eisenhower, D. 169, 174
Elias, N. 172
Elysée Peace Treaty 174
emancipation 113
emergency measures 145
emotion 68–70, 74, 136–7, 142, 146, 172, 177
Empedocles 36
England 20, 169, 174

English language 104, 174
Enlightenment 108, 113
enmity typology 86–7, 90
Enron 27
Equal Rights Amendment 123
equality 2–4, 6, 19–21, 27
  care theory 118–19, 122–3, 126–9, 133, 137–8
  institutions 168
  politics 42
  reasons 51–64
  responsibility 68, 73, 77
  revolution 106
Erasmus, D. 108
Europe 65, 83, 87, 93
  care theory 123, 131, 137
  institutions 168, 174, 177
  revolution 102–3, 106, 108, 113
  trust 143
European Union (EU) 149, 159
evolution 11, 26
exchange value 118
existentialism 65

Fabians 1
Falklands 148, 155
fascism 37, 176
favouritism 121, 128
fear 24, 37, 43, 103, 109, 121–2, 129, 132
feminism 118, 122–5
Ferguson, A. 123–4
fêtes 168–71
feudalism 128
Ficcino 108
Figueiredo, J. 155
filía politikè 36–8, 45
Fineman, M. 130, 132
First World War 87–8, 173
Fischer, F. 166
Flying University 100, 103
Folbre, N. 123–4
Forman, M. 105
fragile peace 147–8, 150, 161

France 10, 83, 86, 167, 169, 172–7
Franco-American institutes 174–5
fraternity 118, 135
Free Trade Area of the Americas (FTAA) 159
free will 23
French Institute 173–4
French language 169
Fréville, H. 174
friendship
  civic 117–38
  equality 51–64
  filía politikè 36–8
  forms 32–4
  institutionalization 165–79
  polemics/diagnostics 83–96
  Polish revolution 99–114
  political 9–29, 31–48
  problem 41–4
  significance 89–92
  status 55–60
  trust 141–62
  typology 89–91
  unequals 60–2
fun 172–3, 177
functionalization 37
fundamentalism 25, 47, 89–91, 108, 111
futile politics 92
future generations 19, 126

game theory 28
Gaullists 173–4
Gaya 104–6
Gazeta Wyborcza 112
Gdansk shipyard 109
Gemeinschaft 42
gender 119, 124–5, 135, 137
General Agreement on Tariffs and Trade (GATT) 158
genetics 12, 23
Geremek, B. 110
German language 40
Germany 167, 169, 171–4
ghetto 112

Giants 172, 177
Gilligan, C. 128
global warming 10
globalisation 44, 90
Goethe institutes 174
Goodman, N. 177
Gorbachev, M. 104
grace 53
Grass, G. 103
Great Depression 10
Greeks 25, 32, 41, 60, 118
guerrillas 10
Gueusquin, M-F. 172
Gwiazda, A. 109

Habermas, J. 42, 84
Hardt, M. 42
harm minimisation 127
Havel, V. 109
Heaney, S. 107
Hegel, G.W.F. 129
Heidegger, M. 34
Held, V. 125
Herbert, Z. 107, 112–13
hermits 125
hierarchy 2, 28, 52–3, 135, 142–3, 177
Hitler, A. 92
Hobbes, T. 41, 93
Hobsbawm, E. 168
Holocaust 83
homophily 54
Hoover, H. 10
human rights 121, 154
humanism 37, 107–8, 112–13
Hume, D. 5
Huston, T.L. 54
Huysmans, J. 83

identity 91–2
imperialism 174
inclination 68–73, 76–7
indicators 150–1
inflation 158
infrastructure 155

insecurity 146, 148
institutions 150, 153, 156, 158, 165–77
interdependence 150, 153, 157, 159
interests 43, 70, 121, 142–3, 153, 156
International Atomic Energy Agency (IAEA) 158
International Relations (IR) 141–4, 152, 156, 165, 167, 171
Iraq 33
Irigaray, L. 34
Israel 10, 148
Italy 43, 83, 169

Jacobins 111
Jansenists 112
Jedynka, C. 106
Jefferson, T. 108
Jews 19, 22, 25–6, 100, 104–5, 110
Joint System of Accountability and Control 158
joint-stock companies 27
Judaism 25

Kacowicz, A.M. 156
Kant, I. 121, 166
Kielanowski, J. 104
Kierkegaard, S. 3–4, 25, 65–80
King, P. 1–6, 9–29
kinship 11–12, 34
Kittay, E. 125, 130–2
Kocowicz, A.M. 149–50
Kodak 175
Kołakowski, L. 107
Koselleck, R. 171
Kowalska, A. 102, 106
Kuroń, J. 99–100, 102–9, 111, 113–14

labour 33, 61, 118, 122–5, 130–2, 134, 137
Laelius 44
laissez-faire 10
language theory 145–8
Lasswell, H. 1
Latin America 154, 158

Latvia 106
Lenin, V.I. 28, 39, 88
Leninism 89–90, 92
Levi-Strauss, C. 11
Levinger, G. 54
Lewis, C.S. 36, 38, 43, 57
liberalism 32, 37–8, 42–3
    care theory 123–4, 126, 137
    institutions 176
    polemics 84–5, 89–90, 92–3
    politics 45–7
    revolution 111
    trust 147, 152–4
liberty 13, 37, 121, 168
Lipiński, E. 100, 104
Lipski, J.J. 104, 107
Lithuania 106
Lityński, J. 103–4
Locke, J. 42
Luther, M. 108
Lux, G. 173
Lyotard, J-F. 35

McCarthy, M. 44
Machiavelli, N. 1, 41, 105, 108
Macierewicz 104, 106
MacKinnon, C. 124
Malvinas 148, 155
market economy 5–6, 42, 124, 131–2
Marshall Plan 174–5
Marx, K. 123
Marxism 42, 110, 121, 123–4, 174
masons 100
Mayans 10
Mazowiecki, T. 110
Mearsheimer, J. 143
media 10, 103, 109, 112
Menem, C. 158–60
mentorship 134
Ménudier 174
Mercosur 144, 159–60
meta-politics 44
Michnik, A. 100, 102–8, 110–14
Middle Ages 89

Middle East 10
Mikolajska, H. 104
military 6, 10, 33, 89
  care theory 127, 135–6
  revolution 108
  trust 142–3, 147, 149, 153–5, 157
Mill, J.S. 52, 55–8, 165
Miłosz, C. 107, 114
modernity 13–29, 78
money 6, 13, 124, 131, 177
monotheism 38
Montaigne, M. de 44, 48
Montgascon, M. 173
Moore, M. 33
More, T. 143–4, 160
Motorola 175
Mouffe, C. 38–9, 46, 48
multiculturalism 111, 119
Muslims 10, 19
mutual care giving 133

Napoleon 87
narcissism 119
national service 135
NATO 174
Nazis 83, 93, 127, 137
negative liberty 37
negative peace 147–9, 151–3, 160–1
Negri, A. 42
neighbours 66–7, 73, 76–7
  care theory 118, 133–6
  revolution 103
  trust 145, 153, 157
neoclassicism 166
neoinstitutionalism 166
neoliberalism 152–3
neorealism 141–3, 152–3
nepotism 5, 20
networking 13, 44
New Evolutionism 107
Noddings, N. 128
North 5
nuclear technology 88, 154–5, 158–9
Nuremberg trials 93

Oakeshott, M. 94–5
OAS 155
Oelsner, A. 6, 141–62, 165
Okin, S. 124, 130
old boys' networks 43
Organisation d'Armee Secret (OAS) 86
Orwell, G. 92
Other 4, 13, 65–80
overpopulation 126
Owenites 1

Pajdak, S. 104
Palestine 148
paradiplomacy 167
Paraguay 155, 159
Paraná, River 154–5, 158
partiality 67–8, 73, 75–6, 120–1
participation 133–4, 161, 169, 172
partisans 84–90, 93–4, 111
partners 22
Pascal, B. 112
peace 141–62
peasants 123
philanthropists 16
Pico 108
Pious XII, Pope 169
Plato 36, 40–1, 45, 47, 54
  care theory 120–1
  responsibility 72
  revolution 102, 112
The Players 99–104, 106, 108–13
pluralism 45–6, 48, 112, 121
  institutions 166
  trust 146, 148–51, 157, 161
pluralistic security communities 148–9, 161
Poland 5, 99–114
Polemarchus 120
polemics 83–96, 111
police 99, 101, 104–6, 108–11, 113
Polish Institute of National Memory 99, 101
Polish Security Police 99, 101, 105–6, 110–11

Index 189

political
  definition 35
  nature 38–41
  notion 46–7
  typology 91–2
politicians 13–15, 34, 44
politics
  antipolitical 103
  definition 35
polytheism 47
pop stars 14
Pope 109, 169
Popper, K. 2, 24
Portuguese language 159
positive liberty 37
positive peace 147–9, 151, 157, 160–1
postmodernism 65
praxis 118, 123, 125, 129–30, 133, 135, 137–8
preference 67–8, 74, 76–7
privatisation 44, 130, 132
productive labour 118, 124
Programme for Economic Integration and Cooperation (PICE) 158–9
proletariat 101, 103
protectionism 158
Protestants 25–6
Proudhon, P. 110
psychiatrists 13
psychology 23, 65, 102, 110
public opinion 10, 155, 157, 161

Radio Free Europe 103
Radius, R. 173
Rank Xerox 175
rapport 20
rapprochement 144, 153–5
rationalism 152–3, 155
Rawls, J. 42, 46
realism 141–4, 152–3
reciprocity 4, 15–26, 52, 54
  care theory 118–19, 122, 128–9
  responsibility 68–9, 73–7
  trust 152, 157–8

reductionism 34–5
regional peace 141–62
reimbursed private care 130–5
Renaissance 108, 113
Rennes Institute 174–5
repression 24, 101–3
reproductive labour 118, 122–5, 132–3, 135, 137–8
Republic of Friendship 103
republicanism 37–8, 43
Republicans 19
resistance 43, 106, 109–10, 113, 145
responsibility 65–80
revolution 87, 90, 99–114
Ricardo, D. 165
ritual 168–71, 176–7
Robotnik 103, 109
robots 11
rogue states 47
Romans 15, 43, 107
Romaszewski 104
Round Table Agreement 111–12
Rumsfeld, D. 11
Russia 173
Russian Orthodoxy 42
Rybicki, J. 104

St Augustine 4, 13, 25, 165
Salan, R. 86, 91
Sarney, J. 157–8
Sartre, J-P. 17
Scheffler, I. 177
Schmid, C. 173
Schmitt, C. 3–4, 32, 34, 38–41, 45–8, 83–96, 171
Schwartz, D. 3, 51–64
Schwarzenbach, S.A. 6, 117–38
Scipio 44
Scotland Yard 106
Searle, J. 166, 169, 172, 177
Second World War 10, 88, 104, 106, 174, 176–7
securitization 144–51, 155–6, 161
security 6, 99, 101, 105–6

care theory 132, 136
institutions 165
revolution 110–11
trust 142, 144–8, 150–1, 156–7, 159, 161
selfishness 69, 71–7
Seneca 31–2, 36
shareholders 27
similarity 53–5
Simmel, G. 177
sin 11
sincerity 34
slavery 11, 60, 120, 123, 128, 137
Slomp, G. 3–4, 83–96, 165
Slote, M. 128
Smith, A. 5, 132, 165
Smith, G.M. 1–6, 65–80
social security 129
social services 118, 133
socialism 37, 102, 104, 106–7, 111, 123–4, 131, 174
Society of Friends 1
sociology 28, 54, 110, 166
Socrates 36, 102, 106
Solidarity 99–102, 107–12
sophists 105
South 5
South America 144, 147, 161
South Atlantic 155, 158
Soviet Union 106, 110, 121, 148, 161
Spain 175
Spanish language 159
Spanish Wars 87
Special Units 106
stable peace 148–51, 157, 160–1
Stalin, J. 28
Staniszkis, J. 110
state role 137–8
status 51–61, 85, 119, 130–1, 165–6
Steinbergowa, A. 106
Student Committee of Solidarity 103
Stuttgart Congress 173
subsidies 130–1
substantivization 34

suffrage 123
superpowers 158
supraterritoriality 44
sustainability 137
syncretism 107–9

taxation 120, 130
technology 87–90, 137, 154, 159
Tharradin, M. 173
theology 26, 38, 47, 53, 65
Third World 124–5, 129, 177
timocracy 61
Tlatelolco Treaty 154, 159
Tocqueville, A. de 176–7
tolerance 26, 29
Torah 25–6
tourism 11
Towarzystwo Kursow Naukowych (Society of Scholarly Courses) 103
trade unions 104, 132, 174
Tripartite Agreement 155
Tronti, M. 84
Tronto, J. 127–8
trust 6, 28, 31, 141–62
twinnings 167–73, 175–7

Ukraine 106
unemployment 11, 101, 124, 129
Union Internationale des Maires (UIM) 173
United Nations (UN) 155
United States (US) 5, 20
care theory 123, 127, 131, 135–6
institutions 174–5
trust 148–9, 154
unstable peace 147–8, 150, 154, 161
Uruguay 159
Uruguay Round 158
USSR *see* Soviet Union

Van der Zweerde, E. 2, 31–48, 165
Van Gennep, A. 171
vendettas 33
Vichy France 176

Videla 154
Vietnam War 174
Vion, A. 6, 165–77

Wæver, O. 144–5, 150
Wajda, A. 105
Walentynowicz, A. 109
Walesa, L. 109
Walterowcy 106
Walzer, M. 177
war 6, 10, 32–3, 39, 41–2
  care theory 136–8
  institutions 172
  polemics 84, 87–9, 92–3
  revolution 113
  on terror 88
  trust 142–3, 145–50, 152–4, 157, 161
Warsaw University 105
Warsaw Uprising 103, 106
weapons of mass destruction 88

Weber, M. 12
welfare state 20
Wendt, A. 141
West 41–2, 101–3, 107, 110, 112–13
West Germany 100
Westphalia Treaty 87
Wielowieyski, A. 110
Wild West 10
Wilde, J. de 144–5
William, Judge 71–2
Witoszek, N. 5, 99–114
Wolfers, A. 142, 144, 156–7
Worldcom 27
Wyler, E. 173

Zbindon, H. 173
zero-sum games 154
Zieja, F. 104
Zitrone, L. 173
Žižek, S. 35